AF560150

India : A Time of Change

Gilles Boquérat et al.

India Research Press

India Research Press
Flat-6, Khan Market, New Delhi – 110 003.
Ph.: 24694610; Fax : 24618637
contact@indiaresearchpress.com; bahrisons@vsnl.com
www.indiaresearchpress.com

2007

ISBN thirteen: 978-81-8386-003-1
ISBN ten: 81-8386-003-6

Cataloguing Publication Data

India : A Time of Change
Gilles Boquérat et al.

Includes references and index.
1.India 2. Economic Reforms 3.Globalization
4.Development/Culture 5. Decentralization
I. Title II. Author

Printed for *India Research Press* at Focus Impressions, New Delhi-110 003.

Contributors

Dr. Gilles Boquérat, is an associate researcher at the Centre for Indian and South Asian Studies (CEIAS) in Paris and is currently visiting fellow at the Institute of Strategic Studies, Islamabad. He was Head of the International Relations Division at the Centre de Sciences Humaines (CSH) in New Delhi (1999-2003). He writes on different regional issues linked to international politics.

Pierre Chapelet, formerly affiliated to the CSH, is currently completing his PhD in geography at the University of Rouen, France. He is also a consultant with the Committee for International Cooperation in National Research in Demography (CICRED), France.

Dr. Gilles Chuyen, a former research fellow in political science at the CSH, has been exploring Indian culture through academics-research project on contemporary Brahmin identity and performing arts.

Camille Deprez, is a Ph.D student completing a dissertation on the Indian film industry at the University of Sorbonne, Paris. She is finalising a book on Indian television.

Dr. Frédéric Grare, was Director of the CSH (1999-2003) and is ently a visiting scholar at the Carnegie Endowment for International Peace, Washington D.C. He also served in the French Embassy in Pakistan. He has written extensively on security issues, energy security, Islamist movements and sectarian conflict in Pakistan and Afghanistan.

Dr. Girish Kumar, is on the faculty of the Indian Institute of Public Administration, New Delhi. He was a Senior Fellow and Head of the Political Science Division at the CSH.

Dr. Eric Leclerc, until recently coordinator for regional dynamics in South Asia at the CSH, is an associate professor of geography at the University of Rouen, France. He has notably worked on the role of the expatriate Indian communities as agents in the construction of a world society.

Dr. Joël Ruet, is Fellow in Economics at the Development Studies Institute, London School of Economics and teaches at HEC-Paris. He was Head of the Economics Division at the CSH. He specialized in the study of infrastructure reforms and state-industry relationships in India.

Dr. Dipankar Sengupta, a former research fellow at the CSH, currently teaches in the Department of Economics at the University of Jammu. His areas of research include problems of transition economies, international economics, industrial organization theory and the political economy of South Asia.

Sachchidanand Sinha, is a socialist thinker, a political activist and author of several books; he has written extensively both in English and Hindi.

Preface

Looking back at India in the nineties leaves us with the feeling of considering unsettled times when the country was referred as an "emerging power" but with a question mark. The time was not ripe for catchphrases like "Shining India" or "India everywhere". If one is entitled to take this type of image-enhancing formula with a pinch of salt–to which the verdict of the voters in the 2004 general elections bears testimony–the fact remains that India's leaders exhibit a new-found confidence and the country has come a long way to invalidate negative prognoses. Its profile internationally has risen dramatically, and only a few will contest, in principle, India's aspiration to be counted among the permanent members of the United Nations Security Council. The upper classes have more to boast than just crowns won at international beauty contests, and relish the praise showered on the new global power by foreign dignitaries attracted by the perspective of a self-sustaining high growth trajectory and oblivious of the "third world" which the majority of the population still inhabits. While India was lectured on the need open its markets not long ago, the Western world now has to reconcile itself to the idea of Indian companies making a host of takeovers abroad. When the country is promoted as a symbol of a harmonious plural society, one would be quite forgiven to forget that communal riots occurred in the not-so-distant past and that, on a different plane, "crossing the Rubicon" was not-so-evident now that India is acknowledged as a *de facto* nuclear weapon state. For all that, one can argue that the affirmation of a global ambition has seen India falling back into line rather than drawing inspiration from the fairly distinctive voice it once assumed to alter an unequal world order.

The scope of this book is to substantiate and critically analyze some of the changes India went through in the decade post-1991. 1991 was a watershed year in contemporary India even if one could argue that the premises of this landmark are to be found before; especially when Prime Minister Rajiv Gandhi tried to break away from traditional Congress policy orientations. On the political front, the Congress Party could not gather enough votes to rule on its own, foreshadowing harder times and new political alignments at work, with the rise of regional parties and the empowerment of hitherto-marginalised segments of society. On the economic front, India, facing an unprecedented financial crisis, verging on a default in payments, was not in a position to further delay the structural reforms which were supposed to allow India to emulate its East Asian neighbours, and consign the famed "Hindu rate of growth" to a bygone era of state-sponsored development. An economy driven by the private sector which generated rapid growth would give the population a "taste of the market". The willingness to open a process of liberation may not have been as compelling if, at the same time, the Soviet Union had itself not been slowly vanishing, burying with it not only a competing ideological system which had inspired the political economy of post-Independence India, but also the "time-tested" friendship" of a strategic ally. The bipolar world in which a non-aligned India had gained room for manoeuvre gave way to a uni-polar domination by the US, requiring foreign policy adjustments. It also created new opportunities resulting from the lifting of Cold War strategic barriers. Ultimately, it is not just the economy which was induced to open up more to the outside world during this defining decade, but also the foreign policy establishment and society at large. These essays explore this crucial and fascinating intervening process.

Gilles Boquérat

May 2006

Contents

A decade reviewed

Gilles Boquérat

'*Under the winds of change* a land inhabited by 380 million people, one sixth of humanity, is waking up, stretching limbs stiffened with the slumber of centuries'. This was the opening line of a book written by Taya Zinkin in the mid-fifties about 'a generation in transition' and presenting a personal assessment of the changes Independent India was going through.[1] India was then laying the foundations which were to guide government policies for the coming decades under the patronage of the Congress Party, especially the promotion of a secular society, a State-regulated and inward-looking economy and a non-aligned foreign policy. During the defining decade under review (1991-2001), precisely these foundations were called into question. At the end of it, it was common to hear the refrain to hear that India had indeed changed. The early nineties witnessed events which were to leave a deep imprint on the social fabric, the standard of living of its population and India's place in the world. 1991 is a landmark in the history of Independent India, and not just because a package of economic reforms covering trade, industrial and exchange rate policy regimes was initiated in this year. The year also witnessed, internationally, the formal end of the bipolar world with the disappearance of the Soviet Union, putting a question mark over the future of non-alignment of which India had been a torch-bearer. India had to adjust to the new global environment of its own volition, if only not to have such changes forced upon it. On the domestic front, though the Congress Party came back to power, it was a declining party, unable to get a majority of seats in Parliament. Another epoch-making event was the much-debated implementation of the Mandal Commission recommendations in favour of the 'Other Backward Classes' which had been decided the year before by the then government of V.P. Singh. The Indian polity had hardly recovered from the crisis over the issue of reservations, than it was soon engulfed in another traumatic development when Hindu extremists tore down the Babri Masjid in Ayodhya in December 1992, jeopardizing communal harmony. In the years to come, India's decision-makers had to address a new set of challenges, with the ascendancy of backward castes, inescapable coalition politics with increased leverage of regional parties (never had so many parties from across the political spectrum been associated in government at the Centre than during this decade), inevitable integration with the global economy, competitive market dynamics, and an international environment characterized by the domineering conduct of the United States. This book is an attempt to explore some of the responses to these new challenges, how they led to changes representing a clear break with the past and which may well have a profound bearing on the future of the country.[2] It is based on the contributions of past and present French and Indian researchers at the Delhi-based *Centre de Sciences Humaines.*

In this introductory chapter, we will look at where India stood in 1991 and where it stands ten years later. Before any other considerations, India is often first viewed in demographic terms since it factually makes up 16 per cent of the world population. At the end of the decade, India crossed the one billion mark. Between the two decadal census of 1991 and 2001, India's total population has increased by about 180 millions inhabitants (from 846 millions in 1991, to 1027 in 2001); an annual increase about the same as the total population of Australia or Sri Lanka. This was an overall figure far in excess of the approximately 800 million inhabitants estimated by the end of the century, on the basis of the 1950s rate of increase and which, 'according to Malthusian laws... will never be reached'.[3] The comforting factor is that the population growth rate has further come down compared to the previous decade, a reflection of a lower total fertility rate, from 3.9 births per woman to 3.0, which also translates into a smaller percentage of the population under the age of fifteen (1991: 35.8; 2001: 33.7).[4] In their contribution, Eric Leclerc and Pierre

Chapelet ('A Census Decade in India: The One Billion Threshold', pp. 00) help us to comprehend the evolving demographic patterns during the nineties, notably region-wise and gender-wise, producing for this purpose detailed cartographic representations.

The slowing down of the population growth rate—from 23.8 per cent (1981-91) to 21.3 per cent (1991-2001)—and a higher GDP growth per annum helped to increase the per capita net national product between 1991 and 2001 by about 40 per cent, and to bring down the percentage of the population below the national poverty line from 36 per cent in 1993-94 to 28.6 in 1999-2000. A measure of India's performance is the transition from the low human development category where it stood in 1992 (134 out of 174 countries with an index of 0.439) to the medium human development category (127 in 2001 out of 175 countries with an index of 0.590), indicating a moderate improvement in socio-economic indicators. In absolute terms, there is no doubt that India matters. At the turn of the millennium, India's economy was the eleventh-largest in the world in GDP terms, and it was ranked fourth in terms of purchasing power parity. Any regular visitor to Indian cities will have noticed the phenomenal increase in vehicles plying the roads and all the trappings of consumerism, reflecting the emergence of a significant middle class.[5] But even for the middle class household, non-stop electricity or water supply remains a dream except the very few who can afford to have a generator or a water-booster directly extracting groundwater.

The post-reforms average annual growth of the GDP was marginally higher in the nineties than it was in the eighties, moving upwards from 5.47 per cent (1981-1991) to 5.68 per cent (1991-2001), and certainly not sufficient to propel the country out of mass poverty in spite of the fact that the reforms were also directed to deal with improving the well-being of the people at large.[6] An encouraging development was that growth in the nineties did not involve large and debt-creating borrowings from domestic and external resources, contrary to what happened with the expansionary fiscal strategy of the eighties which significantly contributed to the 1991 balance of payment crisis. Foreign exchange reserves have strongly recovered from the time they stood at $5.8 billion in Spring 1991, forcing India to mortgage some of its gold reserves to avoid defaulting on international obligations, to attain $42.3 billion in March 2001. Another positive indicator of India's external financial position, the debt service ratio (as a percentage of exports of goods and services) has declined from 27.7 per cent to 12.6 per cent. Still, it is a matter of concern that in 2001, India's human development index was twelve ranks below the GDP per capita (PPP US$) rating, indicating uneven development, notably in relation to health and education. Universal primary education remained an elusive objective with a youth literacy rate (age 15-24) of 73.3 per cent in 2001 (1990: 64.3 per cent). This situation brought Parliament to enact in 2001 the 93rd Constitution Amendment that made basic education a fundamental right, and required the states to provide free schooling for all children between the ages of six and fourteen. If the stockmarkets boosted by economic liberalization have been bullish with market capitalization rising from 12.2 per cent of the GDP to 23.1 per cent during the nineties, rural India, where 72 per cent of population still lived in 2001, remained largely exposed to poor living conditions except for a few farmers with large land holdings availing of the fact that agricultural incomes are largely outside the tax net. If 84 per cent of the population had access in 2000 to improved water sources (68 per cent in 1990), only 28 per cent could avail of improved sanitation facilities (16 per cent in 1990). In 2001, only 51.8 per cent of households had 'pucca' houses and only 55.9 per cent households had electricity as a source of lightning.[7] Per capita energy consumption is a mere 355 kilowatt-hours (2000) compared to 827 kwh for China. Besides, hardly any dent has been made on the prevalence of under-nourishment, which was at 24 per cent of the population in 1998-2000, one point less than in 1990-92. A tragic irony is that food sufficiency, with bulging stocks of foodgrains, co-exists with food insecurity for part of India's population.

A report of the National Sample Survey Organisation titled *Employment and Unemployment Situation among Social Groups of India, 1999-2000* suggested that the Other Backwards Classes (OBCs), who were in the political limelight during the nineties, are still a long way from catching up with the élite socio-economically. Caste is never very far from politics in India and the empowerment of the lower strata of the society is an argumentative subject. Girish Kumar ('Ascendancy of Lower Backward Castes in Indian Politics: Implications for Coalition Governments and Democracy', pp. 00) dwells upon the fact in a study broaching historical and regional premises, that the nineties witnessed an unprecedented horizontal mobilisation of backward castes leading to alignment and realignment of social forces. No major party can ignore the lower castes so much so that over time, they have acted to enlarge the reservation net. This question is also addressed by Gilles Chuyen in *Caste and Politics in the Context of the 1990s: Identity and Otherness among Deprived Populations and Brahmins* (pp. 00) where he deals with the political activism and the strengthened influence of the Dalits and the OBCs, and how they contested the supremacy of upper castes in Indian society and politics. It resulted in insecurities among the 'dispossessed' Brahmins who could always take a leaf out of the lower strata in bringing forward their identity and mobilize themselves into pressure groups, a kind of process of 'sanskritization in reversal'. If capturing power across the states can be seen as a healthy sign of democratic representativeness, Girish Kumar calls to mind that its benefits have not been equally distributed and that it has not led to programmes aimed at social and economic upliftment in the long-term.

If development has not improved social opportunities for all, it has also not necessarily led to a relaxation of regressive social norms, especially for women. For instance, one of the disturbing trends of the nineties has been the increase of female foeticide. The sex ratio has, in fact, declined in 13 out of 25 states of the Union. If sex determination of the foetus has been made illegal with the Pre-Natal Diagnostic Techniques Act of 1994, the practice continues, and is not restricted to rural areas, leading to an imbalance in sex ratios. The female child deficit is even higher in urbanized parts of the country, notably in the cities of some comparatively well-off states like Punjab and Haryana. The male-to-female ratio for the 0-6 age group is 1,000: 903 for urban India and 1,000: 934 for its rural counterpart.[8]

Post-reforms economic growth has not been uniform in geographical terms. Regional imbalance tends to increase with the less developed ones growing not just at levels lower than the national average, but at a slower rate than they did a decade before. This is thus true for Assam, undivided Bihar, undivided Uttar Pradesh, Orissa, whereas state development product (SDP) at constant prices of Goa, Gujarat, Karnataka and even West Bengal grew at over 7 per cent per annum between 1990 and 2000. In SDP growth per capita, it is the Western coastal states which performed the best in the nineties, exceeding the national average, along with Tamil Nadu and West Bengal on the Bay of Bengal rim.[9] No wonder that the most backward districts are found in Bihar, Uttar Pradesh, Jharkhand, Orissa and to a lesser extent in Madhya Pradesh,[10] a situation worsened by the financial sickness of those states and the Centre's increasingly hard-to-come allocation of assistance for capital formation. For, if the fiscal deficit of the Central government has slightly come down over the years, largely and regrettably because of a reduction in public investment (capital expenditure as a proportion of total government expenditure has declined from 30.2 per cent in 1990-91 to 21.8 per cent in 1998-99 or from 5.5 per cent to 3.6 per cent as a proportion of the GDP) not compensated by incremental investments in the private sector, the combined fiscal deficit of the Centre and the states of the Union remains high at around 10 per cent of GDP, about the same level as on the eve of the 1991 balance of payments crisis (9.4 per cent). As a result, public resources need to be used more efficiently and delivery mechanisms for public services need to be reformed. Democratic decentralization has been given a boost with the enactment of the 73rd Constitutional Amendment Act, passed in

1992, in order to give local bodies a driving role in identifying local needs and in ensuring better accountability and monitoring of development and welfare programmes. Dipankar Sengupta (*Globalisation, Competitiveness and Political Decentralisation*, pp. 00) discusses the conflict over the distribution of powers between the Union, the states and its weakest claimants, the Panchayati Raj Institutions (PRI). In the name of economic rationality in a market economy integrating with the global economy, of sustainable development and of employment-generation in relation to public goods requirements relevant to the needs of local people, he argues in favour of empowering the PRIs with more decision-making capacities and resources; a complete turnaround in comparison to what was the earlier centralized, heavy industries first strategy, and the onerous capital intensive model of development.

Inadequate job creation is an acute problem with the unemployment rate increasing in spite of a higher overall growth rate than in the eighties.[11] Employment growth has declined much more sharply than the growth of population, from an average of 2.50 per cent annually for 1987-1994 to 1.07 per cent during 1994-2000, whereas the labour force swelled by an average of 1.31 per cent per annum during the latest period. Furthermore, much of this limited increase in employment occurred outside the organised sector, challenging the notion that the State can be the agent of economic upliftment for the deprived sections of society. As a matter of fact, the policy of reservation extended to the OBCs with the objective of increasing opportunities for employment in public administration and public sector undertakings (the public sector contributes for 5.8 per cent of total jobs) is confronted by a decrease in public employment induced by large-scale fiscal deficits and the disinvestment policy.

India has not been immune to the global trend favouring privatisation/disinvestment, but the politically-sensitive process, started in 1992 with the sale of minority stakes in some public sector enterprises, had not really picked up during the decade. Poor management of public sector enterprises was often the justification for getting the private sector – domestic or foreign - more actively involved, notably for much-needed upgrading of infrastructure. The power sector is a textbook case with unfulfilled production targets, large losses encountered at the post-production stages, erratic distribution, and bankrupt state electricity boards, and was a prime target for restructuring. Some state governments have undertaken often half-hearted reforms without convincing results. The objective of the Electricity Bill, 2001 passed in Parliament in June 2003, was to provide the means of improving the performance of the power sector by encouraging greater competition and by deregulating generation, transmission and distribution. Joël Ruet (Economic reforms and a new public-private development model in India, pp. -) gives its own perception of the relationship between the public and the private sector in the post-reforms era, arguing that it is not so much private investment that a state needs, but a change in methods of management to induce a change of paradigm in the management of resources. In this regard, the success encountered in the telecommunication and IT sectors can give some ideas for other sectors of activities.

Economic growth in the nineties has been more than anything driven by the services sector which in 2001 came to account for almost half of the GDP (49.4 per cent, a seven point increase compare to 1992). The share of the agricultural sector has shown a downward trend from 30.9 per cent in 1992 to 25 per cent in 2001. The growth rate of value added in this sector was less than in the previous decade and the growth in employment was nil in 1994-2000. As a result, the share of agriculture in total employment declined from 60 per cent to 57 per cent during this period. The share of the industrial sector (value-added as percentage of GDP) remained constant at about 27 per cent, yet the decadal growth rate of the industrial sector has also come down. This is in sharp contrast to China, which has emerged as the world's manufacturing centre with industry accounting for half of the GDP, thanks to large overseas investments. Services was the only sector which really expanded, from 6.8 per cent in the eighties to 7.6 per cent in the nineties. No sector has attracted more media attention media than information technology (IT). Understandably, much pride has been derived (especially for an elite taking a distinctive gratification from the country's intellectual achievement) from the rapidly-growing IT sector, with leading companies like Infosys and Wipro, which altered for the better India's image abroad. In a rather short time, India has to offer for export a wide range of IT services including software, database creation, financial back offices, and business process outsourcing. The software and services workforce has rapidly increased, bringing also substantial balance of payments benefits and giving an opportunity to exploit a low-cost, educated English-speaking workforce. From total revenue of less than $200 million in 1990, the computer industry earned over $8 billion by 2000-01, with 75 per cent of the revenue coming from exports.[12] But the information technology sector still makes only a minor contribution to the GDP, of around 2 per cent, and it is not an answer to the country's broader labour sector woes, since IT professionals make up for only about 0.1 per cent of India's labour force. The fast-growing number of internet users, essentially in cities, which jumped from 1.4 million in 1998 to 7 million in 2001 and more than doubled the following year, still means that only 1.6 per cent of the population was online in 2002, far behind China (4.6 per cent) and Indonesia (3.7 per cent).[13] More widely spread out has been the telephonic connectivity in a sector now largely deregulated, even if disparities still exist, with a telephone density of 0.49 per 100 in Orissa to 2.07 per 100 in Gujarat.[14] Telephone mainlines per 1,000 people have increased from 6 in 1990 to 38 in 2001 and the proliferation of ISD/STD phone booths has brought people closer. The pharmaceutical sector also came of age in the nineties and achieved global recognition for production of low-cost, high-quality generic drugs.

A major aspect of the liberalisation and deregulation process has been the transition of a regulated import-substitution economy focused on the domestic market to a free-market economy with entrepreneurs ready to take on competitors at home and abroad. The share of exports of goods and services as a percentage of GDP doubled from 7 per cent in 1990 to 14 per cent in 2001. Indian enterprises were to be made more performing in terms of productivity as well as quality-wise not only by dismantling the 'licence raj' in order to allow private companies to be their own masters, but also by facing competition from foreign goods. As a part of its commitments under the WTO regime, tariff barriers were significantly lowered from 79 per cent (simple mean tariff) in 1990 to 30.9 per cent in 2001. Non-tariff barriers were progressively phased out and the process of removing quantitative restrictions was completed by March 2001. Foreign trade in 2000-01 accounted for 21.8 per cent of GDP compared to only 15.6 per cent ten years before. However, India's share in world trade has only marginally increased, from 0.53 per cent in 1991 to 0.7 per cent in 2001. The attitude towards Foreign Direct Investments (FDI) has evolved from suspicion to expectation. By 2001 there was a policy of automatic approvals for all but a few industries. Net FDI inflows accounted for 0.7 per cent of GDP in 2001, a figure higher than the net disbursements of official development assistance (0.4 per cent). Apart from being non-debt creating, FDI was expected to spur local industries and services into global competitive efficiency and develop export industries and labour-intensive manufactures. The nineties have seen a change in the composition of external resource flows, with a reduction in the relative importance of long-term debt and grants in favour of private capital flows such as FDI and portfolio equity flows with the appearance of foreign institutional investors in the Indian capital markets. FDI inflows increased from $133 million in 1991-2 to a peak of $4.7 billion in 2000-01. India's share of FDI inflows to developing countries rose from 0.5 per cent in 1992 to 3.3 per cent in 2001. However, this performance is not on the scale of India's economy. The share of exports of goods and services, as a percentage of GDP, has doubled from 7 per cent in 1990 to 14 per cent in 2001.

Integration with the global economy was one way of saying to the world that India does matter, and has the potential to be a major actor in the international community. Another way was the nuclear tests of 1998. Gilles Boquérat and Frédéric Grare (*The Long and Winding Road: From Potential to Great Power Status,* pp. 00) remind us of the soul-searching which followed the end of the Cold War and of the ways and means explored to preserve a capacity for independent decision-making in a unipolar world. In this regard, the BJP-led government opted for nuclearization in order to improve India's security and enhance its prestige. This presupposition was soon put to the test by a bellicose phase in Indo-Pak relations. They discusses whether the government's stand was vindicated, whether it fitted into a quest for a multipolar world, or pursued other objectives and ultimately question the repercussions on India's world status at the dawn of a new millennium.

The First Gulf War marked not just the beginning of the unrivalled US domination over world politics, it was also the first war which could be watched on TV worldwide, sometimes through live broadcasts. Some eight years later, at the time of the Kargil conflict, Indian viewers were also able to watch on their TV screens journalists reporting from the theatre of operations. In the meantime, there had been a visual media revolution in India with the monopolistic state television– Doordarshan–forced to compete with numerous private TV channels promoted by satellite and cable television. Politicians were grilled in public debates and some academics taking part in TV programmes found a new audience for their expertise. Ads and TV serials brought to urban and rural households images of unknown behaviour, as Camille Deprez shows (*Indian Television–A Model of Cultural Appropriation in the Context of Globalization,* pp. -). She also demonstrates that globalization does not necessarily mean homogeneity, and that foreign media, to succeed in India, have to adapt to local cultural forms. The more things change, the more they remain the same?

Notes

1. Taya Zinkin, India Changes !, London: Chatto and Windus, 1958, 233 p.
2. It goes without saying that this book does not pretend to give an exhaustive picture of the significant changes which occurred in the nineties. For instance, the greater role played by the judiciary as an arbitrator and player in Indian political life or the rediscovery of the overseas Indians by the political establishment in the nineties could have deservedly found a place among the subjects treated in the next chapters.
3. Taya Zinkin, India Changes !, op. cit., p. 66.
4. Except when differently mentioned, data used in this introductory chapter are drawn from :

   World Development Report 1993, World Development Report 2003, The World Bank, New York: Oxford University Press; World Development Indicators 2003, The World Bank, Washington; Human Development Report 1993, Human Development Report 1995, Human Development Report 2003, UNDP, New Delhi: Oxford University Press; Economic Survey 1998-99, Economic Survey 2002-2003, , Ministry of Finance, Government of India, New Delhi: Govt. of India Press; Asian Development Outlook 1996 and 1997, Asian Development Outlook 2001, Asian Development Bank, Hong Kong: Oxford University Press; India Development Report 2002, Kirit S. Parikh, R. Radhakrishna (eds), New Delhi: Oxford University Press, 2002.
5. The number of passenger cars (per 1,000 people) has more than doubled from 2 to 5 between 1990 and 2000. It is about the same for two-wheelers, from 15 to 29 per 1,000 people.
6. Calculation based on the annual growth rate of gross national product at factor cost/ at 1993-94 prices (See, Economic Survey 2002-2003 , S-4). Pro-reforms supporters often take 1992 as the starting date because of the exceptionally low growth rate recorded in the transition year 1991-92, and consequently the percentage for 1992-2001 goes up to 6.18 per cent. But then it does not do justice to the fact that the recovery of the early years was also a result of the low percentage attained in 1991-92.
7. The Indian Express, 29 October 2003.
8. www.censusindia.net
9. BB. Bhattacharya & S.Sakthivel, "Regional Growth and Disparity in India: Comparison of Pre-and Post-Reform Decades",Economic and Political Weekly, 6 March 2004, pp.1071-1077.
10. See, Bibek Debroy and Laveesh Bhandari, District-level Deprivation in the New Millenium, New Delhi, Konark Publishers, 2003.
11. Surveys of the National Sample Survey Organization on employment and unemployment, Quoted in: Economic Survey 2002-2003, op. cit., p. 218.

12. South Asia Development & Cooperation Report 2001/02, Research and Information System for the Non-Aligned and other Developing Countries, New Delhi: RIS, 2002, p. 127.
13. The Hindu, 28 February 2004.
14. South Asia Development & Cooperation Report 2001/02, Research and Information System for the Non-Aligned and other Developing Countries, New Delhi: RIS, 2002, p. 124.

A Census Decade in India: The One Billion Threshold

Eric Leclerc & Pierre Chapelet

To assess the changes India experienced during the last decade through the study of the evolution of its population is challenging. As far as technical aspects are concerned, this process is simple, since India's entry into a new era of economic reforms lines up with the periodicity of Indian censuses. On the other hand, theoretically speaking, rhythms of demographic evolutions as well as changes in economic policy fit together in two time scales: short-term for the latter, and mid-term for the former. For this very reason, it would be farfetched to think that the recent economic reforms have their translation in demographic behaviour. It is, however, possible to discern trends, especially inflexions in the multi-decennial trends, as revealed by census datasets. We will, therefore, focus on diachronic aspects rather than synchronic ones. In spite of the relative inertia of demographic evolution, we cannot avoid laws of statistic thresholds.

The fourteenth decennial census (2001) confirmed that India's population has crossed the threshold of one billion inhabitants. Officially, this landmark took place two years earlier on May 11, 2000, when a little girl was born in the state-run Safdarjung Hospital in New Delhi. Significantly, May 11 was also the National Technology Day, celebrating the second anniversary of the nuclear test at Pokharan (Rajasthan), thus joining symbolically demographic power with military might. Moreover, the politically-motivated choice of a baby girl sent a powerful message in a male-dominated society characterised by one of the lowest sex ratios in the world (933 women to 1000 men).[1] At the end of the census, on March 1, 2001, the country had a population of 1,027,015,247 persons, split into 531,277,078 men and 495,738,169 women.[2] It is with a certain pride coupled with anxiety that Indian demographers predict that around the year 2050 India's population will overtake that of China. Since 1991, 180.6 million new births have added to the Indian population. Nevertheless, this represents a decline of 10.3 million births as compared to the earlier decade. There is indeed a paradox apparent from the latest census, which shows that at the very moment that India is catching up with China in absolute terms, it is also witnessing a slowdown in the rate of its demographic growth. India had witnessed its maximum population growth during the period extending from the 1960s to the 1980s (See Figure 1: decennial growth 1901-2001), thereby accumulating a very high demographic potential.

Figure 1 : Decennial Growth 1901-2001

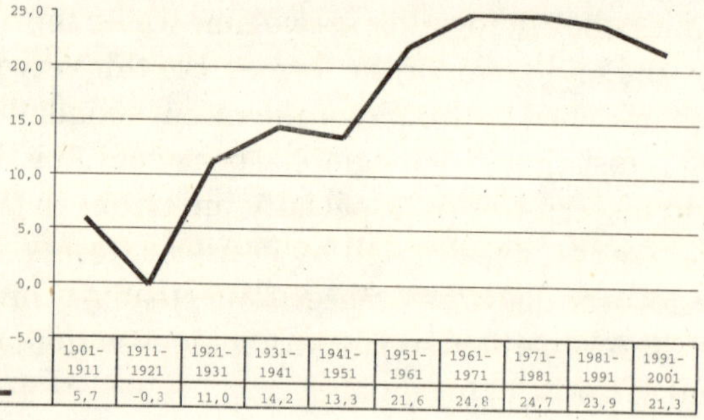

	1901-1911	1911-1921	1921-1931	1931-1941	1941-1951	1951-1961	1961-1971	1971-1981	1981-1991	1991-2001
—	5,7	-0,3	11,0	14,2	13,3	21,6	24,8	24,7	23,9	21,3

© Chapelet P. CSH, Leclerc E. UMI

Before drawing a picture of India at the start of the 21st century through a series of maps, it is necessary to emphasise the magnitude of the exercise that has been taking place on a regular basis since 1872. Two million census agents and inspectors had to be mobilised to question the 220 million households spread over 5,161 towns and nearly 640,000 villages. The counting was conducted between February 9 and 28, 2001, with a period of verification which extended upto March 5. Census operations took place earlier in the foothills of the Himalayas (September 2000) to forestall adverse climatic conditions. In Kashmir, turmoil disturbed the operations to the extent that the information gathering had to be stretched till December 15, 2000. But, above all, two unexpected events complicated the entire process. The first was politico-administrative with the creation in November 2000 of three new states: Uttaranchal, Jharkhand and Chhattisgarh. The second factor was the earthquake which devastated Gujarat on January 26, 2001.

Despite the magnitude of the task, the first results were obtained within just three weeks, thanks to the work of the enumerators who communicated their manually-calculated totals right up to New Delhi, which needs to be underscored. State-wise results as well as preliminary reports were also available on the Census of India website (www.censusindia.net). In just nine months, the provisional results for the 593 districts were at the disposal of the public in digital form. This outstanding technical performance confirms the Indian entry in the information technology era during the last decade. These preliminary results[3] make it possible to draw up the new demographic scene in India through district-level maps, providing a sharper image than the state-wise projection whose extreme heterogeneity is well-known.[4]

Rather than sketch a map of population density whose distribution has not changed fundamentally since the last census[5], we have preferred a map of the total distribution of the population combined with the rate of urbanisation (See Figure 2: Total population 2001 and urbanisation). Comparing with 1991 census data, contrasts in population remain, particularly the North-South dissimilarities. In the North, we find a large zone of the continuously-populated Gangetic valley, where the basically rural character of the middle valley (Bihar and south-east Uttar Pradesh) becomes apparent. However, at the two extremities of the Gangetic valley, there is a progressive transition towards urbanisation. First in the north-west of Uttar Pradesh extending towards Punjab, with the capital, New Delhi in the centre and, then, in the lower part of the valley, in West Bengal, were we find again very high human concentrations, albeit with large city/countryside contrasts.[6] The rest of India gives a different picture. Opposed to the diagonal vacuum from Rajasthan to Orissa, there is the contrast of the more populated southern states whose patterns are very varied. But in any case, dissimilarities between these states are so numerous that the widely-held view of a North-South opposition must be used with care. As opposed to the very densely populated coastal Kerala is the emptiness of Karnataka or even of fairly-urbanized

Figure 2 : Total Population 2001 and Urbanisation

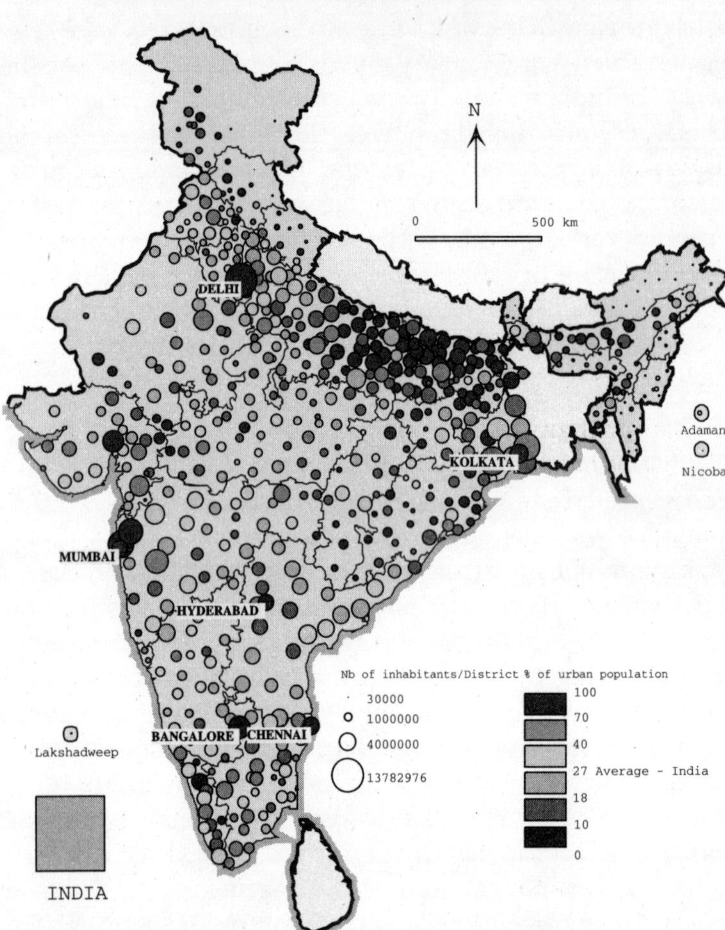

Southern Maharashtra. Andhra Pradesh presents the picture of a high population evenly spread, predominantly rural, with some urban cores (Hyderabad, the Krishna delta). Tamil Nadu is more urbanised but less populated. These differences in population distribution between towns and countries, according to their level of concentration, represent structural constraints for India's economic development. If one takes, for instance the much-needed modernisation of the transport network, privatisation of networks will lead to regional disparities as profitability implies a minimum demographic threshold for their building.

This scene, though rich in perspectives, must be completed by a diachronic approach which we have done in two stages: first by using a decennial perspective, studying the demographic growth between 1991 and 2001; second by using a comparative approach between the last two decennial trends (1981-91 and 1991-2001).

By combining the total population in 1991 with the decennial 1991-2001 population growth rate (See Figure 3: total population 1991 and growth 1991-2001), we discover another spatial configuration. A prolific India is found to contrast with an India undergoing a demographic transition following a very distinct Mumbai-Kolkata line which, therefore, neither ties up with the earlier spatial distribution nor with the rural-urban divide. These different spatial configurations must be interpreted with caution. It reflects the complexity of the local systems, where the interplay of structural inertia and the dynamics of trends are mixed in variable proportions. The imprint of the urban factor is not any less absent on this map, with cities growing faster than their rural environment (Bangalore, Hyderabad or Mumbai). The development of New Delhi, on the other hand, is slowed down by a regional configuration characterised by a high population growth which could probably be explained by a more homogenous economic development in this area in the long term. In India, as a whole, the demographic growth is fairly even in space with a tendency towards a higher growth at the periphery of urban centres.

The unity of South India stands out particularly prominently, with a very homogeneous growth for the four states, which smoothes out singularly well the differences in population concentrations observed earlier. A decreasing North-South gradient covers the entire Deccan in which Maharashtra appears as a state in transition.

To put into perspective the trends that have been brought out, we have used a residual-versus-predictor analysis, allowing us

Figure 3 : Total Population 1991 and Growth 1991-2001

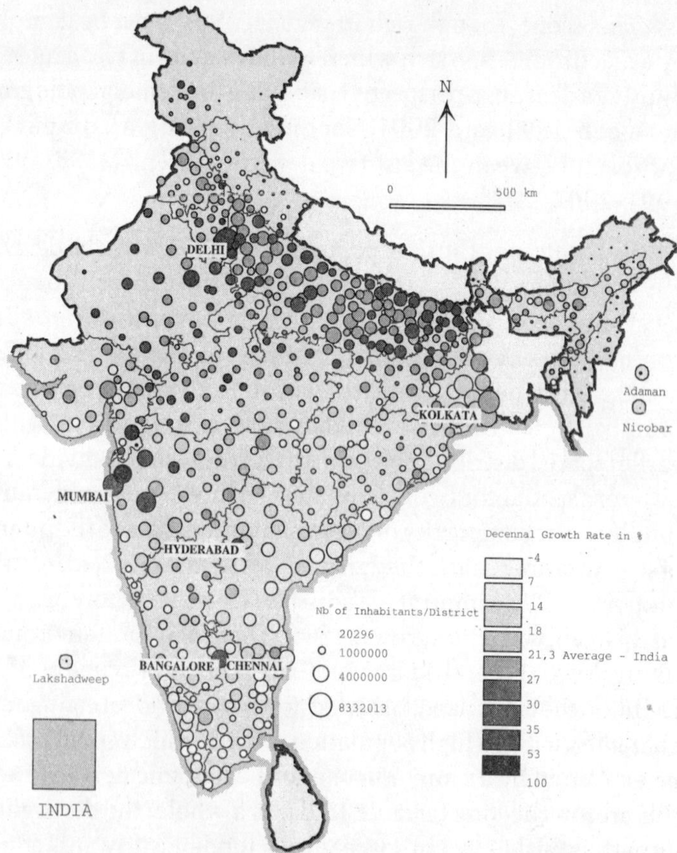

to compare two interlinked phenomena: we have compared the decennial growth of the last two censuses by using a linear regression model on 1981-1991 and 1991-2001 datasets. In that case, it is the time factor which stands as the causal link. The mechanical transmission from one demographic pattern to another constitutes the structural effect, while residuals unveil changes in the trend. By calculating the values of population growth for 1991-2001 as a function of the values taken for 1981-1991, we will thus be able to verify if the trends have continued from one decade to the next. The equation of the regression line is as follows:

$$Growth[1991-2001] = (0.80 \times Growth[1981-1991]) + 2.33$$

The positive value (0.80) of the line slope (See Figure 4: Linear adjustment of the 1991-2001 rate of growth by the 1981-1991 rate of growth) indicates a direct relationship between high growth from one decade to the next. Conversely, the districts where there was low growth between 1981 and 1991 witnessed the continuation of these trends between 1991 and 2001. However, the quality of this statistical model is poor as the determination

Figure 4 : Linear Adjustment of the 1991-2001 Rate of Growth by the 1981-1991 Rate of Growth

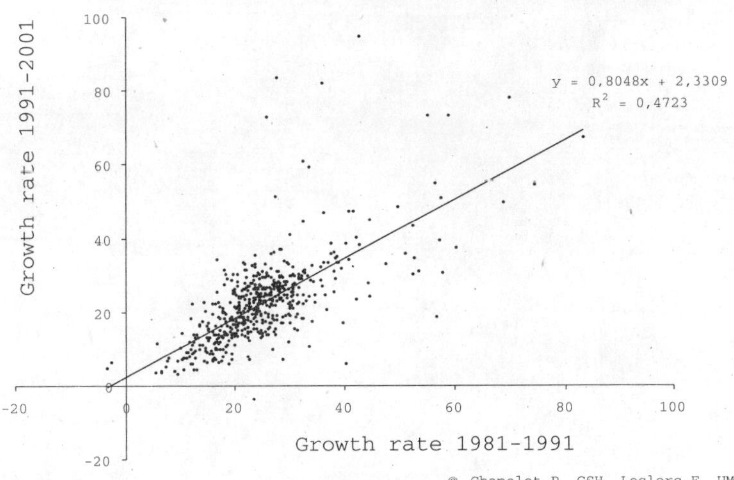

coefficient of the adjustment is below 50 per cent (0.47). In other words, 53 per cent of the calculated variation in the 1991-2001 growth rates is not explained by the growth rate of the earlier decade. This proves that a reversal in trends took place between the two periods.

To identify these, we calculated and mapped (See Figure 5: Difference between observed/estimated 1991-2001 growth) the residuals of this linear adjustment, that is to say the difference

Figure 5 : Deviation Between Calculated and Observed Population Growth Rate in 1991-2001 according to 1981-1991 Growth Rate

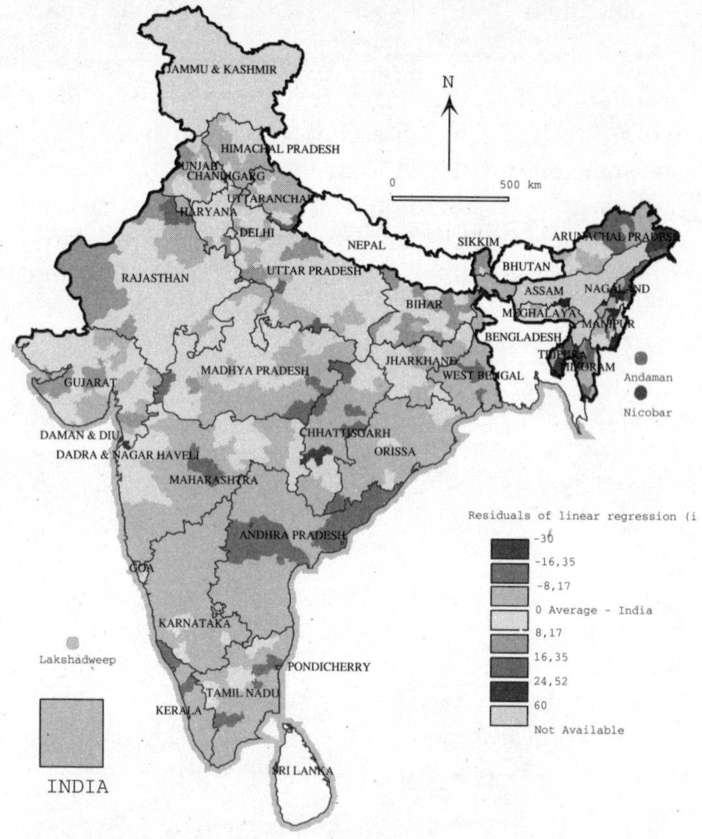

between the observed 1991-2001 growth rate and the one calculated in the model. For instance, the districts which have witnessed a growth that is lower than was calculated appear in the negative. The map of the residuals is, on the whole, well-correlated to that of growth, which brings out a basic trend, somewhat disrupted, however, by some local variations. We find again on this map the Mumbai-Kolkata line undergoing a small shift towards the north for West Bengal.

North India and South India are very homogeneous except in the North-East which combines high negative (Arunachal Pradesh, Tripura and Mizoram) and positive (Nagaland, Manipur) residuals. Considering the small numbers of the population in these areas, these results are more random in nature and these large contrasts may be explained by the high degree of migrations as well as by political tension. The situation in the Gangetic valley is very homogeneous from Haryana to Uttar Pradesh. Bihar stands out once again with values showing a higher growth than the national average during the last decade. A very interesting phenomenon to point out is the shape of the northern border of the newly-created Jharkhand, which clearly follow the north-south population growth division of undivided Bihar. Conversely, a crown-shaped slowdown (Uttaranchal, Himachal Pradesh, Punjab and even northern Rajasthan) surrounds the upper Ganges valley, a probable sign of a reversal trend.

South India stands out for its negative trends, confirming the widening of distinctly greater divergences in comparison with North India. In this overall unit, Andhra Pradesh and Chhattisgarh make a better showing than Kerala or Tamil Nadu. This highlights a latter phenomenon of transition in these two states, the high negative values underscoring a reversal in trend and a catching-up with the southern states situation. These values finally show a widespread homogenisation of the demographic trends throughout South India.

To understand the demographic breaks observed above, we have built up a map of sex-ratio which reflects the state of the demographic structure. We then combined this snapshot at the dawn of the new millennium with its evolution between 1991 and 2001 (See Fig. 6). This approach introduces supplementary elements which confirm the earlier hypotheses, but also reveals new situations: we find there, once again, the Mumbai-Kolkata axis, but the different zones on either side of this line are much

Figure 6 : Sex Ration 2001 and Evolution 1991-2001

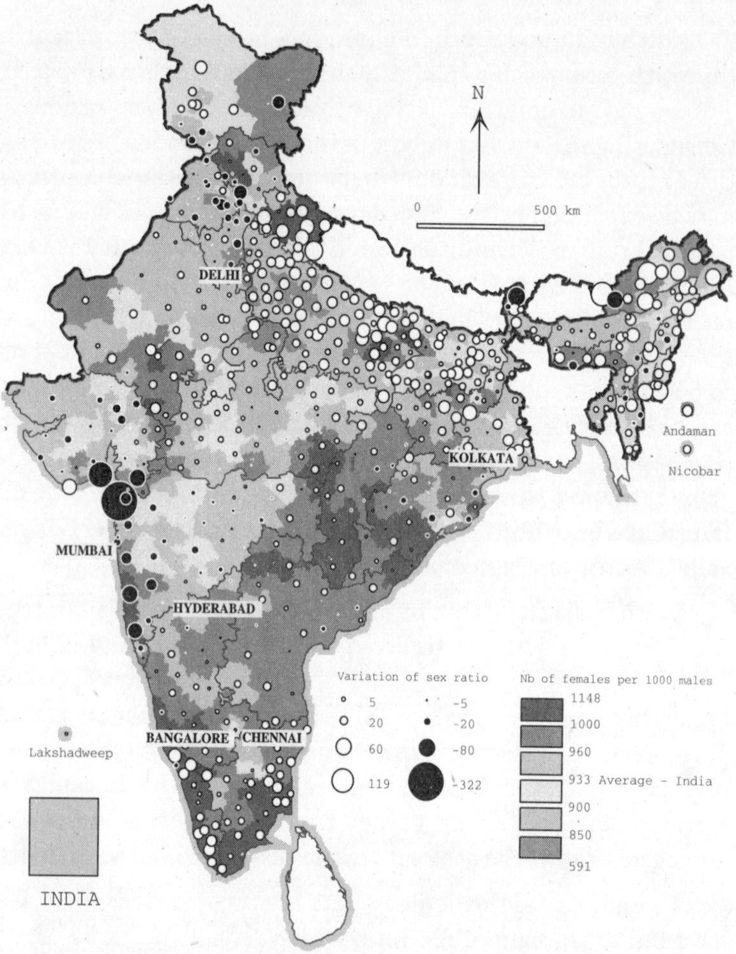

© Chapelet P. CSH, Leclerc E. UMR IDEES, 2002

Source: CENSUS OF INDIA 20C

less homogeneous (they result from a much longer time scale). The map unveils here all its relevance as a heuristic tool for research, underlining new trends outlines. Subject to verification that these results may not be artifacts of statistical analysis, this map could allow us to identify fieldworks for complementary investigations in order to understand these new trends. However, one of the main difficulties in analysing this map comes from explanatory elements of the observed variation of sex-ratio. Indeed, sex ratio variations not only indicate a gender inequality but can also highlight phenomenon like migrations, traditionally male migrations in India, which decrease female percentage in destination places and increase it in departure places. Because of the lack of datasets at this time, the inability to quantify the migration effects on sex-ratio is a restrictive factor in the understanding of observed phenomenon.

Firstly, the long term trend: while India's low sex-ratio confirms the sluggish trends described by Amartya Sen[7], we observe, nonetheless, some completely unexpected situations. Thus, there appears in the south-eastern part of Uttar Pradesh, north of Varanasi, a nucleus in which the sex-ratio values come close to the woman-man balance. More predictable is the case of the mountainous state of Uttaranchal where high number of females per male is a consequence of male migration towards the cities in the plains. Conversely, in the upper Ganges valley and right up to Haryana, the situation remains one of an imbalance disadvantageous to women. In the India of high sex-ratios, we face again the predictable cases of Kerala and Tamil Nadu, as also the tribal zone of Chhattisgarh. Andhra Pradesh, on the other hand, with a near-balanced situation, has not yet reached the records achieved by the neighbouring states, confirming the still-recent nature of the new demographic model which has not yet spread over the entire society. Maharashtra remains the state with the greatest contrasts, with the coastal areas reproducing the North-South model, and the hinterland which have not yet tilted towards the new demographic pattern.

Diachronic aspects of this map allow us to relativize the widely admitted North-South partition. If it confirms a trend of sex-ratio harmonisation, it also unveils unexpected reversals of trends. It throws up greater surprise as the zones of high sex-ratio progression do not tally with the geographical patterns described above. The situation becomes more favourable to women both in the Gangetic valley (except in Punjab and Haryana) as well as in the southern extremity of the peninsula (Kerala and Tamil Nadu). The former development signifies perhaps a reversal in trend heralding a demographic model merging with that of the South, while the latter is continuing its march towards feminisation.

The peculiarity of the two states that have been the forerunners of the Green Revolution (Haryana and Penjab), in which the man-woman gap is expanding, appears more clearly by using an indicator as sex-ratio evolution. Some more refined analyses have shown that this reversal in trend is particularly noticeable in the 0 to 6 years age group[8]. The transition towards a smaller family model is accompanied by a strengthening of the preference for the boy child. In spite of the presence of very strict regulation, the latest sex determination techniques are being used to verify the sex of the unborn child to eventually prevent its birth.

The most astonishing discovery is the West-East contrast in the middle Deccan, whereas the situation in Maharashtra deteriorates all along the coastal region, even in the south previously characterised by high sex ratio levels (>1000 women per male). Supplementary data might enable us to find similarities with the situation in Haryana and Punjab. In the eastern part of the Deccan, the male-female imbalance evolves only very slowly as is seen in Andhra Pradesh. The map also shows a divergent evolution between the tribal zones of the Deccan and those of the North-east, the latter witnessing a higher rate of catching up in favour of women while the former are stagnating. The combination of the sex ratio and of their evolution during the last decade therefore suggests some very complex situations that show the need to look beyond a simplistic North-South divide.

The maps, as a whole, draw a very qualified portrait of the one billion of India. The demographic transition, which appeared first in Kerala, is becoming a reality for the country as a whole but at very uneven speeds. Indeed, the BIMARU states seem to somewhat lag behind.[9] But divergent trends are not rare within these large masses. Some Southern states, such as Andhra Pradesh, seem to be catching up with their neighbours at an accelerated pace while Maharashtra appears to be marking time. Haryana and Punjab make one ponder over the impact of economic development on human development: better equipment and infrastructure does not necessarily translate into greater equality between men and women. Conversely, in Tamil Nadu and Kerala, more progressive socio-economic policies ensure the marriage age is being pushed back as well as that the man-woman balance is improving. A new family model is in the process of being forged with young women being married around the age of 22 and getting themselves sterilized at the age of 27/28, immediately after the birth of their second child. The idea of an Indian development model, therefore, needs to be viewed in its various dimensions, taking into account the uneven diffusion of new demographic behaviours. As C. Z. Guilmoto has demonstrated in a convincing manner with regards to demographic transition, the influence of local communities remains crucial when analysing these trends.[10]

Notes

1. Officials of India's Health Ministry and of the United Nations Population Fund (UNPF) selected the place, the time and the sex of the child, thus making Astha Arora the billionth individual in the country.
2. Census of India 2001, Provisional Population Totals. Series-1, Paper– 1 of 2001. Registrar General & Census Commissioner, India, 2001.
3. The difference between the provisional and the final results is not expected to exceed 1 per cent, that is, to say, a population, on March 1, 2001, of around 1.040 billion.
4. If we take note of just the 28 states, leaving aside the 7 Union territories, the surfaces vary by a ratio of 1 to 100 (Goa and Rajasthan) and the populations by 1 to 300 (Sikkim and Uttar Pradesh).

5. Except for an average increase of population pressure by 57 inhabitants per square kilometer (i.e. a general average of 324 persons/km^2).
6. The seven districts of New Delhi have been joined into a single whole as the urban population exceeds 70 per cent. On the other hand, the other areas carry less weight on the map as they are cut up into several administrative entities, or then their periphery merges into the adjacent rural districts.
7. Amartya Sen has pointed out this break-up of India into two parts and who has made use of the idea of the 'missing woman' by comparing the Indian sex-ratio to a normal sex-ratio of 1022 women to 1000 men so as to arrive at an assessment of the deficit between the two sexes. 'Many faces of gender inequality', Frontline, vol. 18, no. 22, 27 October-9 November 2001, pp. 4-14.
8. A. K. Nanda, J. Véron, 'Child sex ratio imbalances, son preference and fertility behavior in India: Recent evidence from Haryana and Punjab'. Unpublished paper presented at the seminar 'One billion Indians' organized by the INED (Institut National d'Etudes du Développement), 23 May 2002, Paris.
9. Denoting Bihar, Madya Pradesh, Rajasthan and Uttar Pradesh, 'bimaru' meaning 'sick' in hindi.
10. C. Z. Guilmoto., Rajan S. Irudaya, 'Spatial patterns of fertility transition in Indian districts', Population and Development Review, vol. 27, no. 4, December 2001, pp. 713-738.

Ascendancy of Lower Backward Castes in Indian Politics: Implications for Coalition Governments and Democracy

Girish Kumar

'The movement for change is not a struggle to end caste; it is to use caste as an instrument for social change. Caste is not disappearing, nor is casteism – the political use of caste – for what is emerging in India is a social and political system which institutionalizes and transforms but does not abolish caste'.

— Myron Weiner, 1999

The decade in focus here, the 1990s, will be remembered for several tumultuous happenings : the decline of the longest ruling party - the Congress and its near equivalent governmental stability ; the emergence of the Bharatiya Janata Party (BJP) as a key political player on the national scene and the corresponding rise of the coalition politics both at the centre as well as in states; the politics of economic (liberalisation and privatisation) and political reforms (*à la* seventy-third and seventy-fourth constitutional amendments) ; and to cap it all, the growing upsurge and ascendancy of the backward castes in politics. Although the 1967 Assembly elections had heralded an unfettered entry of backward castes (Other Backward Castes – OBCs in official parlance [1]) into state level politics (Frankel 1990: 251-52, 1991) their country-wide presence was felt only after the Janata Dal led minority coalition government came to power at the centre in 1989. The subsequent victory of the Janata Dal and similar political formations in several state Assembly elections in 1989 / 1990 as well as the acceptance of the Mandal Commission's recommendations (reservation of 27 percent seats for OBCs in central government services) accelerated the growing political clout of the ascending backward castes in India. In fact, the 1990s witnessed a massive horizontal mobilisation of backward castes leading to alignment and realignment of social forces. Clearly, the resurgence of the movement of OBCs was different from the co-option of ambitious lower caste elite as loyal subordinates to upper caste elite within the folds of the Congress party.

Slowly but gradually, the politics of elite accommodation, designed and perfected under the dominant Congress culture, has almost disappeared from the Indian political landscape. What has emerged on its place over the years is the growing power of hitherto disadvantaged backward castes, fiercely engaged in an open and democratic competition for capturing political and state power across the states and at the centre.

Considering their numerical strength[2] and its significance for the electoral outcome, no political party can afford to ignore them. Rather, practically all political parties try to appease them to win over their support. It is apparent from the fact that even a party like the BJP, to which the caste based political mobilisation was anathema until recently, was forced to choose a 'Lodha' – an upwardly mobile backward caste- leader, Kalyan Singh to head its first government (1996) in Uttar Pradesh, the most populous state in the country. By introducing a system of reservation for the extremely backward and most backward castes (EBCs and MBCs), the last BJP government in UP, though headed by an upper caste leader, Rajnath Singh confirmed the continuation of the same electoral strategy. Similarly, the Shiv Sena - the party which is given credit to form the first real non-congress government (in coalition with the BJP) in Maharashtra in 1995[3] - was forced to bring a Maratha leader, Narayan Rane to replace its Brahmin chief minister, Manohar Joshi on the eve of the next assembly elections, held in 2000. Even in a southern state like Kerala, widely known for its impressive social development records (in terms of the highest women literacy and lowest infant mortality rates and also for having the first elected Left Front government in 1957 itself) is not immune from what is referred to as the caste politics. The defeat of the Left Front in the latest Kerala Assembly elections held in March/April 2001 is also attributed to the alienation of 'Ezhwa' caste[4], which provide the bulk of the rank and file of the left parties in general, and the CPI (M) in particular.

Interestingly, the state of Tamil Nadu, where the anti-Brahminical movement started as early as in 1920s and where caste based contradictions were supposedly resolved long back, has lately woken up to the recent changes in its political equations following the emergence of the Pattali Makkal Katchi (PMK) in the state. This is primarily a party of MBCs who were not accommodated in the folds of both the DMK and AIADMK during the last four decades or so. In fact, given the deepening grip of lower castes, including OBCs, MBCs and EBCs over electoral politics during the last decade, a keen observer of the electoral scenario has described it as 'the distinct attribute of the 1990s', albeit with a caveat that reads 'if one goes by the popular accounts'(Yadav, 1999).[5]

The issues involved with the empowerment of OBCs are many; more so because of their varying strength and hold over the political power across the states. Against this backdrop, the paper will address the following questions: (a) To delineate the process of empowerment of the backward castes and to what extent they have been incorporated into the political system? (b) To what extent the policy of positive discrimination has facilitated the empowerment of MBCs and EBCs? (c) Why the increasing empowerment of lower backward castes has not led to policies and programmes aimed at creating economic opportunities and increasing their access to better education and health facilities? (d) What would be the implications of increasing polarization on caste basis for coalition governments and the democratic polity as a whole?

In terms of its scope the paper has limited ambition. Although a modest attempt would be made to give a pan-India picture, the study would be obviously focused on the developments taken place during the last decade in the Hindi heartland states. For, caste as a factor in politics, the southern states had witnessed long back. According to a leading political scientist, the phenomenon—the ascendancy of lower backward castes into politics and power—essentially represents a south Indianization of Indian politics (Varshney, 1996).

Political Empowerment

Although the present spate of political empowerment of lower castes has its origin in Mandal Commission's report, it is a century old phenomenon dating back to the British period.[6] After independence, the Constitution recognized the need of reservation for OBCs, but unlike the case of the Scheduled Castes (SCs) and Scheduled Tribes (STs), the specific measures to be adopted was left to commissions to be constituted by the Union government for the stated purpose. During the last five decades, however, only two Commissions were set up by the Union government. First in 1953, known as Kaka Kalelkar Commission[7] and the second was Mandal Commission, set up in 1978.[8]

It needs mentioning however that the state of Tamil Nadu (then Madras) had enunciated its reservation policy in 1950s itself.[9] Two decades later, Vokkaligas, a prosperous peasant caste in Karnataka claimed and received the benefits of a quota based reservation in 1971.[10] Prior to that, in 1966, the then Congress government in Andhra Pradesh headed by Brahma Nand Reddy had provided reservations 'for the backward classes of 25 percent to all degree granting courses and to posts in state government' (Frankel & Rao, 1989: 510).

Later, several other states had followed suit. Bihar, for instance, implemented its reservation policy in 1978.[11] In 1981, Gujarat went one step further as not only it constituted its second Backward Class Commission but quickly implemented its recommendations for an 18 per cent increase in then existing quota of 10 per cent, though the then state government was subsequently forced to withdraw the stipulated increase following a prolonged violent agitation against this decision. In the southern states, barring Tamil Nadu, the quota was by and large in tune with the size of the backward caste population (a state-wise reservation for OBCs is given in Appendix-I). On the other hand, such provisions do not exist in several states including Rajasthan, West Bengal etc; and of course, the north eastern states but excluding Assam.[12]

Who are these lower castes or the OBC (to put the lower castes in the Mandal Commission's language)? All the intermediary castes, placed between the upper castes and shudras (untouchables) are referred to as the OBCs.[13] Internally, these castes are also divided on sub- caste and class lines. The cultivating castes, including both landowners and tenants, among them are relatively prosperous, therefore upwardly mobile. On the other hand, there are service castes (carpenter, blacksmith, barber, oil-man, washer-man, potter etc.), shepherds, those who earn their living as agricultural labours, earth cutters and similar other menial occupations. They comprise about half of the total population in the northern states; they are 42 percent in UP and 52 percent in Bihar for instance.[14] As compared to these northern states, the numerical strength of OBCs, however, varies in the southern states since unlike north, "the 'twice-born' castes are represented almost entirely by Brahmins alone, and even their numbers were small" (Frankel, 1991:228).

Notwithstanding the numerical supremacy of the OBCs and SCc taken together, the upper castes have been dominating the politics and society in all respects, historically, culturally and economically. The upper castes are: Brahmins, Kshatriyas, Vaishyas/Banias and Kayasthas.[15] Their number as well as status also varies from one state to another.[16] For instance, Baniyas are not considered as an upper caste in Bihar, whereas they have occupied a prominent position in Gujarat politics and society.[17] This is true of UP too. For centuries, the caste- based hierarchical social order remained entrenched in the country.

The overall dominance of the upper castes started weakening only from the first quarter of the last century, largely because of the reform movements that brought awakening among the lower castes.

Nadars and Thevars in Tamil Nadu, Jats in western UP particularly, Marathas in Maharashtra, Vokkaligas and Lingayats in Karnataka, Patidars in Gujarat, Reddys in Andhra Pradesh etc were the first to challenge the domination of the upper castes (read Brahmins in southern states and Maharahtra, Brahmins and Baniyas in Gujarat, combined with Thakurs in UP) in their respective regions/states, to be joined later by Yadavs and Kurmis in UP and Bihar.

In Tamil Nadu, for instance, the Brahmins were the first to be exposed to the Western (read english) education which facilitated their entry into government jobs on a very large scale. The non-Brahmins followed the same route but, unlike Brahmins, they found their entry into government jobs blocked as Brahmins, comprising only 3 per cent of the total population under entire Madras presidency, had almost monopolized all the possible avenues of employment.[18] Other traditional discriminatory social practices targeted against the non-Brahmins, particularly the SCs were already in vogue. The ire against the Brahmins ultimately took the form of an anti-Brahmin movement led by the Justice party, later by the Dravida Kazgham (DK). The basic objective of this movement was to bring an end to the monopoly of the Brahmins over the possible avenues of vertical mobility in the society such as higher education, government jobs and other professions such as doctors, managers, contractors et. al. 'The anti- Brahmin movement provided impetus for legislative interventions to address issues of social justice and access to power for the backward communities; it dramatically pruned Brahmnical hegemony and dominance in post-colonial politics' (Hasan, 1998: 134; Frankel, 1991: 232). The DMK and AIADMK are off-shots of the original DK. This also led to the social mobilization of the backward castes such as Nadars (toddy tappers in southern states) who were mobilized to overcome their social backwardness (Manor, 1989; Washbrook, 1989).

In contrast to the south, the northern Indian states, more particularly the Hindi heartland did not witness an anti-Brahmin tirade for several reasons. First, instead of single upper caste dominance, here the resources and power were distributed among diverse group. Apart from Brahmins, there were Kshatriyas, Kaesthas, even Banias (vaishyas), as well as elite among Muslims such as Ashrafs. Second, this assorted group was also numerically large, comprising about one fourth of the total population. Third, the internal division among backward castes was another factor that prevented their horizontal social mobilization. In UP, for instance, 'the lower OBCs and Yadavs, Kurmis, and Lodhas were hostile to each other' because of their antagonistic economic interests. 'The latter were not economically exploited but they were deprived of political power' (Hasan, 1998: 135). The OBC leadership also emerged from these strata, therefore from the very beginning they were after capturing political power and using it to their own advantage (read property making). Their numerical preponderance worked as a magnet, attracting all political parties.

The non-Brahminical movements both in Tamil Nadu and Karnataka were not seeking radical changes, rather were aimed at gaining greater share in power structures such as bureaucracy, local bodies, state legislatures. Although the avowed objective of the Dravidian movement in Tamil Nadu was destruction of the caste system itself, in practice, however, 'it used caste as a means of political mobilization and ultimately increased the political importance of caste' (Washbrook, 1989: 207). In the same way the upper caste Congress leaders spoke against castes but went on creating caste specific vote banks. Gradually, it became an inalienable part of the democratic system and in the process, 'it created an incentive for political mobilization along the lines of caste, religion and language. Indian politics became the arena within which group identities were sharpened, and individuals sought material benefits through group membership. Factions and parties were often based upon these identities' (Weiner, 2001: 198). So much so that political leaders would vie with one another while invoking such group identities for their partisan ends. In sum, this turned out to be an unintended, 'unhappy outcome of the democratic process in the country' (Ibid.).

With their numerical strength, the upper castes, comprising 20 per cent of the total population in UP for instance (Hasan, 1998: 124; Frankel, 1991:230), maintained their hold over the Congress party, which was the main instrument of the political mobilization in the northern India. It managed to maintain its radical postures through the fifties by the abolition of *zamindari* in BIMARU states particularly.[19] The subsequent land reforms measures were not seriously implemented. Yet the Congress party succeeded in maintaining the illusion of openness of the democratic system. It must be emphasised, however, that the principal beneficiaries of the first phase of the land reforms measures were the former tenants among Jats, Yadavs ,Kurmis, Koeris, - all belonging to the upper crust of the backward castes. Interestingly, it was the legislatures of these caste groups that 'took the lead in blocking all subsequent attempts at reform designed to benefit the marginal farmers and the landless who usually also belonged to castes and groups further down the hierarchy' (Jain, M., 1996: 138). Their spokesman was Chaudhry Charan Singh who 'held that such moves would reduce efficiency in agricultural production' (Ibid.). It is worth noting that by then the Congress party had accommodated a broad spectrum of the OBCs, yet they were not given leadership position either in the government or in the party. 'In the 1962 Uttar Pradesh Legislative Assembly, for example, almost 63 per cent of the Congress MLAs belonged to the elite classes and only 6.8 percent of the backward castes. In the same year the Congress ministry in Bihar had 58 percent cabinet ministers from the forward castes and 8 per cent from the backward castes' (Jain, 1996:137).

Emergence of OBC Leadership

They emerged as an autonomous political force in 1967 only when the Congress riven with internal dissension for the first time lost in the fourth Assembly elections in as many as nine states, including all northern Indian states. The defeat of the Congress in the 1967 elections was largely due to its inability to accommodate the emerging political forces into its fold. 'Politically, the rise of the middle farmer was the single most important cause of the decline of the Congress in North India. Despite its electoral dependence on the forward castes, scheduled castes, tribes and minorities (Gopal Krishna, 1967: 55), till 1967 the party was also successful in incorporating sections of the backward castes even though they did not serve as its vote bank' (Jain, M., 1996: 41). Yet when Charan Singh, by then recognised as an important leader and the 'pre-eminent spokesman of the rural interests', left the Congress in 1967 on being denied chief ministership, the doors of the party remained open for these newly mobilized groups. At the same time, the Congress refused to give them primacy in the state politics (Ibid.).

The year 1967, however, turned out to be watershed in the backward castes' quest for power. It was for the first time that intermediate caste leaders took over as Chief Minister in Bihar (B.P. Mandal, Daroga Rai, Karpoori Thakur et. al), Haryana (Rao Birendra Singh), Madhya Pradesh (G.N. Singh) and Uttar Pradesh (Chaudhry Charan Singh).[20] The ministries headed by these backward castes leaders had had sizable presence of their caste brethrens. The backward castes, for instance, represented '30 per cent of the ministers in Charan Singh's government and 34 per cent of the B.P. Mandal's ministry in Bihar. Forty-five percent of the ministers in Rao Birendra Singh's government in Haryana were Jats' (Jain, M., 1996: 142). The presence of backward caste leaders as minister, no doubt, ensured the increasing 'participation of hitherto deprived groups, progressive and radical transformation has not been the defining feature of this upsurge, rather has produced an expansion of political participation and satisfied their craving for greater representation in government by changing the personnel of the government' (Hasan, 1998: 122).

The defeat of the Congress party in two most populous states, Bihar and UP, however, 'set the stage for a chaotic competition for power between rival politicians, factions and parties' - all fighting with each other in order to draw support from numerous lower castes. It finally led to a phase of political instability during 1967-1971. The Yadavas reaped maximum benefit of this fluid political situation as they cornered 'a larger share of ministerial posts in the name of all exploited groups. After all, the Yadavas had emerged as the second largest caste group after the Rajputs' (Frankel, 1991: 253). In the 1967 Bihar Vidhan Sabha, the numerical strength of Yadava MLAs was 11.6 per cent as compared to 17.2 per cent Rajputs (Robin, 2001).

The chief ideologue of the non-Congress coalition of the OBCs, Dr Ram Manohar Lohia, gave a socialist orientation to its activities which was rooted into twin programmes - promotion of Hindi and reservation for OBCs. However, the most important element of the process of empowerment of the lower castes has been the 'politicization and transformation of (lower) castes under the impact of competitive politics and democracy. This process is further encouraged by the vernacular political discourse, growth of Hindi and the ascendency of OBCs, whose main purpose, however, is not the abolition of caste system but the establishment of a political practice committed to the removal of upper castes from power and provision of special support in education and employment to caste-based deprived social groups. This has entrenched conflict between upper castes and OBC in the political system. This political process has provided a favourable ground for social mobilization, on the one hand, and intensification of conflicts, on the other' (Hasan, 1998: 122).

The struggle waged by the upcoming OBC leaders, not only in Bihar and UP alone, even elsewhere, had the following components: First, replace the upper castes as political leaders in the state legislatures; and second, through instruments of reservation weaken or dilute their 'monopoly over senior posts in the state services'. For, entry into these positions was perceived by the backward castes 'as the only avenue for overcoming the caste disabilities that prevented them from achieving equal dignity and power in society' (Rao and Frankel, 1989: 512).

In post-1967 period, the short lived Karpoori Thakur government in Bihar took a bold step by implementing reservation policy for OBCs in the educational and government services. Although his reservation policy (based on the Mungeri Lal Commission's recommendations) was basically meant for OBC, he also extended the benefits of reservation to women and the poor, irrespective of the caste they belonged to. In other words, he had tried to strike a balance by considering gender and class factors along with caste. Although Bihar witnessed a lot of anti-reservation backlash, Thakur took another step for the empowerment of OBCs; amidst widespread protests he made announcement for holding panchayat elections that was long over due.

True, he wanted to widen the social base of the (ruling) Janata party. But unlike the Congress party which had a long history of retaining power essentially through the prominent upper caste men with the elite among the OBCs, SCs & STs co-opted as their loyal subordinates, Thakur wanted to build the mass base of his party. He realized that political mobilization of the downtrodden of the society was a must and in order to do that he took the above mentioned two steps. In fact, he partly succeeded as large number of his supporters, whom he wanted to mobilize, won the panchayat elections by defeating the old, upper caste dominated panchayat office bearers. As he had to resign in 1979, he could not get time to pursue his policies. Yet his policies paid rich dividends in course of the Assembly and Parliamentary elections held between 1980 and 1985. For, it was noted that only Thakur's Lok Dal (an off-shoot of the Janata Party) managed to institutionalize itself with popular support base, i.e. institutionalization of the party as a strategy for mobilization of the under-privileged people (Blair, 1990: 133). It also confirms that his concern for panchayats had its roots in his anxiety to institutionalize the power base of rainbow coalition of the backwards.

In the post-1967 phase, almost similar attempts were made in Karnataka but, unlike in northern states, under the Congress dispensation, particularly when Devraj Urs was at the helm of affairs (1972-80). At first, at the cost of Lingayats and Vokkaligas (the two dominant peasant castes),[21] he favoured the lower castes, scheduled castes and Muslims by selecting their representatives as the Congress candidates. Then, in order to sustain a broad base coalition of the disadvantaged groups, Urs, like Karpoori Thakur, adopted the same strategy: reservation for the backward classes. Included among them, were the Muslims and virtually all castes, except the Lingayats, and it comprised also a range of welfare schemes for them (Frankel and Rao, 1989: 511).

The strategy for mobilisation is now completely changed, at least in northern Indian states. Its progenitor was Kanshi Ram, the founder of the (BSP) Bahujan Samaj Party. Subsequently, most of the backward caste leaders seem to have taken a cue from him. The BSP's only strategy has been 'to attack its opponents in as militantly and aggressively transparent a language as possible. It has spared no effort in being absolutely crude and unconventional in its electioneering and has restrained from wasting energy on efforts aimed at revolutionising the dalit social consciousness' (Maurya: 1996, cited in Pai, 1998). Kanshi Ram, equates political power with 'the key by which any lock can be opened' (Ibid.). As a matter of fact, practically all the formerly disadvantaged groups have sought upward mobility through incorporation in the established (politico-administrative) system, rather than through changing it. Accordingly, the strategies adopted by the lower caste leader involve the following steps :

- Reshuffle of bureaucracy to put the right kind of officers on key positions;[22]
- Installation of the statues of their icons;
- Renaming of universities, newly created districts or naming roads, parks, rural development/ social welfare schemes after a dalit/backward caste heroes/historical figures—all aimed at creating political fervour and sensitising masses;
- Heavy reliance on the state machinery to implement its agenda

- Public humiliation of senior officers to demonstrate how the upper caste establishment has been tamed, though this carefully crafted posture is often attributed to the arrogance/short tempered attitude of leaders (Kumar, 1999).

Practically all the chief ministers from mandal quota have resorted to these mechanisms. This includes Laloo Prasad Yadav, Mulayam Singh Yadav, Ram Naresh Yadav, Mayawati, even Jayalalita. Indeed, 'the election of Laloo Prasad Yadav or Mayawati has of course been of immense symbolic value for Indian society', a decisive step ahead of 1970s, when a politician like Jagjivan Ram, the longest serving SC cabinet minister in successive union governments, was denied the highest position in the country for 'no other discernable reason than an implicit upper caste consensus against him' (Kaviraj, 2000 : 113).

The strategy of caste based mobilization converges on control of the state machinery and such strategy can destabilize the political system but, to them, it appears necessary to achieve justice for lower caste groups. Even V.P. Singh, the former premier who is credited for 'mandalisation' of Indian politics, had candidly confessed it: 'Through Mandal I knew we were going to bring in changes in the basic nature of power. I knew I was not giving jobs, Mandal is not an employment scheme, but I was seeking to replace people in the instrument of power through the use of governmental power'(Mustafa, 1993).

Empowerment of MBCs and EBCs

Described variously as MBC (most backward castes), EBC (extremely backward castes) or lower backward castes, a host of such social groups are still deprived of representation, if not participation. Owing to their profound social and economic deprivation the most backward castes failed to reap the benefits of the reservation per se. An overwhelming proportion of them still happen to be landless, as they were centuries ago, and to a large extent they are still to come out of their traditional occupations with which they had gained their identity long back... Included among them are large numbers of service castes such as *Dhobis* (washermen), *Lohars* (blacksmiths), *Gadarias* (shephards), *Kumhars* (pottery makers), *Kewats* (boatmen), *Nai* (barbers), *Madari* and *Nat* (nuts), *Sonar* (goldsmith), *Vanniars*, etc. In fact, as compared to MBCs, several castes among SCs are in better placed conditions–thanks to the reservation available to them for a long period.

In the north, during the last two decades a substantial chunk of neo-rich have emerged from the upper layer of OBCs, such as Yadavs, Kurmis and Koeris, particularly in Bihar and the eastern part of UP. The Yadavs, as we have noted earlier, had emerged as the second largest group (comprising 11.6 per cent of total MLAs) in the Bihar Assembly in 1967. A decade later, in 1977, they accounted for 15.4 per cent of the total legislators and by 1980, they earned the distinction of being the single largest caste group(13.8 per cent while the corresponding figure for Rajputs had come down to 11.4 per cent) in the Assembly. In the 1985 Assembly elections 41 Yadav MLAs (out of total 324) were elected. In 1990 and 1995 Assembly, the strength of Yadav MLAs reached to 19.1 and 25.8 per cent respectively. Only in 2000 election, their position was reduced to 20.7 per cent. Besides, during the last three decades, four Yadav chief ministers, including the current incumbent have presided over the destiny of Bihar (Jain, 1996:146-148; Robin, 2001). Over the years, they have become part of the patronage network, making them able to siphon off development funds. Earlier this role of the middle men was played by the upper castes, they are now replaced by the OBCs. Again, within the ranks of the OBCs, as long as the Kurmis and Koeris were willing to play the role of second fiddle, the caste equations worked well. But as soon as they sought parity with Yadavs in running the affairs of the state, crack started appearing in their informal ties. For, the Yadav leadership was not prepared to share political power with them at the state level. In a way, Yadavs tried to treat other backward caste leadership the same way upper castes had treated them, i.e. forcing them to accept the subordinate role. Summing up the treatment they received within the folds of the Janata Dal, Nitish Kumar, the foremost leader of Kurmis who was instrumental in the formation of the Samata party, argued: 'The entire backward castes along with Muslims voted for the Janata Dal. Was there any need to search for a core group among the OBCs? Laloo is a casteist, a neo-Brahmin who wants to make his caste-the Yadavs - the nucleus of his support, and others are simply doomed to be on periphery' (*Pioneer*, 5 February 1995, cited in Jain, 1996: 149).

Why do they do so? 'Caste majorities are by nature permanent', argues a perceptive analyst, 'and obviously any permanent majority would make democracy unbearable for other groups', which is akin to what Tocqueville had described as 'elective despotism'. In essence, exercise of political authority acquired through caste based mobilization has often been to 'deny access to others rather than make it universal' (Kaviraj, 2000: 110-111). This explains the split in the Janata Dal in Bihar and emergence of the Samata party with Kurmis and Koeris on the forefront. This also means that the process of the political empowerment of the lower castes is a long drawn and it would not be completed unless all the caste groups are accommodated in the political system. The recent happenings in the eastern part of the state confirm the trend.

The 1995 Assembly elections in Bihar for the first time witnessed a different kind of polarization of castes which was 'not on the lines of the upper and backward caste divide but it was around the two axes of backward caste politics' (Kumar, 1999). Among the upwardly mobile OBCs, the Kurmis and Koeris had switched over their loyalty to the newly formed Samata party, once they realised that their proportionate representation in the political system was not going to be honoured by the Yadav driven Janata Dal. Moreover, for the first time the upper castes found themselves totally marginalized. Interestingly, the same Laloo Yadav, the supremo of the Janata Dal, who had received flack for neglecting the development and by extension, not doing any thing to improve upon the economic condition of the poor, received maximum support from the poor? Why did poor vote for him? For many of them, he was largely instrumental in bestowing '*izzat*' (self respect/honour) to them. In a major election survey conducted in Bihar, many backward caste voters candidly confessed that their material condition had not improved during the first five years of Laloo Yadav's regime but they had preferred to vote for him second time (1995) since now upper caste people could not dare abuse them. Many of them (backward caste voters) had for the first time in their life saw a ballot paper and voted also (CSDS, 1995). This also explains that why after a division within the folds of backward castes, Laloo Yadav still holds the key to power. Most importantly, the formation of the Samata party, with Kurmi and Koeris on the fore front, has demonstrated that if caste specific groups want their voices to be heard, they have to form their own party; they must have their own leader. It is on this count the MBCs suffer the most; they neither have their own political party nor their own established leader, not even proxy leader.

The lower backward castes or the MBCs constitute about 32 per cent of the total population in Bihar (Blair, 1980) It comprises more than hundred backward castes (104 out of total 128 backward castes) such as *Mallahs* (fisher folk), *Kahars* (pumpkin carriers/ water men), *Nunia*/ *Beldars* (earth cutters), *Lohars* (blacksmiths), *Tatwa* (Hindu weaver), *Teli* (oil men), *Hajjam / Nai* (barber) etc. No doubt, they are dotted throughout the state but numerically they are large in the eastern part of Bihar, such as Katihar, Naugachia, Purnea, etc. In the northern part of the state, they are concentrated in a few districts such as Madhubani and Sitamarhi. Fisher folks among them is relatively numerous and they also have a state level leader - Captain Jai Narain Nishad.

Similarly, since 1993, a few MBC leaders[23] are engaged in organising *rath yatra* in the eastern districts particularly, to raise the awareness of communities living at the lower rung of society. It should be noted that the formation of the Samata party too was preceded by a '*kurmi chetna maha-rally*', organised at Patna. In order to impress upon the masses they [Samata leaders] had proclaimed it as a party of '*Lav* and *Kush*' (the twin sons of Lord Ram and Sita; interestingly, they ended by becoming a junior ally of the party that swears by the name of Ram, that is, the BJP).

Ostensibly, the purpose is the same, that is, to raise the consciousness of EBCs and ensure their mass mobilisation. In sum, they are preparing the ground for the empowerment of the most backward caste people. But there is a difference, that is, the emphasis is on community; they are not focussing on a particular caste. Their slogan is '*Jat se Jamat ki Or*' ('Moving away from the idea of specific caste identity to their community').[24] There could be two possible reasons for the same. One, unlike Yadavs or Kurmis-Koeris combine, a single caste or even a group of most backward castes does not have adequate numerical superiority over the others within this category of castes to claim the leadership. Two, the emerging leadership is also cautious not to rake this issue, recalling the way Janata Dal and Samata party had cheated the most backward castes as a whole (if OBCs other than Yadav could not find respectable place in the Janata or the Rashtriya Janata Dal, they were treated the same way by the Samata party which is monopolised by the Koeri-Kurmi combine). Otherwise, the medium is the same, so is the message: that they have to unite; close ranks and sink differences; they are told about their numerical strength and also that over the years they were cheated by the party of the forward castes, read the Congress. Even the upper backward castes have just used them but have not given them their due share.

This is true of the Tamil political system where the Dravidian parties have remained in power since 1967. The scheduled castes are still at the receiving end, notwithstanding their relatively improved economic condition, at least a section of them who have availed benefits of reservation have moved upwards. Ironically, those SCs who rose to occupy key positions in local level institutions like panchayats, thanks to the 73rd constitutional amendment that ensured reservations for SCs & STs in panchayati bodies, are facing ire of the dominant peasant castes like Thevars. Even some of the SC Sarpanchas who went to play an active role - duly ordained by the constitution - were brutally murdered by the de facto holders of power in the rural areas in the state (Panchayati Raj Update, October 1995). To cap it all, the rise of the Pattali Makkal Katchi (PMK- literally it means a party of the toiling masses and it essentially represents Vanniyars, one of the most backward castes in the state) has become an added factor in the Tamil electoral politics.

The PMK was launched in early 1980s as 'Vanniyar Sangam' in the northern part of Tamil Nadu. But then it should be recalled that apart from Vanniyars, Dalits and Muslims (both having sizeable presence in this part of the state) were also brought into its fold. However, once the Sangam succeeded in winning over a substantial chunk of Vanniyars in a decade or so, it gradually started neglecting its two other constituents. In late 1980s , it re-christened itself as PMK. By alienating the Dalits from its fold, this party not only has consolidated its base among Vanniyars, it has rather fought dalit's assertion in its base area. The Muslims, on the other hand, could not pose a challenge to it because they are confined to a couple of districts only. In 1998, the PMK aligned itself with the BJP. The PMK's complete hold over the Vanniyars, however, was amply demonstrated in the 2001 Assembly elections when it succeeded in transferring its vote in favour of the AIADMK led front, capturing a large number of seats in as many as six districts, out of eight, in the northern Tamil Nadu. 'It has now become unambiguously clear that the Vanniyars in northern Tamil Nadu hold the key for the success of any alliance' (Thirunavukkarasu, 2001). A more than willing gesture of both the DMK and AIADMK to forge electoral alliance with the PMK during the successive parliamentary and assembly elections since 1995 testify to the growing clout of the Vanniyars led party. It also confirms the similar pattern of the mobilisation of the deprived sections of the society.

Most importantly, the rise of PMK has once again re-established the fact that such mobilization helps a particular social group to corner maximum benefits. This also shows that once a group becomes visible and demonstrates its capacity to capture the votes of the group it stands for, it starts treating the other groups below it in the caste hierarchy the same way it was treated earlier by the superior caste groups. If this on-going political mobilization of hitherto excluded groups has led to the birth of caste-specific, small localised parties, it has also resulted into a depletion of votes for larger parties.

Interestingly, in southern Tamil Nadu the dominant OBC communities like Thevars, Nadars, and Yadavs (all belonging to the upper crust of OBCs) form the support base of the AIADMK. On the other hand, some other OBCc like Kallars, Udayars and Vellas are distributed among all the major parties of the state. Similarly, the Telugu speaking Naidus, along with a few other OBCs, comprise the MDMK which was formed by an expelled leader of the DMK. Besides, the Left parties are firmly rooted among the landless labourers belonging to Dalit communities. The point to be noted here is that the 1960s witnessed the assertion of the backward communities, notably Thevars in the state. In the next two decades their political mobilization and consolidation of votes reached its peak, giving way to political formations of other backward castes. The parties like the PMK, Pudhiya Tamizhagam (PT), Makkal Tamil Desam (MTD) are testimony to this fact. The former is the party of Dalits whereas the latter belongs to the Yadavs. It also needs mentioning that during the last two decades the southern region of Tamil Nadu has witnessed many caste riots and Pallars — a Dalit community having sizeable presence in this region — has been among its worst victims. The PT is essentially a party of Pallars.

That EBCs are rising, it is a fact now. It is not a coincidence that both the BSP and RJD have an EBC cell within their folds. In fact, after the formation of the Samata party, the impression was gaining ground that a section of EBCs might desert the Janata Dal.

In order to forestall such eventuality, Laloo Yadav went to induct six EBC leaders as members of the Legislative council. Further, of the remaining 9 per cent ST quota, (following the bifurcation of Bihar, the Scheduled Tribe quota was sliced from ten to one percent), four percent was reallocated to MBCs, three percent to OBCs, and the rest one percent was added to the SC quota (Bihar Times, Patna; 25 May 2001). All these steps are obviously directed at mollifying MBCs and keeping them in good humour. But the fact remains that in all likelihood MBCs may not rest until they form a party of their own. After all, the game is to capture the state power, if not alone, then in association with other social groups. It is equally clear to them that larger is the strength of their own legislatures, greater would be the size of their cake, i.e. the benefit accruing from the state power.

Evidently, the objective of capturing the state power is property making. This is what the upper castes have done and so have the upper OBCs. If the EBCs follow the same route, it would not be surprising. Rather, that would be quite natural for them since unlike the forward and upper backward castes, a great majority of them do not own any asset, including land. In fact, given their level of deprivation for generations down the line, majority of them have no sense of what is called the ownership right. Or, what it means to own something.

Recent developments in Uttar Pradesh

Apart from Bihar, UP is another state in the Hindi heartland which is in the vortex of the caste politics. Again, here is a state where OBCs have a party of their own called Samajwadi Party (SP) led by Mulayam Singh Yadav. The same is true of Dalits; they have the Bahujan Samaj Party (BSP). But the fact is that the SP is monopolised by the Yadavs/Ahirs and the Jatavs/Chamars control the BSP, leaving a large number of other backward and scheduled castes out of the frame of these parties. Not surprisingly, the fear of numerically insignificant backward castes being swamped by the dominant castes has led to the formation of caste specific parties such as Apna Dal and Pragatisheel Manav Samaj Party in the post-Mandal phase.[25] Although these parties are small and confined in the eastern part of the state, their vote share has steadily increased during the last decade (SG, 1999). All these factors have led to an intense polarisation of votes on caste lines in the state. Consequently, no political party has been able to gain majority in any Assembly elections held in post-Mandal phase: in 1991 (May-June), 1993 (November),1996 (September-October), 1999 (January- February) and the last, in 2003 (February). So far only certain caste groups have cornered maximum benefits of reservation in the government services. In order to end the virtual monopoly of these caste groups patronised by the SP and the BSP, the Rajnath Singh led (last) BJP government made an abortive attempt to introduce a more equity–based quota system as recommended by the Social Justice Committee.[26]

According to this Committee report, the Yadavs, for instance, have disproportionately availed 34 per cent of reservation benefits whereas they comprise only 19 per cent of the total population in UP. Much more than Yadavs, Jatavs have virtually monopolised all the benefits meant for the SC quota. Within SC category also, '22 dominant Dalit castes constitute 56 per cent of the total Dalit population in the country and the remaining 44 per cent account for about 1000 small castes. This makes it strategically easier for these more numerous castes to carve out a disproportionate share of reservation for themselves. Thus the Chamars (Jatavs and Kureels), the Malas, the Ramdasias (mazbis) and the Mahars more or less monopolise the benefits given to the Dalit population in UP, Andhra, Punjab and Maharashtra, respectively (Kumar, 2001).

Accordingly, the UP government proposed to divide the omnibus list of other backward castes into three separate lists by putting them in three distinct categories—OBCs, MBCs (most backward castes) and EBCs (extremely backward castes). Likewise, by introducing a list of the most backward scheduled castes (MBSCs), the SCs were also divided into two categories. Although the Committee 'recommended a one percent increase in overall reservations for OBCs, the reservation pie has now been trifurcated : with the Yadavs and the Ahirs being given a mere five percent. The rest has been divided into Most Backward (9 per cent) and Extreme Backwards (14 per cent) categories. Similarly, the Jatavs have been restricted to a ten percent share in reservations for scheduled castes'(Ibid.).

If one goes by the logic of the affirmative action, then there was nothing wrong with this step. Although the government was blamed for running with break-neck speed in completing the whole exercise, a political motive was attributed to it; all the more rather since updated caste based census details are not available. Besides, a proper yardstick is yet to be found to distinguish extremely and most backward from just backwards only. It may be noted that practitioners of the caste based politics always want to maintain such ambiguities which prompt them to oppose caste census. Notwithstanding these shortcomings, however, there was a merit in this initiative of the BJP government in UP. No doubt, with this step, the BJP put both the SP and BSP in a difficult situation. In the proposed scheme of things, quota had been reduced for both Yadavs and Jatavs who separately wield the baton for these two parties respectively. Yet, fearing the resentment of the rest of backwards and scheduled castes, neither of them could afford to oppose this move of their common foe.

The reservation system for SCs was introduced half a century ago but only a very small segment of this category reaped its maximum benefits. It is also true of the OBC category, though the quota system for them was introduced about a decade ago. In fact one of the major drawbacks of the Mandal Commission was that it did not try to distinguish between the more backward and less backward castes.[27]

The Yadavs , for instance, were the 'least backward as they were relatively richer, had access to power because of their numerical preponderance and were educated. Small wonder that they began cornering the benefits of the 27 per cent reservation for the other backward castes' (editorial in the *Indian Express*, 3 September 2001). It is more or less true of Jatavs among SCs in the state. So far, the OBC leaders have managed to ward off such initiatives. Even, the directive of the Supreme Court to identify the creamy layer from within the OBC category and remove them from the purview of reservations has not been honoured by many states.

The reverberations of the steps taken by the UP government will not remain unnoticed in the Andhra Pradesh where the Madigas, along with the Rallies and the Adi-Andhras have for long demanding a separate sub-quota for themselves within the general SC quota. It should be noted that the Malas, like Jatavs in UP, the most dominant Dalit caste in Andhra, has disproportionately cornered the reservation benefit.

Untouched Sources of Inequalities

The mobilization of lower castes through electoral politics has, to a large extent, reduced the traditional caste discrimination. However, an overwhelming percentage of lower caste, particularly MBCs and EBCs people somehow eke out their living as there has hardly been any improvement in their economic condition. Nevertheless they seem to draw satisfaction from symbolic acts of their leaders.

As legislatures, they are empowered to enact reform legislations and execute them through state agencies. But this does not seem to be happening. What could be the possible reasons ? Why their leaders have not touched the institutional sources that breed inequality in society, such as access to education and health, nutrition and literacy etc.?

The money spent (measured in terms of rupee per capita) on primary education, for instance, in Tamil Nadu and Karnataka, the two southern states where the lower castes rose to power earlier than the northern ones, are not more than those of Gujarat and Maharashtra (Weiner, 2001 : 213). Similarly in Andhra Pradesh, where the non-Brahmin Telugu Desam party is in power, the corresponding figures are very low. In UP, when a Dalit woman rose to occupy the post of chief minister, she did hardly any thing to improve the primary education system for SC children, instead she used state resources, manpower and materials for the construction of Dr Ambedkar's statute in thousands of villages. In Bihar, a Yadav chief minister had earlier played all gimmicks in the name of promoting social justice but did precious little for the economic uplift of the lower castes. It is equally true of a Lodha chief minister in UP. 'The middle classes within the lower castes promoted their own interests and for the rest there was little more than the psychological benefit promised by the Mandal Commission' (Ibid.).

Apparently, backward castes leaders usually manage to get what they want and even that too at the cost of their poor brethren. For instance, a great majority of backward caste people happen to be agricultural labourers, tenants and small landholders. Yet their leaders do not demand hike in daily wages or credit facilities for marginal peasants or tenancy reforms. On the contrary, they demand subsidies for fertilizers, irrigation, electricity, pesticides or increase in procurement prices of food grains. For the very simple reason that their leaders-come usually from the better off among the peasant proprietor families. In sum, it is the rich landowning Yadavs, Kurmis and Koeris who have reaped material benefits of reservation whose interest clash with the poor, agricultural labourers of their communities. 'By emphasizing the importance of caste political solidarity the richer peasants among the OBCs mobilise the poor section of their castes to further their own class interests' (Weiner 2001, 214). This is not to deny the implementation of welfare programmes by several state governments. But the fact remains is that Dalit politicians, bureaucrats, political parties or Dalit associations 'have had little impact on public policies' (Ibid.).

Structural reforms aimed at attacking the very roots of inequality have not figured on the agenda of backward castes.

What they have managed instead is to incorporate formerly excluded groups into establishment and allowed the diversion of public resources to their benefits. This is illegal, unlawful but they do not care, to them it is the easiest and shortest route to enrich them (Hasan, 2000: 172). Indeed, 'the process of wealth creation is in itself apt to be pursued by cornering political power and government contracts, grabbing land and distribution of largesse' (Rangrajan, *Seminar*, January 1997).

It also needs mentioning that during a very long pre-reform period, when the authority and powers of the state were constantly increasing with matching resources at its command, the state could do very little to remove the inequality of this type. Now in the era of economic reform the 'resources and legal authority to act upon these sectors are being wrenched from the state's grip', the symbolic politics of this kind will be equally ineffective' (Kaviraj, 2001: 114).

Over the years, 'the politics of lower caste assertion has, in a sense, retreated from a more mundane reformism to a spectacular exchange of symbolic acts. Symbolic exchanges do not have the power to affect the level of primary distribution of access goods, concentrating on a spectacular redistribution of prestige on a very small scale. Thus this politics can create enormous spectator interest through the parliament and media, but the satisfaction drawn by lower caste groups is primarily symbolic and episodic. It does not touch the institutional sources which reproduce inequality in society' (Ibid.).

Implications

The on-going process of the political empowerment of the OBCs, which started in late 1960s, reached its crescendo during the last decade. In most of the states, the OBC (and SC in case of UP) leaders came to occupy the centre stage of politics earlier monopolised by the upper caste politicians. The process is yet to be completed since the political churnings have brought to the fore new claimants of power. In their quest of power, these new claimants - the MBCs / EBCs - have adopted the same strategy what OBCs had deployed earlier. But unlike the upper crust of backward castes, the MBCs comprise numerous small groups and they are equally divided among themselves. So far their leadership has not emerged from their ranks who could articulate their grievances. They have not been able to economically assert themselves either. This explains why they lack social and political empowerment. The experiences of upper OBCs have shown that economic empowerment follows political empowerment. The question arises here is: what is the road map of the MBCs empowerment?

There are two possible routes of the political empowerment of a caste group. One, the natural emergence of political leadership from within its own fold; and two, the political system creates leadership from the select groups, albeit for its partisan ends. In case of MBCs both routes are likely to be followed. We have noted earlier that the mobilization of these numerous but small groups have already begun, though on a small scale and confined to small pockets/certain regions e.g., eastern part of Bihar and UP, even northern Tamil Nadu for that matter. Given the social churnings it is likely to intensify in other parts of the country.

The Rajnath Singh led BJP government's move to enlist support of MBCs and a section of Dalits , however, failed because a stay order was clamped by the Supreme court (*Indian Express*, 5 June 2002). However, a major chunk of the marginalised sections of both the OBCs and SC caste groups have already aligned themselves with the parties of the upper Hindu castes like the BJP and the Congress. The electoral compulsions will also force other parties, such as SP and BSP, to give due representations, if not equal, to upcoming local level MBC leaders. Therefore, after a couple of more Assembly elections, there would be sizeable numbers of MBC legislatures. Bihar will not be far behind. Not even Andhra Pradesh and Maharashtra where similar demands have already been made.

What would be its implications for the coalition government in the centre? And, by extension on the democratic process in the country? The widening of reservation policy that aims at providing proportionate benefits to numerous social groups in itself, at least immediately, is not going to affect the coalition government at the centre.

The reasons are obvious. First, no political party can afford to oppose this policy, even if it goes against their immediate interest. It is one of the compulsions of electoral politics, or call it political expediency, that they have to fall in line. This includes practically all the minor or major constituents of the ruling NDA. Second, even if it goes contrary to the immediate interest of the upper castes which otherwise dominate the BJP, they, like other constituents of the NDA, will succumb to the demands of electoral equations. Third, if the outcome of Assembly elections due in 2003 would necessitate internal re-arrangements, that would be done without any major problem. The formation of the BSP-BJP coalition government in UP following the 2002 Assembly election is a pointer to this direction[28]. After all the BJP or its alliance partners, none has any moral compunctions in accepting/rejecting any thing at the cost of their lust for political power. Ideology has already been pushed to backwaters by the Indian political class to the extent that politics today stands for nothing or, to put differently, for anything.

Now, as far as the democratic processes are concerned, it would become more flexible rather bent to accommodate the up-coming social forces. By nature and inclinations too, these hitherto oppressed social groups are not democratic, nor do they believe in equality either, therefore they would bend the rules, as their predecessors and role models have had done earlier, to use political power to make property. Or to do whatever suits their convenience. So in the immediate course of the political march of the most and extremely backward castes, there is every possibility of democracy reduced to the level of farce, more blatant and crude in its form. But in the long run the political mobilisation and consequent empowerment of these hitherto politically excluded castes might help deepen and consolidate democracy in this country. After all, once this long march is completed there would not be any need to create enabling conditions of empowerment since by then everybody would become honoured participant in the political game. Rather, they would like to see the game gaining respectability, therefore, the rule of law, which is the first causality of the political expediency, would be uphold supreme by the players.

Postscript (February, 2004)

The political fight for the reservation pie has lately taken a strange turn with the two biggest mainstream parties- the Congress and the BJP- seem to be scrambling with each other in alluring the gullible voters. Months before the assembly elections last year (December 2003), the Rajasthan government decided to bring Jats within the folds of the OBCs. The Madhya Pradesh government enhanced the OBCs quota to 27 percent. Both these governments were ruled by the Congress party. The former (Rajasthan government) also urged the Centre to consider 14 percent reservation for economically poor amongst the upper caste population. This proposition was accepted by the BJP led government in the Centre (but at the behest of the BJP Rajasthan unit) and in fact, the Vajpayee government also announced (before the dissolution of the parliament in late January 2004) to set up a panel to consider this issue. Prior to that the Brahmins particularly in Rajasthan took a lead in voicing the despondency among upper castes whose resources, both political and material have dried up over the years following the ascendancy of the backward castes. "Education was our forte but now, with reservation for OBCs and Dalits, our meritorious students can not get into colleges even with 90 percent plus marks, while less bright students from other castes make the grade... Likewise, jobs are hard to come by. Even traditional sources of livelihood have dried up, with the Supreme Court ruling that non-Brahmins can perform poojas in temples", to quote the president of the *Brahmin Arakshan Manch* (Brahmin Reservation Forum) (*Outlook*, February 3, 2003).

Appendix-I

Details of Reservation for OBCs in States & Union Territories

State	% of Reservation
Andhra Pradesh	25
Assam*	15
Bihar	26
Goa	27
Gujarat	27
Haryana**	27
Himachal Pradesh	N.A.
Jammu & Kashmir	N.A.
Karnataka	32
Kerala	N.A.
Madhya Pradesh	14
Maharashtra***	30
Orissa****	27
Punjab	12
Rajasthan	21
Sikkim	21
Tamil Nadu	69
Uttar Pradesh	N.A.
West Bengal	05
Andaman & Nicobar Islands	N.A.
Chandigarh	27
Daman & Diu	N.A.
Delhi	27
Dadar & Nagar Haveli	27
Lakshadweep	—
Pondicherry	27

Source: Ministry of Social Justice & Empowerment (Official Circular, no. 20012/1/2001 - BCC, dated 23 August 2001), Government of India.

* Among seven north-eastern states, reservation for OBCs is provided only in Assam.

** This is applicable in case of Class III & IV posts but for Class I&II posts, it is restricted to 10 per cent only.

*** Here Vimukta Jatis and Nomadic Tribes are clubbed with OBCs.

**** The matter was sub-judice in Orissa High Court.

Notes

1. The lower castes, placed in between the upper castes and scheduled castes (a term used for Dalits, described as untouchables in ancient Hindu texts, though Mahatma Gandhi gave them another name – Harijan, people/children of the God), in Hindu social hierarchy are described variously as backward castes, other backward castes (OBCs). They are also referred to as 'intermediate or middle castes' because of their middle level placement in the caste hierarchy. Again within this category, there are dozens of castes who vary from each other in all respect. Some are more educated, relatively well developed, propertied, exposed to the outside world and long back they moved out to join secular professions, as against the traditional caste based occupations which the poor, the most backward castes are still condemned to live with. In the official parlance, however, they are described as OBCs. Here, in this paper they are described interchangeably both as OBCs and backward/ lower castes. Besides, to distinguish the most or extremely backward castes, another term MBCs or EBCs have been used. Why caste has remained the axis of politics in India or why is it so much caste focused or, for that matter, whether the caste as a factor in politics is a continuing theme in the Indian politics or lately there is an upsurge of backward castes, including the Dalits in politics – all these issues have remained controversial. The practitioners of caste- politics as well as scholars are divided on this issue. Even there is a section which finds the use of caste in politics as a slur, carrying of primordial identities as opposed to any modern identity and they tend to dismiss the term 'caste' as an anomaly in the discourse on democratic politics. Sociologists, social anthropologists, political scientists, historians - all have looked at this unique traditional institution of caste in their own way. As such there is a plethora of writings on the subject. For a quick grasp of the subject, see, Rajni Kothari (1971), Caste in Indian Politics is an excellent reading on the subject. The same is true of M. N. Srinivas (1996), Caste: Its Twentieth Century Avatar , Francine A. Frankel and M.S.A. Rao (1989), Dominance and State Power in Modern India: Decline of Social Order. All these books are edited volumes. The list, as mentioned earlier, is exhaustive.

2. The exact numerical strength of the backward castes is not available for the simple reason that they are not counted as a separate population category in Census operations. In fact, the methodology adopted by the Mandal Commission to estimate the population size of OBCs was not scientific, therefore, remained controversial. While commenting on this aspect of the Mandal Commission, Radhakrishna wrote (1996: 207): " Its estimate of OBC population is a hotchpotch, arrived at by subtracting from 100 the population percentages for SCs, STs and non-Hindus (22.56 and 16.16 respectively) as per the 1971 Census, and the percentage for 'forward Hindus' (17.58) as extrapolated from the incomplete 1931 Census, and adding to this derived sum (43.7) about half of the population percentage for non-Hindus (8.4) (see

Government of India 1980, Part I:56)". It is roughly estimated, however, that OBCs comprise anywhere between 40-50 percent of the total Indian population. And state-wise their numerical strength varies; rather the percentage of OBC population is relatively on higher side in the southern states.

3. The first non-Congress (coalition) government formed in 1979 was led by Sharad Pawar, then leader of a break away group of the Congress which after sometime merged with the mother party. It was essentially a Congress government, though its outer appearance was temporarily modified.

4. See, Amrith Lal, "Why Kerala is not Bengal', Indian Express (Delhi edition), 16 May 2001.

5. Going beyond this popular belief, the author has given an account of what has been happening in electoral arena since the first general election held in 1952 wherein the caste of the candidates would be a deciding factor in distribution of party tickets. See, Yogendra Yadav (1999).

6. For the origin of backward classes educational categories in Tamil Nadu, see, P. Radhakrishnan (1990a).

7. Article 340 of the Constitution authorizes the President of India to set up a commission 'to investigate the conditions of socially and educationally backward classes, and to make recommendations to improve their condition'. The first backward class commission was appointed on 29 January 1953. It was headed by Kaka Kalelkar. Inter alia, the commission 'was to determine the criteria for identification of the backward communities'. The commission adopted the following criteria: a) Low social position in the traditional caste hierarchy of Hindu society; b) Lack of general educational advancement among the major section of a caste or community; c) Inadequate or no representation in government services; and d) Inadequate representation in the field of trade, commerce and industry'. On this basis the commission identified 2399 backward castes in the country and appended a list of them with its report submitted in 1955. Interestingly, the members themselves were not unanimous in accepting 'caste as a basis for backwardness' or considering economic determinants, the union government did not act upon the report. For details see, Dahiwale (2000).

8. For a quick review of the reservation policy of the Government of India as per the Mandal Commission recommendation, see, Kameshwar Chaudhry (1990), also see, B. Sivarammaya, 'The Mandal Judgement: A Brief Description and Critique' and P. Radhakrishnan, 'Mandal Commission Report: A Sociological Critique' in Srinivas (ed.) (1996), and Seth (2000), 'Changing Terms of Elite Discourse: The Case of Reservation for 'Other Backward Classes' in Zoya Hasan (ed.2000), Politics and the State in India, volume 3 of a series on 'Readings in Indian Government and Politics'.

9. Much before the acceptance of the Mandal Commission's report, Tamil Nadu has made use of the provisions for preferential treatment to backward caste given in the constitution. In 1951, it was protested in a famous court case (Champakkam vs. State of Madras) which ultimately necessitated the very first constitutional amendment to accommodate caste based admissions. See, Radhakrishnan (1990a).

10. It should be noted that the reservation policy of the Karnataka government was not based on any rational criteria. For instance, another dominant caste Lingayats were kept out of the purview of the reservation benefits, thanks to Hanavur Commission report. It did not have any other logic except the fact that the then Chief minister, Devraj Urs, wanted to 'isolate Lingayats and win over the Vokkaligas. Subsequently, when Hegde came to power, the Lingayats were included. The acceptance in 1990 of the Mandal Commission recommendations only nationalized what was already happening in large parts of south India. These developments did not take place in isolation but in active interaction. With the Yadavas, Kurmis and Koeris now becoming beneficiaries of backward caste reservations, there is no question of holding back quotas, or even of revisiting them. The schedu led castes and tribes are therefore the indirect beneficiaries of the Mandal Commission and Hanavur Commission and all that happened between those two events. Kaka Kalelkar's inability to designate backward castes on any firm set of criteria was forgotten as being too academic'. See, Dipankar Gupta (1998)also, Radhakrishnan (1990 b).

11. See, Seth (2000).

12. Ibid. Explaining further as why such provisions do not exist, say in West Bengal and Rajasthan, the author of the paper said: The Marxist regime in West Bengal considers caste as a retrogressive factor , therefore they refuge to recognize it. On the other hand, the reverse is true of Rajasthan where because of the entrenched feudal order, presided over by the upper caste dominated ruling hegemony, OBCs did not have voice. The north eastern states are tribal dominated states. Hence, there is no reservation policy for OBCs as such in these states. (Personal Communication, dated 10 August 2001). A circular of the Ministry of Social Justice and Empowerment, Government of India, however indicates that reservation for OBCs is also in vogue in West Bengal and Rajasthan (perhaps accepted reluctantly and that too lately), though the year of implementation is not provided. See the Appendix-I. Besides, following the 73rd Constitutional amendments that ensured the continuity of Panchayati raj Institutions (of third tier of governance), several states have provided reservations for OBCs in these three-tiered bodies.

13. Ramashroy Roy (1970)'Caste and Political Recruitment in Bihar' in: Rajni Kothari (ed.), Caste in Indian Politics. See also, Seth, op. cit.; especially pp. 261-63

14. An authentic count of caste-wise population is not available since the last caste based census was held way back in 1931. Leaving aside scheduled castes and tribes population that have been covered in all decennial census operations, data related to any other caste group are simply assumptions, based on 1931census report. However, following the 73rd Constitutional Amendment a quick caste survey was done in some states including both Bihar and UP to ensure quotas for the backward castes in local government institutions. But the way this limited caste census was carried out in both the states, it raised doubts about its authenticity. Therefore, the estimates of OBC population are vague. Hasan (1998), for instance has cited 42 per cent OBC population in UP, whereas a Delhi based influential newspaper says 'Backward castes form 54.05 per cent. See, UP: Caste-wise employment and new reservation policy'. See, special supplement of the Indian Express, 28 September 2001

15. In the ancient Hindu texts, not castes but '*Varnas*' find mentioning. Accordingly, Hindu society was composed of fourvarnas- Brahmins, Kshatriyas, Vaishyas and Shudras. These varnas have been interpreted as generic terms from which the castes derived their names.

16. In fact, the status of castes within a State has also gone on varying from time to time. The Kolis, for instance, in Gujarat struggled for long to acquire the status of Kshatriyas and took as affront if they were called by their original caste name. Of late they have started taking pride in introducing themselves as Kolis. Explaining the 'u turn', Ghanshyam Shah says: 'They have realized that they will not get any material benefit by calling themselves Kshatriyas'. On the other hand, they [lower castes] feel 'that they could improve their social status and gain political power by improving their economic condition rather than by acquiring Brahmin and Kshatriya status'. See his 'Caste in Contemporary India' in: Desai, I.P. et. al.(ed. 1985). This paper gives a good account of functioning of caste as an institution and also highlights welfare activities of the caste associations as well as use of these institutions to further the political agenda of caste leaders.

17. Apart from their impressive presence in business and secular professions like law, medicine, engineering, Banias have been prominent in the state politics in Gujarat. It is apparent from the fact that of the first four chief ministers in the state two were Banias (and the remaining two were Brahmins). See the Gujarat chapter in Ghosh and Kumar (2003).

18. It is apparent from the fact that a little over two-thirds of the students (67.5 per cent) who graduated from the Madras university in 1918 were Brahmins alone. They held 55 per cent, 82 per cent and 72.6 per cent of posts open to Indians among deputy collectors, sub-judges and district munsiffs (1912). For details see, Frankel, 1991: 232-35.

19. The word BIMARU is used both as an abbreviation and also as a connotation in Hindi which could be roughly translated as 'perpetually sick', that is, an

individual/organisation that can not compete with the healthy ones owing to continued sickness. As an abbreviation it stands for Bihar, Madhya Pradesh, Rajasthan, and Uttar Pradesh. All these four states represent the Hindi heartland of the country and in terms of both social and economic indicators they are far below as compared to the relatively developed states in the southern and western part of the country. From this stand point, these four states are treated as permanently sick states. Hence, they are referred to as Bimaru states.

20. Along with several other states in the northern India, the Congress was dislodged from power in Bihar also in 1967 elections. But the defeat of the Congress did not mean a smooth sailing for the opposition. In fact, 'none of the opposition parties was in a position to form a government on its own strength. The result was the emergence of coalition politics based on narrow political gains of various factions. Between 1967 and 1972, Bihar had to bear with as many as nine Chief Ministers, three separate spells of President's rule, and one mid – term election'. Politically, thus, the state became highly unstable, but 'the backward castes began to make their presence felt in the legislature and the government. Even while distributing tickets for 1967 elections, the Congress party itself – which was previously almost monopolized by the upper castes – had to make major concessions for backward castes. It is not a coincidence that out of nine governments formed during this period, seven were led by men of backward or Harijan Castes' (Prasad, 1976: 66, cited in Ghosh and Kumar (2003).

21. Lingayats and Vokkaligas, the two dominant peasant castes, taken together comprise about one third of the total population in Karnataka. And like Marathas in Maharashtra or Reddys in Andhra Pradesh, they had been controlling the Congress party in Karnataka. It is apparent from the fact that before Devraj Urs, Karnataka had witnessed only Lingayat and Vokkaliga Chief Ministers. In fact, 'every Chief Minister before Karnataka unification in 1956 (when Vokkaligas outnumbered Lingayats) was a Vokkaliga, and every single one from 1956 until 1972 (when Lingayats outnumbered Vokkaligas in the enlarged state) was a Lingayat'. See, Manor (1989: 342).

22. During March – September 1997, when Mayawati (first woman Dalit Chief Minister) was in power in Uttar Pradesh, she set a record by transferring 1,400 civil and police officials. Even 'some district magistrates and civil servants of the rank of secretary were transferred and posted as many as four to six times during those six months'. Her two predecessors from OBC quota had earlier effected 521 transfers in 1991-1992 and 814 transfers in 1993-1995. See, Pranab Bardhan, (2001: 235-6). Mayawati assumed chief ministerial position third time on May 3, 2002. Within first three days of her rule she transferred 'as many as 106 senior civil servants ... Even as several parts of UP reel under power-cuts lasting 10 hours and more, Mayawati's priority are different'. Within a week in office, she resurrected her pet

project– construction of the Ambedkar park which 'she had inaugurated in her second stint as chief minister. The project was estimated to cost Rs. 18 crore (180 million rupees) but is still lying incomplete after around Rs. 110 crore have been spent on it' (EPW, 11 May 2002: 1773).

23. Practically in all the districts mentioned in this context, there are local level organizers only. The MBCs do not have a party of their own. It is still a movement so far spread in a few pockets only. Nevertheless, among the noticeable leaders of this movement are Kishori Das, Kedar Mandal. They are well known in the wider political circle in Bihar, but not outside the state. This information was collected in course of an informal interview (15 October 2001) of Shashi Bhushan - a Patna based economist cum political activist and the founder general secretary of Bihar People 's Union of Civil Liberties - who has addressed some of the rallies at Purnea, Katihar, Sitamarhi etc.

24. Ibid.

25. The decline of the Congress in post-Mandal phase, the disintegration of the Janata Dal and subsequent rise of the Samajwadi party has led to greater split into OBC vote bank. The BJP has managed to win support of two powerful backward castes, Lodhas and Kurmis who are opposed to both Yadavs and a section of MBCs. The Apna Dal, for instance is a party of Kurmis and the Pragatisheel Manav Samaj Party of Binds, a community belonging to MBCs. The supporters of these parties feel that it provides them 'a channel of self-assertion, a way of ensuring that castes—which are either numerically small or lower down the social ladder—are not swamped by the dominant social groups'. For details see, SG (1999).

26. Initially it was stalled on account of a stay order by the Supreme Court, later the Mayawati Government did not pursue this matter in the court for obvious reasons. Hence, the case was turned down by the court.

27. In fact, in a sole dissenting note appended to the Mandal Commission report, one of the members of the Commission had recommended 'separate quotas of 12 per cent and 15 per cent for the less backward intermediate castes and the MBCs respectively'. It is equally important to note that this dissenting note was submitted by the only SC member of the Commission. The remaining three members and the chairman of the Commission were from the other backward castes. See, Kumar, 2001.Varshney, Ashutosh (1997), 'Three Master Narratives of Indian Politics',Seminar January: 45-7.Washbrook, D.A. (1990), 'Caste , Class and Domonance in Modern Tamilnadu: Non-Brahminism, Dravidianism and Tamil Nationalism, in Frankel and Rao, ed (1990).Weiner, Myron (2001), 'The New Struggle for equality: Caste in Indian Politics' in Atul Kohli, (ed. 2001) The Success of India's Democracy, Cambridge University Press, Cambridge.Yadav, Yogendra (1999), 'the Third Electoral system', Seminar, August:14-20

References

Bardhan, Pranab (2001), 'Sharing the Spoils: group equity, development and democracy' in Atul Kohli, ed (2001), '*The success of India*'s Democracy', Cambridge University Press.

Blair, Harry W.(1990), 'Electoral Support and Party Institutionalisation in Bihar: Congress and the Opposition, 1977-1985' in Richards Sisson and Ramashray Roy (ed. 2000) Diversity and Domonance in Indian Politics, vol.1, SageChaudhry, Kameshwar (1990), 'Reservation for OBC: Hardly an Abrupt Decision), *Economic and Political Weekly (*henceforth EPW), 1 September: 1929-35.

CSDS (1998), 'State of Democratic Institutions: A study of Bihar Assembly Elections, 1995', Mimeo, Centre for the study of Developing Societies, Delhi.

Dahiwale, S. M. (2000), 'Identifying Backwardness in Maharashtra', EPW, 9 September: 3293-7

Desai, I.P. et. al.(1985),'Caste – conflict and Reservation ', Mimeo.,Centre for Social studies, Surat.

Frankel, Francine R. (1991), 'Middle Classes and Castes in Indian Politics' in Atul Kohli,(ed. 1991)India's Democracy: An Analysis of Changing State-Society Relations, Orient Longman, New Delhi.

Frankel, Francine R. and M.S.A. RAO, ed (1990), Dominance and State Power in Modern India: Decline of a social Order OUP, New Delhi.

Frankel, Francine R., Zoya Hasan, Rajeev Bhargava and Balveer Arora (2000),ed. *'Transforming India: Social and Political Dynamics of Democracy*, OUP, Delhi.

Ghosh, Buddhadeb, Girish Kumar (2003), State Politics and Panchayats in India, Manohar, Delhi

Gupta, Dipankar (1998), 'A question of quotas', Seminar, November, 57-62.

Hasan, Zoya (1998), Quest for Power:Oppositional Movements and Post-Congress Politics in Uttar Pradesh, OUP, Delhi.

—— ed.(2000), Politics and State in India, Sage, New Delhi

Jain, Meenakshi (1996), 'Backward Castes and Social Change in UP and Bihar' in M.N.Srinivas, ed. (1996) Caste:Its TwentiethCentury Avatar, Viking, Delhi.

Kaviraj, Sudipta (2000), 'Democracy and Social Equality' in Frankel, Hasan et.al (ed, 2000),

Kothari, Rajni (ed. 1970) Caste in Indian Politics, Orient Longman, New Delhi.

Krishna, Gopal (1967),'One Party Dominance Development and Trends' in Party System and Election Studies, Allied Publisher, Delhi.

Kumar, Sanjay (1999), 'New Phase in Backward Caste Politics in Bihar: Janta Dal on Decline', EPW, August 21-28, 2472-80.

Kumar, Pradeep (2001), Reservations Within Reservations: Reai Dalit – Bahujans, EPW, September 15, 3305-7.

Manor, James (1989), 'Karnataka: Caste,Class, Dominance and Politics in a Cohesive Society' in Frankel and Rao, ed (1989).

Mustafa, Seema (1996), The Lonely Prophet: A Political Biography of V P Singh, Wiley Eastern, Delhi

Pai, Sudha (1998), 'The BSP in Uttar Pradesh', Seminar, November:38-42

——(2001), 'Phoolan Devi and Social Churning in UP', EPW, August 11: 3017-20.

Radhakrishna, P. (1990a), 'Backward Classes in Tamil Nadu :1872-1988',EPW, 10 March:509-520.

——(1990b), 'Karnataka Backward Class', EPW, 11 August: 1749-54

——(1996) ' Mandal Commissuion Report: A sociological Critique' in M.N. Srinivas (ed. 1996).

Rangrajan, Mahesh(1997), 'The Politics of Transition' Seminar, January: 41-44

Robin, Cyril (2001), 'From the Upper Castes to Backward Caste Politics in Bihar: The Bihar Paradox, Mimeo, CERI, Paris.

Roy, Ramashray (1970), 'Caste and Political Recruitment in Bihar" in Kothari (ed. 1970)

Seth, D.L. (2000), ' Changing Terms of Elite Discourse: The Case of Reservation for Other Backward Castes' in Zoya Hasan (ed. 2000).

SG (1999), Uttar Pradesh: Rise of Smaller Parties, EPW, October 9: 2912-3.

Shah, Ghanshyam (1985), 'Caste in Contemporary India' in I.P.Desai, et.al. (ed.) Caste Conflict and Reservation, Mimeo, Centre for Social Studies, Surat.

Sivarammaya, B. (1996) 'The Mandal Judgement: A Brief Description and Critique' in M.N.Srinivas (ed.,1996)

Srinivas, M.N.(ed.1996), Caste: Its Twentieth Century Avatar, Viking, 1996, New Delhi.

Thirunavukkarasu, R.(2001), 'Tamil Nadu Election 2001: Changing Equations, EPW, July 7:2486-9

Varshney, Ashutosh (1997), 'Three Master Narratives of Indian Politics', Seminar, January: 45-7.

Washbrook, D.A. (1990), 'Caste , Class and Domonance in Modern Tamilnadu: Non-Brahminism, Dravidianism and Tamil Nationalism, in Frankel and Rao, ed (1990).

Weiner, Myron (2001), 'The New Struggle for equality: Caste in Indian Politics' in Atul Kohli, (ed. 2001) *The Success of India's Democracy*, Cambridge University Press, Cambridge.

Yadav, Yogendra (1999), 'the Third Electoral system', Seminar, August:14-20

Caste and Politics in the Context of the 1990's: Identity and Otherness Among Deprived Populations and Brahmins

Gilles Chuyen

The nineties have been a very rich period as far as political identities are concerned. The post-1947 period had set the trend of exploration of political pluralism in a country where forerunners of the Independence Movement had put unity forth. 'Secularism' was one of the key words brought in with the nationalist movement. Yet, the partition with Pakistan took place on communalist lines and thereafter religion, caste, and politics got further intertwined on a large scale. Indeed, exclusive and closed ways of defining the nation or the reference group have developed during the second half of the twentieth century, nurturing intolerance, and social fragmentation.[1] Beyond their extremist aspect these socio-political phenomenons remain, in fact, an expression of the undeniable Indian cultural diversity.

What happened to these identity expressions in the Indian society of the nineties? The monopoly of the Congress to shape Indian social dynamics, in its appeal to the unity of all Indians beyond caste or creed, came to an end, being any way already spoiled by numerous strategic uses of communitarian vote banks by the party. The nineties represent the time of a real reconfiguration of the Indian political scenario. The decade witnessed, along with the decline of the Congress, the rise of the *Bharatiya Janata Party*, the regionalization of politics and the narrowing of political mobilization basis. Correlated with this ideological shift, the empowerment of deprived sections of society needs to be highlighted. This paper aims at addressing the issues of such empowerments in the framework of institutional and electoral evolution. The notion of identity is here central to understand the variation of the repercussions of political decisions according to the groups that perceive them.

The building process of a group social identity is made of perceptions and analyses of political events touching this particular group or other bodies related to this group. Summing up this essential dialogue, Paul Ricoeur says that the experience of being alone would not be totally possible without the intervention of the other that helps to gather, strengthen and maintain one's identity.[2] Each and every social group will define its characteristics, aims, aspirations and strategies in accordance with those of its competitive groups. In this framework, we are looking at the impact of the moving social, political and economic scenario of the nineties on three sections of the Indian society: the Dalits, the OBCs (Other Backward Classes) and the Brahmins.

Intertwined social readings of these groups will be highlighted through the analysis of two major processes: the implementation of the Mandal Commission report's recommendations and the assertion of the Dalit identity through politics. The use of caste as a political instrument has been central in the context of the nineties. The dynamics through which caste has been used as a tool to struggle, for deprived populations will be explored here. The identity reactions of populations that suffered from such a process, especially the Brahmins, will be articulated thereafter.

Economic and political empowerment of the Backward Classes

The issue of the social advancement of Backward Classes has been the core of political debates in India during the nineties. At the beginning of this decade, the implementation of the recommendations of the Mandal Commission report has been definitely a major step in this regard. However, it is necessary to put this decision in the perspective of the actual socio-economic and political evolution of deprived populations since the sixties.

The Mandal landmark: the quest for social justice

The nineties as far as socio-political issues are concerned can be called the 'decade of Mandalisation'. After the failure of the Kalelkar Commission in 1953, the Mandal Commission got the sensitive task to work on the socio-economic situation of the Backward Classes. Implemented in 1990, its recommendations stand as a landmark in the field of reservation policies. Key word of the Indian democracy, since the beginning, social justice has been used as the ideological framework in the Mandal Commission report. Positive discrimination and equality are the two points we study to evaluate the impact of such recommendations on Backward Classes.

Defining policies based on a process of any discrimination requires detailed studies of the social background for which these policies will be formulated. The question of defining the populations to protect has to be coupled with issues pertaining to the nature of the policy to implement. The term of 'Backward Classes' itself has to be specified. It can be understood according to different meanings, among which two main ones are used.[3] It is a generic term covering all deprived populations such as Scheduled castes and Scheduled Tribes as well as Shudra depressed populations. It can otherwise include only the last category, known as OBCs. We will be using it in this last definition.

Backward Classes, as their denomination indicates it, are socially backward but are placed above the 'Scheduled Castes'. These populations gathered today under the category of 'Scheduled Castes' share a very low status in the traditional Hindu hierarchy, born out of the stigmitization of untouchability. The Constitution of Independent India is a major document concerning policies in their favour. Scheduled Castes and Scheduled Tribes were in focus at the times of its drafting, for social improvement and protection from injustice and exploitation. Their economic and educational interests are taken into account in this document (art. 46). Beyond the concern of following up of their situation (art. 164 (1), 338, 339), numerous actual policies have been implemented: reserved seats in assemblies at the Union level (art. 330) and at the state level (art. 332) and access favoured to government services (art. 335).[4]

For the Backward Classes, the political context in south India has been the privileged background for appropriate measures. Two major decisions from the Supreme Court in April 1951 got the debate running around this category.[5] They were aiming at giving limitations to the use of article 16 (4) of the Constitution. These decisions created a great upheaval in south India and entailed the creation of the alinea 4 of the article 15, first amendment to the Constitution. This alinea comes indeed as a clarification of the expression used in the alinea 4 of the article 16 for the definition of the populations entitled to apply for reservations: 'any Backward class of citizen'. Article 15.4 specifies that backwardness is to be understood at both the social and educational levels, to avoid any misuse of such policies by forward communities, taking advantage of vague criteria of definition.[6] Still, no policy at the Union level got defined after these constitutional improvements and various regional practises have been developed.

The Kalelkar Commission was in charge of finding guidelines to propose a harmonized policy. However, its report faced major criticism, due to its focus on caste as the major criterium of identification for backwardness. This approach was indeed considered dangerous, in the sense that it could lead to a strengthening of caste divisions and thus caste discrimination and social backwardness for which it was supposed to find remedies.[7] The Mandal Commission, yet conscious of such an issue, kept the caste belonging as the major tool for the selection of Backward populations.[8]

Justifications for this method were extensively developed in the report itself. Quoting Rajni Kothari, it is explained that 'those in India who complain of 'casteism' in politics are really looking for a sort of politics which has no basis in society'[9]. Further more, in the Chapter IX on evidence by Central and State Governments, results of a survey show that the majority of State Governments favour caste as an important parameter for evaluation of educational and social backwardness in their policies.[10] Similarly, nearly 78 per cent of the public, polled through questionnaires were considering caste as a criterion for identifying backwardness.[11] In this framework, the Mandal Commission recommended a reservation of 27 per cent for OBCs in Government services and technical and professional institutions, both in the Centre and the States. This quota has been limited to 27 per cent, because of the existing 22.5 per cent in favour of SCs and STs and of the constitutional limitation of reservation to 50 per cent, under Articles 15(4) and 16(4).[12]

These policies got implemented, even if in the education field, no national harmonization has been organized. In Tamil Nadu, for example, the Union directly finances institutions like the Indian Institutes of Technology and to the contrary of other regional engineer colleges who practice an exceptionnal 69 per cent of reservation, they do not have quotas for Backward Classes but only for SCs and STs.[13] Otherwise, at a larger social level, the whole decade of the nineties became indeed for various communities, an arena to grasp the 'Backward label' in order to have access to the reservation measures. The example of the Jat community is a characteristic example of such a race.

Since the beginning of the twentieth century, the Jat community was involved in the search for a Kshatriya descent, in the double context of a group conversion to the ideology of the Arya Samaj and of the assertion of its identity in the army. In favour of references to the Varna system, less narrow-minded than the jati system, Dayanand, founder of the movement, encouraged the community to claim Kshatriya origins, so as to counter stigmatization coming from upper castes.[14] From elements of the past, such as the 1857 revolt, Jats have been creating a 'natural' identity, warlike, anterior to the British rule and opposed to any analysis of their potential low status.[15] Nevertheless, in the wake of Mandal, the access to reservation schemes became a central issue for the community, so as to be part of this new dynamics of social and economic advancement.[16] Working at getting a Backward status in their public sphere, to enjoy the reservation system, Jats and other similar communities remain attached at the same time to a Kshatriya affiliation in their private sphere.[17]

Operating in a completely opposite dynamics to the process of sanskritization, the mandalisation has led communities to claim a low status in order to have access to resources. During the nineties, this issue of reservation became one of the main social axes of political mobilization. Aiming at decreasing social inequalities, the recommendations of the Mandal Commission enhanced caste-based positioning, thus focusing debates on the meaning of equality in Indian society.

Equality before law, as defined in article 14 of the Constitution is one of the most precious democratic rights for Indian citizens. But speaking of equality of opportunities in the educational and professionnal fields is quite utopic, if one takes into account the old and clear disparities, characteristic of Indian society. Merely stating rights to freedom and equality does not automatically lead to an equitable society. The Mandal Commission was in charge of this pursuit of equity, so as to make the legislation evolve in favour of the other deprived sections of the population, apart from SCs and STs, namely the OBC.

In the name of equality, treating unequal individuals in an egalitarian way, in fact perpetuates inequality. In a genuine approach for social justice, deprived sections of the population have to be part of positive discrimination schemes. This is the view supported by the Mandal Commission.This approach defending social advancement as a whole clashes with the interests of any individual claiming his right to be treated as equal as any other citizen. This opposition of principles is not new and was very much part of the debates which occurred during the discussions around the first amendment to the Constitution in 1951.[18]

The Mandal Commission report is indeed the expression of the pre-eminence of social advancement against potential individual claims, because of the highly hierarchic nature of Indian society. Overrepresentations of forward communities in higher education and government services constituted undeniable proofs of the necessity of a general policy aiming at discarding such differences. Intellectual debates, before and after this Mandal Affair were aiming at justifying the pros and cons of such a policy.

Anti-Mandal diatribes were numerous. Apart from André Béteille and Veena Das who would criticize the reservation process as a reproduction of the colonial 'divide and rule', other researchers, such as M. N. Srinivas, A. M. Shah and B.S. Baviskar would insist upon the deepening of social inequalities thus entailed.[19] Many other arguments against positive discrimination would address for example the illusion of socio-economic equality through legal equality and the questions of individual merit and maximisation of skills.[20] However, the underlying issue concerns the use of caste as a political tool. Many viewpoints can be adopted to discuss this problem. First, it is a fact that caste as a criterion for identification of backwardness is not always accurate. Both the Kalelkar and Mandal Commissions faced heavy criticism on this regard and the alternative of class has been ofsten put forward.[21] Another point is that the circumstances under which the Mandal Commision report has been implemented is not a very good example of the political use of caste.

Representing a strong issue during the elections of 1977 in the political agenda of the Janata Party - core of the anti-Congres forces after the Emergency implemented by Indira Gandhi, the question of the Backward Classes was indeed put forward by the new Prime Minister, Morarji Desai. In February 1978, the decision to formulate a Commission in charge of this topic, presided by B.P. Mandal was taken. However, with the Congress coming back to power, the report submitted in 1980 went unheeded. After ten years, when the next anti-Congress coalition came to power, the recommendations of the report were finally implemented. But more than an ideological statement, the implementation of the report played as a strategic electoral tool for the Prime Minister V.P. Singh, to fight the rise of the competing peasant movement led by Devi Lal, becoming dangerously popular among OBCs from North India.[22] But on the other hand, various intellectuals asserted strongly their views of a positive effect of such a political use of caste, apart from these electoral strategies.

Ashgar Ali Engineer explained that caste conflicts are part of the democratic dynamics of confrontation of identities, would they be based on religion, geographical origins, or caste[23]. In the same approach, Harold A. Gould, in his study of the relations between caste and politics, explains in his introduction, that conflicts and adjustments between specific groups of interests are not the result of a failure in modernization, but a logical process contributing to the formation of a modern State. In the Indian context especially, caste, religion, and regional identities are functional; they are part of the contemporary social dynamics.[24] Rajni Kothari is the thinker who brought the most acurate views on the subject, because of his long-standing interest in the relations between caste and politics.[25] As soon as the Mandal issue started, he had set caste as a possible tool for social justice. He considered caste as a tool through which social dynamics can evolve to either of the two extremes - absolute hierarchy or contesting of this hierarchy. In this argument, Kothari highlights the historical failure of the attempt to eradicate caste since Independence. Further, he fights the views, according to which an automatic movement would be at work, coupling a decrease of communalism and casteism with a rise of secularism and egalitarianism. Caste based mobilization movements have the potential to promote secularism and democracy through a defence of pluralism.[26]

This debate is still central in Indian society today. The issue of trying to avoid caste as a political tool for social advancement was raised recently in reference to caste related information in Indian census. Blocking a political use of caste here tends to deny the importance of such pieces of information in a more precise fight against social inequalities.[27] The nineties indeed had the spotlight on caste and politics and highly charged debates on social justice in Indian society ensued. The implementation of the Mandal Commission report had great repercussions on intellectual arguments about the nature and evolution of Indian democracy. Nevertheless, as far as the benificiaries are concerned, our study would be incomplete if we do not look at the actual evolution of the social conditions of Backward Classes, before and through the nineties.

Actual improvement of the deprived populations

The Mandal Commission is indeed a landmark in the history of defending the rights of the deprived. This should however not prevent us from looking at the historical evolution of the conditions of such populations. Social statuses have been through large transformations in the last decades in India. A focus on the economic and political status of the Backward Classes will enable us to understand new trends at work in contemporary India.

Economic situation of the Backward populations in the nineties needs to be analysed keeping in mind the impact of both liberalisation and implementation of new schemes of reservations. To evaluate the actual impact of reservation policies on deprived populations, one must begin with the situation of the Scheduled Castes and Tribes, because of much longer span of time attributed to them, as compared to the OBCs.

Scheduled Castes and Schedules Tribes have been suffering from economic distress linked to a system of exclusion. For tribes, this exclusion comes from their situation of cultural and geographical isolation. As for Scheduled Castes, exclusion is a conseqeunce of the hiearchical base of the caste system. From this principle of separation, Ambedkar started claiming a status of separate electorate for these populations. Major debates happened in the thirties around this topic, especially between him and the Mahatma. Nevertheless, after Gandhi's emotional blackmail through his fasting, the Poona Act in 1932 ensured that the issue of separate electorate was kept out of the agenda. Scheduled Castes would be taken care of through reservation policies only.[28] When we look at the evolution of the socio-economic situation of Scheduled Castes after the Independence, when reservation policies were actually at work, the picture is rather disappointing.

Reservations in fact became a tool for social transformation, especially with the failure of development programmes. Through reservation policies, the Government worked at providing education and job opportunities for the SCs and STs to gain social resources. But the situation of discrimination because of a separation from the rest of the society has not disappeared.[29] When one focus on the specific condition of Scheduled Tribes, the scene is even worse. First, STs have not taken advantage of the reservation facilities as much as the SCs did. However, the scenario has to be analysed here in terms of lack of abilities. Education level is an issue that development programmes really failed to tackle properly for these populations. STs suffer also from specific drawbacks, compared to SCs for the improvement of their conditions. Their cultural, linguistic and geographical isolation coupled with a lack of large identities prevent a positive social dynamic to take place, which can open these communities to change.[30]

The core of the debate lies in the different forms of equality. In the Indian context, it is quite an utopia to think that implementing equality through laws will automatically entail a real socio-economic equality between citizens of such a hierarchical society. Finally, we have to take into account the last parameter that completely changed the social scenario of Backward populations in the nineties - privatisation. While new schemes of reservations were being implemented in the public sector following the recommendations of the Mandal Commission, the Indian Government decided to disinvest public sector undertakings, opening the country to international investors, thus completely changing the socio-economic scenario for deprived populations. Government policies were aiming, since Independence at providing social resources to these populations by facilitating their access to public education and services. But the rapid expansion of the private sector completely redefined the problem.

Many aspects must be looked at. The whole scenario of globalization has various impacts according to social stratification. For the poor, it means very often that socio-economic gaps get wider. As far as education is concerned, fields such as biotechnology and information technology for example are highlighted in the process. But this kind of development is largely out of reach of the SCs and STs. Apart from the level of education, the issue of the cost of such trainings is also a hindrance, for both reasons of privatization of education in such fields as well as the withdrawal of the state from social expenditures such as education.[31]

Furthermore, there are direct consequences of the New Economic Policy implemented by the Indian Government in July 1991 on SCs and STs. These economic reforms aim at developing economic activities from a capitalistic point of view. Reduction of poverty is considered a long-term consequence but not a paramount goal in this programme. The State was changing its priorities and thus had to reduce its investments in social sectors such as education and health. This directly influenced the quality of life of poor people. In the rural sector, a developing mechanization entailed the unemployment of unskilled labour among SCs and STs. In fact, rural non-agricultural and urban informal employments have suffered the most under the new economic measures, with the SCs and STs being highly involved in such sectors.[32]

Finally, the overall impact of the reservation policies in the public sector looses its value, in such an socio-economic change. That is why some Dalit leaders started to claim the necessity of reservation in the private sector as well.[33]

As far as the OBCs are concerned, they had not been taken into consideration at the time of Independence in anti-discrimination measures. Placed higher in the traditional Hindu hierarchy than the Untouchables, they have not been suffering of socio-religious stigma. But still, they are characterized by a backward standard of living. Even if the recommendations of the Mandal Commission represent a major step in the improvement of their conditions, one must also look at the historical conditions that led to such recognition.

Non-untouchable Backward Castes first benefited from the Green Revolution and the economic reforms related to it in the sixties. From this context, an intermediary class of peasants was able to release surplus and hence modify their socio-economic situation as well as their strategies. They put aside their claiming about land reforms and turned to the State to get advantages in terms of costs and prices. It is because of this economic upsurge that their political influence increased, giving way to a trend of 'new agrarianism'. Rurally based electoral coalitions or new farmers' movements more aloof from politics grew through the sixties and the seventies, as a sign of the economic development of such populations.[34]

Thanks to this dynamic, this upcoming strata of the population then became the beneficiaries of the Mandal policy. What has to be pointed out here is the mixed effect of such a policy. As we explained before for the SCs and STs, reservation policies have a limited impact for populations with such a strong rural background. Moreover, at the time of implementation of these new quotas, the Indian Government opened itself to a totally different perspective with the liberalisation programme in 1991. What can be highlighted today, ten years later is the formation of an élite among these populations, which was able to take advantage of the new scenario, as well in terms of reservations as in terms of the New Economic Policy. This élite has been able to become part of the New Middle Class. This new social category goes beyond the barriers of caste and socio-religious considerations and has been shaped on the lines of new life style linked to modern consumption patterns, ownership of specific economic assets and self consciousness of belonging to such a category. This process is such, that political and cultural attitude is more common within this category than between members of the same caste having different economic background.[35] This élite has also been empowered through the political movements supporting Backward populations. We are going to address this issue herafter.

Apart from a certain improvement in the economic situation of Backward populations, one should look indeed at their political empowerment, especially in the nineties, when both OBCs and SCs and STs enjoyed a strengthened visibility. We highlighted at the beginning of our study, the importance of the Mandal Commission report, as a landmark in the struggle in India for social justice. We also pointed out later that this political recognition in the nineties was the outcome of a socio-economic upsurge of these populations from the sixties. But at the political level, the fact remains that the OBCs as a political category strengthened their position during the nineties.

When one first looks at the evolution of politics in the nineties, it is first obvious that the reservation policy implemented from the Mandal report had huge effects on political mobilization. A certain political sensibility started among leaders of these communities with the work of the first Backward Classes commission, in the fifties, highlighting common interests, source of a potential political base.[36] With the development of the various peasant movements in the sixties and seventies, a political identity started emerging among these populations. But the issue of reservation has been the main trigger in the process of identity building. In a similar way as during census, communities aim at defining clearly their status in the social hierarchy, to legitimate their demands and their access to resources. Two parallel dynamics seem to coexist most of the time. Still involved in the logic of sanskritization in the private sphere, meaning by that the claim for a higher ritual status, Backward communities, in the public sphere, work at getting the 'Backward label' to have access to the reservation resources, as we have already mentioned in the case of the Jats.[37]

The OBC category thus became a treasured vote bank, creating a strong political category in the arena of comtemporary Indian society. This process constitutes the end of the Congress system through which Backward interests were in the hands of upper castes political leaders, in a clientelist web.[38] With this strengthening of the reservation issue, a real 'OBC front' took shape in electoral politics. Communities in north India such as Yadav, Kurmi, Gujar, Koeri and Lodhi and lately Jats were indeed able to focus on common interests so as to form this strong political front. The two anti-Congress coalitions, at the end of the seventies and the eighties were representing such interests. Secondly, there has been also a real transition in the sociological background of political representatives all over the country, with the political rise of the OBCs. Even if this trend is unequal across the country, the nineties are definitely the decade of assertion of such a process.[39] Reservations constitute so strong an issue that socio-political identities have been shaped accordingly.

The decade of the nineties has also been a landmark in the building of Dalit identity. Much before any government policies favouring depressed populations, voices were raised to highlight the precarious condition of populations known as untouchables. The views of Jotirao Phule (1827-1890) were based for instance, on an analysis of Hinduism as an instrument of brahmanical domination. A leading social activist in Maharashtra, he was in favour of the British taking the lead in breaking Brahmins' hegemony in terms of socio-economic advantages and control of the social norms, that formed a real 'brahmanical colonialism' especially harsh on low status populations.[40] Following the same approach, adi movements were active in the twenties, in Uttar Pradesh, Andhra Pradesh, and Punjab to fight discriminations born out of caste segregation.

Various movements aimed at defining the nature of Dalit identity. At the crossroads of culture and politics, Ambedkar fought for Dalits, in a more specific way than the leftist movement. He worked towards a better integration of them in Indian society, through political programmes as well as a new religious approach with Buddhism.[41] Various cultural references such as the Bhakti approach and the performance of *tamasha* became part of a Dalit inheritance.[42] The Dalit Panthers movement has been the figurehead of such a cultural assertion. Founded in 1972 in Bombay, this movement was born off a new generation of writers and poets, in a plural and stimulating context. The rise of education level among Dalits and the economic crisis in the second half of the sixties were coupled to the revolutionary dynamic at the international level, mirrored in the situation in China, Vietnam and Cambodia and the Black Movement in the United States.[43]

However, as far as the unity and the strength of Dalit identity is concerned, the nineties have been a very special period, for the visibility of the Dalit vote in particular. The Dalit vote has been largely held responsible for the decline of the Congress in the nineties. It is also regarded as an important element in the strategy of the BJP to unify all Hindus.[44] The role of the *Bahujan Samaj Party* has been central in this political rise. Founded in 1984 by Kanshi Ram, an Untouchable from Punjab, this organisation aims at the empowerment of Dalits through politics. Different phases can be observed in its approach: from 1985 to 1989, the BSP is a radical movement, opting for socio-cultural mobilization strategies, using agitation campaigns. The Ambdekarite influence is then more sensible with the attempts to get closer to the *Shudras* in a more holistic approach of the issue of backwardness from 1989 to 1995.[45] It is during this second period that the party won its historical victory in Uttar Pradesh, in 1993. Allied with the *Samajwadi Party* of Mulayam Singh Yadav, in favour of OBC, it was successful at keeping the Congress out of the power. This attempt to work hands in hands with the Shudras was without keeping in mind the tremendous differences and tensions existing between these two strata. The attempt to shape a *Bahujan Samaj* as the political expression of the majority, as well as the theory of *Dalitbahujan* of all the deprived populations developed by Kanchah Ilaiah are still disconnected from the social reality, taking the numerous clashes observed between the various elements of this political cluster.[46]

Dalits, more strictly taken as Untouchables, have been asserting, their will to form a united and specific political front, apart from the more general strategies of the Congress and the BJP. The various elections of 1996, 1998, and 1999 are strong proofs of this process. The BSP has been a key tool in this dynamic of identity consciousness. But the electoral awareness of the Dalit voters did not prevent the BSP to try electoral alliances, often very contradictory to its ideological premises.[47] A fact remains. The nineties have been a period of a clear increase in the political involvement of Backward populations, in terms of vote, political activism, and representation. After the very vibrant political scenario of the sixties, the nineties have been named the second democratic upsurge of India, with a strong 'bahujan' character, with Mandal and Kanshi Ram as symbolic figures.[48]

The building of Brahmin identities through politics

Why should one highlight the viewpoints of Brahmins in this debate? It is to notice that the whole history of reservation policies has a strong brahmanical touch. The Mandal Commission comes in the lineage of regional policies in favour of Backward Castes, especially in the south, within the anti-Brahmin movement. In spite of such strong and ancient positive discrimination policies, born out the overrepresentation of Brahmins in education and government services, no reservation policy for Backward Castes had been indeed adopted at the Union level. Indian society has a long history of strong links between caste and social, educational and economic status. Brahmins, at the top of the socio-ritual hierarchy, torch-bearers of the sacred knowledge were strategically keen on maintaining a holistic and rigid caste system, to legitimate the supremacy of upper castes.[49]

At the time of the survey of the Mandal Commission, the status of élite of Brahmins was still obvious. Suren Navlakha, in his analysis of urban élites in the second half of the sixties, focussing on civil servants, industrialists and professors, highlights the fact that Brahmins alone, represent more than 50 per cent of the Hindu élite.[50] The prestigious Indian Administrative Service is a characteristic example of such brahmanical bastions, with 38 per cent of Brahmins against 2,04 per cent of OBC, at the end of the seventies.[51]

The recommendations of the Mandal Commission constitute the present apotheosis in the history of positive discrimination in India, after non-Brahminism and Dravidianism in south India. Considered an identity milestone by many Brahmins, it is perceived by the ones from south, as the first real hostile measure against Brahmins from north India.[52] In the context described in the first part of our paper, we will first look at the range of Brahmin attitudes towards first the empowerment of the Backward and then deal with the specific issue of fragmentation.

From enhanced pride to socio-economic weakness

Attitudes exposed here are based on control mechanisms to ensure the coherence of threatened Brahmin identities. From an assertion of inherent superiority to discourses on socio-economic drawbacks, Brahmins express their fears towards the new socio-political focus on the Backward. Even if the Brahmins who develop an attitude centered on the issue of meritocracy, do not explicitly express a feeling of threat, they do express their fear, by the strength of their identity discourses.

Opposed to reservation policies, Brahmins presented here consider these as passing events, as choices made out of certain political conditions which can not call into question their élite status and their high qualities. They develop an elitist approach on politics.

'You know, in Congress regime, Brahmins were in a dominant position and as long as Brahmin element was dominant in any government, (...) some values were maintained in Indian politics'.

Brahmins are put forward as the real specialists of politics. They are supposed to be the guardians of reference values, as counsellors to the leaders, in particular. Thus their political role as an old historical legitimacy.

'If you see during the independence movement, most of those who were in the foreground were the Brahmins. One reason they were, Brahmins, if you notice... were not a majority part of the government service, they were also not the rulers... so, they had really nothing to lose from the British government, and they were the only ones who could come out very openly, and since they had the intellectual background, they knew how to counterargue and how to fight it all. Therefore, by and large, most of those who were into the independence movement were the Brahmins. So, when it took over, when the independence came in, all those who were there, they were obviously to come into power.'[53]

In this identity type, one vision has developed according to which Brahmins, involved for such a long period in the public affairs, would logically manifest a great interest for the *res publica*. They are considered as members of the 'enlightened élite' who evinces a clear sense of civic responsability.

'As I said, India is a country of many castes as you make a bouquet. So, in a bouquet there are Brahmins and other castes, but above all, we are Indians. This is how we exhibit unity in diversity, and this thinking of mine is because I am a Brahmin.'[54]

Brahmins of this type do not get into narrow-minded visions, meaning that they do not want to give greater importance to the specific interests of their community. Contrary to other social groups, they are not in a position to have to proove anything in society. Particularly characteristic of upper middle class Brahmins, this discourse comes as a result of exacerbated awareness of belonging fully to the élite, from the socio-ritual as well as the economic hierarchy. Thus Brahmins would not indulge in what others would enjoy, in the promotion of casteism.

'When a Scheduled Caste, Scheduled Tribe comes into politics, or bureaucracy, he's overobsessed with the feelings that he and his kinsmen have been deprived, have been kept away from certain things. Therefore, his zeal for putting that right takes presidence over his general doing the right and doing the wrong. And then he tends to do wrong things.'[55]

Brahmins developing such a discourse, often appear as ready to teach lessons, proud of their incomparable brahmanical qualities.

'The Brahmin brain (...), the excellence and being at the top, that can not be diminished by laws, or constitutional amendments.'

According to this attitude, Brahmins are gifted with the highest qualities, enabling them to go through any socio-political context. Educated for generations, strongly established in the best professions, they have no reason to worry about any hostile reservation policy. Brahmins express their views on the inadequacy of such policies for a real social justice. In addition, they point out one of the arguments given by André Béteille against Mandal, based on the great value of merit for a maximised institutional functioning.[56]

'You can never build up a whole society overnight by doing reservations. (...) Most of the professionnal work will still be in the hands of the Brahmins (...). By reservation, the U.P. government was able to give admissions to the Roorkee University to a child with 0 per cent mark, just because the Chief Minister said there were seats for OBCs who have applied. But then, when he went to the university, he would not just understand.'[57]

Distributive justice and instititutional functioning need to be taken into account together. Any society, according to this perspective, even if it gives place to social justice, has to respect and promote individual abilities and skills. Brahmins project this self-image of individuals having the best competence to offer. They are endowed with intellectual superiority, nourrished generation after generation and which is visible today in genetic terms.

'They are born Brahmins, which possibly give them a slight genetic advantage, slight because their forefathers got classified as Brahmins because they had a certain inherent intellectual ability which has filtered down.'[58]

'I do believe the discipline, the hard work of the Brahmin is also an explanation of their being at the top, it is not luck, it is not manipulativeness'.[59]

Brahmins who follow this approach are proud of their talent and abilities, which prevent them from needing any governmental help to have access to education or professions.

'I'm still proud of being a Brahmin, because I am there, out of my own merit. I have not been privileged because I was born in a particular caste'.[60]

These notions of merit and talent have been addressed in the Mandal Commission report, in its chapter VI on social justice, merit and privilege. The example of two children, from two very different backgrounds and competing from the same exam, is given to make a point about the meaning of equality. Merit in an elitist society is a mix of 'native endowments and environmental privileges'. Speaking of equality as an individual right in an unequal society, these Brahmins do, comes to maintain inequalities.[61]

Other perspectives have been developed among Brahmins, about mandalisation of society. Reactions had been violent. Demonstrations and intense debates among intellectuals and students highlighted the discontent of upper castes. Brahmins especially reject these measures as hindrances to their career options as well as a drastic calling into question of the social order.

This new scenario highlights the shaping of a hostile otherness and issues about the socio-economic status of contemporary Brahmins.

When the report was implemented in 1990, many Brahmin students decided to react in a very violent way, setting themselves on fire. Rajeev Goswami, unique son of a Brahmin Punjabi family, initiated this trend. Searching for media attention, the masquerade turned dramatic and Rajeev Goswamy was badly injured.[62] This accident has inspired many youngsters to project their identity crisis, especially among upper castes and Brahmins. At the end of October 1990, 159 suicidal cases were registered all over India, of which 63 were fatal.[63]

We must look at the motivations behind such intense reactions, especially in comparison with the attitude towards SCs and STs. Policies implemented for these populations did not entail such identity assertions. First, the improvement of the life conditions of SCs and STs was part of the nationalist political programme. The legitimacy of such policies could not be really contested with Gandhi's backing and a latent sense of guilt present among upper castes, making the whole issue politically correct. On the contrary, for many Brahmins, OBCs are perceived as the first tyrants against Untouchables.

'*Actually if you find in such states like Bihar, UP, the maximum atrocities on the Scheduled Castes and Scheduled Tribes in India now are committed by the Yadavs, Jats, etc., you know, and that is not the other higher castes, they had committed in the centuries gone but not now, now in India you'll find these other intermediate castes and OBCs, they are the biggest perpetrators of crimes against the Scheduled Castes and Tribes*'.[64]

Many clashes actually happened between Dalits and OBCs in Uttar Pradesh especially, giving an end to the historical political coalition of the BSP and the SP in 1993. Brahmins perceive OBCs here as a vague social category with a clear use as a vote bank.[65] The recommendations of the Mandal Commission appeared as a challenge to Brahmins. It is a sign for Brahmins developping such views of a social decline, evincing Brahmins as out of the social mainstream.

'We were taught when we were young, by our elders that as Brahmins we were the best. However, as the social processes and the political and economic processes have developed in India subsequently, the Brahmin finds that he is encountering a very different kind of reality, which is very different from the self-perception which he has internalised'.[66]

As Dipankar Gupta points out, every notion of hierarchy is relative. No positioning can be universally accepted. Discourses on hierarchy depend on the relation the locutor is fostering with this hierarchy.[67] Brahmins who feel threatened by positive discrimination policies, remain aware of the global elitist image of their community and of the unrealistic claim of a quota for them. Still, they feel offended by such practices.

'Quite obviously there is not and there can not be any quota or reservation in jobs, in the employment market for Brahmins... who are perceived as the perpetuators of an unequal and unjust social system... Therefore, the reservation system for the Scheduled Castes and later on the reservation system for the OBC, is widely perceived as a economic, social offense against the Brahmins and for a lot of Brahmin families, the daily evening discourse over meal time is a whole range of debate on this issue.[68]

The pessimistic approach developed among the Brahmins presented now is based on socio-economic considerations. Members for most of them of lower middle classes, their brahminical origins are not synonymous with élite. In this context, sociologist Jagpal Singh highlighted the extreme poverty of some Brahmins, seen by one of his Dalit interviewees, as the legitimate beneficiaries of reservation policies.[69]

'The poor Brahmin, especially the middle class Brahmin, especially the... intelligent articulate educated but lower middle class Brahmin, especially their girls, their daughters, they find themselves in a great upheaval, and they have great difficulty in

deciding whether they are the best, they continue to be at the top or that the processes have brought them down together, in the political, social and economic level.'[70]

Brahmins should be taken care of nowadays, say Brahmins of these deprived backgrounds.

'*Brahmins should not have so much money because it was the duty of the society to give them finance, to give them food, to facilitate them but the duty of Brahmins was to get knowledge and give that knowledge to other people. Now, there is no such work for Brahmins. He is doing business, he is holding money, other things that he should not do.'*[71]

A discourse is developed according to which Brahmins have been so involved in the public interest, looking down on their individual confort, for so many generations, that the State should acknowledge these sacrifices now. Brahmins from the lower middle classes focus on their overlasting link with knowledge, compared to richer ones more interested in money. This claim puts forward again, the issue of reservation on the basis of caste and not class.

'*Brahmin is generally avoided in the government policies. There is reservation on the basis of caste... There should be reservation on the basis of economic conditions. If a person is weak economically, he should be given reservation to get admission, and starting from the primary school, whatever caste, harijan, or Brahmin'.*[72]

However, steps had been taken since 1990. In August-september 2000, the list of OBCs has been extended and for example, Nayee Brahmins from Andhra Pradesh were included.[73] The Tambras in Tamil Nadu also fought along these lines, aiming at implementing policies towards individuals and not communities.

'*On this reservation issue, we are going to make a very basic plea. The constitution speaks of socially and educationnally backward citizens... It is seven months I hold this post, I went to the all thing and I discussed with lawyers from various communities... what is social backwardness, what is educational backwardness, it is not written there in black and white, it is not quantified. There are no parameters laid for that. So we are going to plead, you lay parameters for what is that, apply it not to caste, and apply it to candidates. Even if you are a Brahmin, if your father was not educated, you must be given the reservation. If you apply this to the candidates, problems will be avoided.'*[74]

This issue of socio-economic differences within communities pushed the Supreme Court to exclude the creamy layer among OBCs from the reservation measures in the public sector.[75]

Professional reconversions among Brahmins became an option to counter the new social dynamic, and some of them left administration services for the private sector, as Tamil Brahmins did, much earlier, during the non-Brahmin movement in south India.[76]

'*I feel good to be a Brahmin, but... today, S.C. and other people like this get more advantages. Brahmins have problems in service jobs. Education was their priority. But today's situation is very bad for Brahmins. Access to service must be by the level of education, not by castes. For Brahmins, it is difficult... no promotions for them. So, we went into business.'*[77]

Yet, business is still looked down upon sometimes, especially among orthodox Hindu families.[78] The relation to money is also ambivalent, with respect for money as such but suspicion towards the people who have lots of it, as a Brahmin was framing it.[79] It remains now one specific issue related to the political rise of Dalits especially that Brahmins related to, in their identity perspective, the issue of fragmentation.

The issue of fragmentation

Having to face a strong and unified Dalit political identity, discourses from Brahmins got crystallised along the same lines, according to the logic of identity and otherness. Strategic mimetism are indeed at work, taken the two levels of the Hindu community and the Brahmin community.

Caste divisions are a kind of taboo for the Hindu nationalists, preventing them from unifying all Hindus against the hostile others, Muslims and Christians. The political strategy of the Hindu nationalists is totally opposed to the one of the Dalits and the Backward parties who deals with restricted caste vote banks. The Hindutva aims at building larger and larger blocks, ending with one constituting an unique reference community - the Hindus.[80] Promoting Hinduism, as a political ideology, cc nsists here, in theory, in negating the caste hierarchy. The lectoral discourse of the BJP targets the SCs, for their inclusion in the large Hindu family.

'The political persons and to a good extent, the distorsions which later came have divided the society, have fragmented the Hindus. Otherwise, with the original caste system, the Hindus together could make a strong society. Because, the caste system was to bring order according to professions. Widening the gap between castes and use caste for political reasons has put India 20 to 25 years' back, because of this political thing. For a strong Hindu society, all castes should come together'.[81]

The BSP and the SP are political enemies of such a programme. Moreover, the implementation of the Mandal Commission report has constituted a real break in the long-term strategy of the BJP. The campaign against Babri Masjid in Ayodhya, in December 1992 is a direct response to the process of mandalisation: it is 'Mandir versus Mandal'.[82] In an interview given to the magazine *Frontline*, Arvind Rajagopal, author of the book *Politics after Television: Hindu Nationalism and the Reshaping of Public in India*, explains the context through which this campaign was built. He takes as cultural reference, the broadcasting of a serial based on the Ramayana, from January 1987, forming an ideological backing for the BJP. Bringing forward the cultural unity of the Nation, this particular audiovisual support became an instrument to highlight strategic themes and symbols. The references to a golden age, the apology of the virtues of the Hindu leaders were coupled to processes that are more explicit. For example, an episode on Ram wanting to get his land back has been created, whereas it is not developed in the *Ramayana* by Valmiki or Tulsidas. Finally, a common iconography is set, visible in the serial as well as in the politico-religious processions, yatra, organised by the Hindu Parivar.[83]

The Hindutva represents indeed the desire to come back to the system of social justice as defined according to the Varna organisation. One gets according to its status. The traditional hierachical structures are legitimized and integrated to contemporary processes of economic and political transactions. The Hindutva aims at building a pan-Indian hegemonic identity, widening brahmanical values and modes of functioning to a larger middle class in the making.[84] This fear of fragmentation is also expressed by some Brahmins, in connection with the specific situation in the Varna.

The debate on fragmentation among Brahmins includes an awareness of common interests and a cristallization of the debate in terms of identity and otherness. The Chaturvedi jati interviewed in Agra is characteristic of such a perspective. Tracing its origins in Mathura, this community is typical of a Brahmin community having to struggle in the contemporary Indian scenario. Highly placed in the socio-ritual hierarchy – they are supposed to know the four Vedas – Chaturvedi Brahmins are mainly members of the middle class and lower middle class. The study of the journals published by their *Mahasabha* highlights the need of togetherness in hard times, involving issues on marriages and assistance for professional matters within the community. Encouraging a network of solidarity has become a necessity. Favouring young Chaturvedi Brahmins is one of the priorities, by financial sponsoring or professional guidance.[85]

At the level of the full Varna, the same topic of fragmentation is addressed.

'*The Brahmins are basically foolish, they are stupid (…), because they don't understand their self-interest, because it is perceived that there is a great fragmentation among the Brahmins, and two segments of Brahmins can not get together to safeguard their common 'brahmanity' cause against the perceived other, whether it is the Dalit or it is the OBC, or the Thakurs or the Jats or whoever... the fragmentation among the Brahmins is so deep... and their corporate identity is very poor.'*[86]

As an extremist expression of common interests among Brahmins, the situation in Bihar is typical. Private upper castes armies, especially linked with the Bhumiyars, a mixed caste claiming a brahmanical status, are opposing Dalits. *Bhoomi Sena, Brahmarshi Sena, Sunlight Sena, Savarna Liberation Army* and *Ranvir Sena* fight for the interests of the upper castes, in a context where Backward are politically supported, with the figure of Laloo Prasad Yadav.[87]

The new strength of Backward group political identities pushes the upper castes and the Brahmins especially to react along the same lines to be able to counter the new social dynamic. The couple identity – otherness is here at work. It is like a reversal of the procesus of sanskritization. Working downwards in the cultural context, sanskritization gives way today to a mimetism process in the political scene, going upwards, from the Backward to the Brahmins. During the Kalyan Singh government in Uttar Pradesh, pro-Backward, Brahmin specific interests became very visible within the BJP, as expressions of the weaknesses of the community, against strong political assertions of the Backward.[88] An anti-Kalyan Singh lobby got developed among the Brahmin leaders of the BJP. In this context, a seminar had been organised in Kanpur to deal with the issue of 'Brahmins and situations of adversity', on 31 January 1999. A Brahmin leader, responding to critiques regarding this meeting, put forward the fact that there is nothing wrong in such a process, when all the other communities have already done the same to defend their specific interests.[89] In Agra, celebrations around *Parashuram Jayanti* are also characteristic of this assertion of brahmanical identity. Parashuram is an archetype of the Brahmin, a model and a symbol of the brahmanical violence for the Dalits. Celebrating this day, 28 April, is seen as a way to build a cultural and symbolical Brahmin inheritance, which has to be promoted.[90]

Conclusion

The nineties have been a decade in which the situation of Backward populations was highlighted, both economically and politically. The context of globalization, perceived sharply in India with the liberal policies of 1991 has had a strong impact on social and economic issues for these populations. Withdrawal of the state from the decision-making process, operating nowadays at a more global level, has strong consequences for deprived populations who need help from a welfare state.[91] But the nineties have also been linked to the process described by Rajni Kothari, as early as in the seventies: the politicization of caste. Starting with an increased political awareness among Dalits and Backward Castes, the process finally reversed towards the upper castes, and especially the Brahmins who were entailed to rediscover their identities, in such a hostile context. Through politics, in a process of rejection and mimetism of the other, Brahmins were pushed to redefine their perceptions and views on hierarchy and social justice in contemporary Indian society.

The dialectics of identity and otherness have been playing a key role in this environment. The nineties have been a mixed period for deprived populations. Suffering from the socio-economic context entailed by the New Economic Policy of 1991, they were granted more advantages through the implementation of the Mandal Commission report. At the same time, political awareness grew among these populations, with the rise of the Dalit movement. One still notices the strategic use of such political awareness for vote bank matters. However, beyond the actual changes coming from this very context, the visibility of such populations has been enhanced, modifying views and perceptions and creating new social dynamics in Indian society. The Brahmins especially, as representing the traditional élite, could not remain neutral in such a scenario. It is indeed the process of identity assertions giving way to expressions of the interests of the other, in the complex context of the NEP on one side and of Mandal and Dalit politics on the other side, which can be highlighted as central to the socio-politically turbulent decade of the nineties.

Notes

1. R. Thapar (ed.), India, another millenium?, New Delhi: Penguin Books, 2000, pp. XIX-XX.
2. P. Ricoeur, Soi-même comme un autre, Paris: Seuil, 1990, p. 384.
3. M. Galanter, Competing Equalities, Law and the Backward Classes in India, Delhi: Oxford University Press, 1984, p. 155.
4. The Constitution of India, Government of India, 1991, pp. 14, 41, 92-94.
5. A.C. Kapur, Constitutional History of India, 1765-1984, New Delhi: S. Chand & Company, 1985, pp. 468-469.
6. M. Galanter, op. cit., pp. 154-167.
7. P. Radhakrishnan, "Caste, Politics and the Reservation Issue" in Harriss-White, B. & Subramaniam, S. (ed.), Illfare in India, Essays on India's Social Sector in Honour of S. Guhan, New Delhi: Sage Publications, 1999, pp. 170-171.
8. J. Mishra, Equality versus justice - the Problem of Reservations for Backward Classes, New Delhi: Deep & Deep Publications, 1996, pp. 49-50.
9. Mandal Commission Report of the Backward Classes Commission, Delhi: Akalank Publications, 1980, p. 23.
10. Ibid, pp. 42-47.
11. Ibid, pp. 48-54.
12. Ibid, pp. 63-64.
13. J. Jayalalitha, the AIADMK leader, fought for such a high quota. She got the right to implement it through the 85th Amendment to the Constitution (Radhakrishnan 1999: 173-179). These 69 per cent (50 per cent for the Backward Classes, 18 per cent for the SCs and 1per cent for the STs) work for government services and training institutions sponsored by the state of Tamil Nadu.
14. C. Jaffrelot, Hindu Nationalist Movement and Indian Politics, 1925 to the 1990's: Strategies of Identity Building Implantation and Mobilisation, New Delhi: Penguin Books, 1996, pp. 11-15.
15. N. Datta, 'Arya Samaj and the making of Jat identity', Studies in History, New Delhi: Sage Publications, 13,1, n.s., 1997, pp. 97-119.
16. N. Datta, 'Jats: Trading caste Status for Empowerment', Economic and Political Weekly, Mumbai, 6 November 1999, p. 3172.

17. Kolis from Gujarat claim the status of a martial peasant community, culturally related to the kshatriya ethos, but opposed to the rich peasants Kanbi-Patidars, thus entitled to be labelled as Backward in the Mandal scenario (Bayly: 329-331).
18. Mandal Commission Report,op. cit., Chapters VI & VII.
19. N.B. Dirks, 'Différence et discrimination - La politique des castes dans l'Inde post-coloniale', Annales - Histoire, Sciences Sociales, Paris, 52 (3), May-June 1997, pp. 611-612.
20. A. Béteille, Backward Classes in Contemporary India, New Delhi: Oxford University Press, 1992, pp. 45-69.
21. S. Patil, 'Should "Class" be the basis for recognising backwardness', Economic and Political Weekly, 25 (50), pp. 2733-2744; G. Mahajan, Identities and Rights, Aspects of Liberal Democracy in India, Delhi: Oxford University Press, 1998, pp. 137-141.
22. P. Radhakrishnan, 'Caste, Politics and the Reservation Issue' in B. Harriss-White & S. Subramaniam (eds), Illfare in India, Essays on India's Social Sector in Honour of S. Guhan, New Delhi: Sage Publications, 1999, pp. 171-172.S. Bayly, Caste, Society and Politics in India from the eighteenth to the modern age, The New Cambridge History of India, IV (3), Cambridge: Cambridge University Press, 1999, p. 301.
23. 'Democracy and identities', The Hindu, 12 December 1997.
24. H.A. Gould, The Hindu Caste System: Politics and caste, vol.3, Delhi: Chanakya Publications, 1990, p. 3.
25. R. Kothari, Politics in India, New Delhi: Orient Longman, 1970; R. Kothari (ed.), Caste in Indian politics, New Delhi: Orient Longman, 1991.
26. R. Kothari, Communalism in Indian Politics, Delhi: Rainbow Publishers, 1998, pp. 171-176.
27. Satish Deshpande, 'Counting on caste for social justice', The Times of India, 20 August 1999.
28. H.H. Dodwell (ed.), Cambridge History of India: the Indian Empire, 1858-1919, New Delhi: S. Chand & Co., vol.6, p. 637. B.R. Ambedkar, Babasaheb Ambedkar writings and speeches (compiled by Vasant Moon), Bombay: Education Department, Government of Maharashtra, vol. 5 (1989), p. 341. G. Omvedt, Dalits and the democratic revolution: Dr Ambedkar and the Dalit movement in colonial India, New Delhi: Sage Publications, 1994, pp. 173-5.
29. G. Mahajan (ed.), Democracy, Difference and Soial Justice, Delhi: Oxford University Press, 1998, pp. 144-145.
30. V. Xaxa, 'Protective discrimination: why Scheduled Tribes lag behind Scheduled Castes', Economic and Political Weekly, 21 July 2001, pp. 2767-2770.

31. G. Guru, 'Dalits in pursuit of modernity' in R. Thapar (ed.), India, another millenium?, New Delhi: Penguin Books, 2000, p. 130.
32. P. G. Jogdand (ed.), New Economic Policy & Dalits, Jaipur: Rawat Publications, 2000, pp. 1-16, 62-64, 206.
33. G. Omvedt, 'Reservation in the private sector', The Hindu, 22 January 2000.
34. See, C. Jaffrelot, La démocratie en Inde, Paris: Fayard, 1998, pp. 179-181; S. Bayly, Caste, Society and Politics in India from the eighteenth to the modern age, The New Cambridge History of India, IV (3), Cambridge: Cambridge University Press, 1999, pp. 282-284.
35. D. L. Sheth, 'Secularisation of caste and making of new middle class', Economic and Political Weekly, 34 (34 &35), 1999, pp. 2508-2510.
36. J. Mishra, op. cit, p. 63.
37. S. Bayly, op. cit, p. 287.
38. C. Jaffrelot, La démocratie en Inde, op. cit., pp. 163-170.
39. C. Jaffrelot & J. Zérénini, 'La montée des basses castes dans la politique nord-indienne', Pouvoirs, no. 90, Paris : Seuil, 1999, pp. 69-73.
40. M. Gavaskar, 'Colonialism within Colonialism: Phule's Critique of Brahmin Power' in S.M. Michael (ed.), Dalits in Modern India - Vision and Values, New Delhi: Vistaar Publications, 1999, p. 88.
41. G. Omvedt, Dalit Visions: the anti-caste movement and the construction of an Indian identity. Tracts for the Times (8), Hyderabad: Orient Longman, 1995, pp. 43-52.
42. G. Poitevin & H. Rairkar, Stonemill and bhakti: from the devotion of peasant women to the philosophy of swamis, New Delhi: D.K. Printworld, 1996, pp. 245-250. E. Zelliot, From untouchable to Dalit: essays on the Ambedkar movement, New Delhi: Manohar Publications, 1992, pp. 317-320.
43. G. Omvedt, Dalit Visions, op. cit., pp. 73-76.
44. Pushpendra, 'Dalit assertion through electoral politics', Economic and Political Weekly, 34 (36), 1999, pp. 2609-2618.
45. S. Pai, 'The BSP in Uttar Pradesh', Seminar, New Delhi, no. 471, Novembre 1998, p. 40.
46. K. Ram, 'Why is Bahujan Samaj dependent in Independent India?', New Delhi: Bahujan Samaj Party, 1997, p. 4. K. Ilaiah, 'Why I am not a Hindu - a Sudra critique of Hindutva philosophy, culture and political economy', Calcutta: Samya, 1996. See also the article by K. Ananth, 'Isolation forces Dalit consolidation', The Hindu, 14 November 1997.
47. O. Heath & Y. Yadav, 'The United Colours of Congress, Social Profile of Congress Voters, 1996 and 1998', Economic and Political Weekly, 34 (34 & 35), 1999, pp. 2518-2528.

48. Y. Yadav, 'Understanding the second democratic upsurge: trends of Bahujan participation in electoral politics in the 1990's' in F.R. Frankel (ed.), Transforming India: Social and political dynamics of democracy, New Delhi: Oxford University Press, 2000, p. 133.
49. Mandal Commission Report, op. cit., pp. 19-22.
50. S. Navlakha, Elite and Social Change - A study of Elite Formation in India, New Delhi: Sage Publications, 1989, pp. 64-66.
51. C. Jaffrelot, La démocratie en Inde, op. cit., p. 219.
52. As collected during a fieldwork in Chennai in 1999 and 2001.
53. Interview done in New Delhi on 27 March 1997.
54. Interview done in Agra on 16 January 1998.
55. Interview done in New Delhi on 10 January 1997.
56. A. Béteille, Backward Classes in Contemporary India, New Delhi: Oxford University Press, 1992, pp. 45-69.
57. Interview done in New Delhi on 27 March 1997.
58. Interview done in Agra, 19 January 1998. A doctor made this comment. Further references in an article on the survey led on genetic differences between low and upper castes in the north-east of Andhra Pradesh, in collaboration with Uttah University: The Indian Express, 18 October 1998.
59. Interview done in Agra on 24 January 1998.
60. Interview done in New Delhi on 24 February 1997.
61. Mandal Commission Report, op. cit., p. 28.
62. India Today, 15 October 1990, p. 15.
63. India Today, 31 October 1990.
64. Interview done in New Delhi on 28 April 1997.
65. J. Mishra, op.cit., p. 3.
66. Interview done in Agra on 15 January 1998.
67. D. Gupta, Interrogation caste - Understanding hierarchy & difference in Indian society, New Delhi: Penguin Books, 2000, p. 130.
68. Interview done in Agra on 15 January 1998.
69. Interview with Jagpal Singh, New Delhi, 13 February 2001.
70. Interview done in Agra on 15 January 1998.
71. Interview done in Agra on 22 January 1998.
72. Ibid.
73. Newstime (Hyderabad), 5 September 2000.
74. Interview with N. Narayanan, President of the Tambras, Chennai, 17/02/2001.

75. Article of P. Radhakrishnan on the history of the Supreme Court decisions on reservation policies at the Centre and in Tamil Nadu, The Hindu, 26 July 2000.
76. 'The shifting sites of reservation', The Hindu, 2 December 1997.
77. Interview done in Agra on 22 January 1998.
78. 'In India, businessmen are seen as villains', The Times of India, New Delhi, 20 December 1998.
79. Interview done in New Delhi on 20 January 1997.
80. P. Van der Veer, Religious nationalism: Muslims and Hindus in India, New Delhi: Oxford University Press, 1996, pp. 52, 134-136.
81. Interview done in Agra on 20 January 1998.
82. S. Bayly, op. cit., pp. 296-297.
83. Interview by Darryl D Monte for Frontline, 18 August 2000, pp. 76-79.
84. R. Desai, 'Culturalism and Contemporary Right - Indian Bourgeoisie and Political Hindutva', Economic and Political Weekly, 20 March 1999, p. 705.
85. Journals of the Chaturvedi, Mahasabha : July 1993 (p. 4), March 1995 (p. 3), June 1995 (p. 8), January - February 1996 (p. 12-14), May 1996 (p. 46).
86. Interview done in Agra on 15 January 1998.
87. *Frontline*, vol.16, n. 5, p. 30.
88. Interview with journalist David Devadas, New Delhi, 30 June 2000.
89. The Asian Age, 2 February 1999; The Telegraph, 3 February 1999; The Hindu, 27 January 1999.
90. Amar Ujala (Agra), 25 April 1998.
91. N. Koshy, 'Political Dimensions of Globalisation', Economic and Political Weekly, 5 May 2001, p. 1516.

Globalisation, Competitiveness and Political Decentralisation

Dipankar Sengupta

The nineties have been a period of dramatic change both for India's polity as well as the economy. Politically, it was the first decade since independence when the Indian National Congress (INC) and non-Congress political formations shared power for an equal period of time at the Union level (in contrast to the previously near total domination of the INC). Economically, this decade finally saw almost all political formations eschew State-led socialism of various shades and hues and embrace private enterprise, free markets and free trade to an extent that had never been seen before.[1] So while the INC had to share power with rivals like the National Front and the United Front and the Bharatiya Janata Party (BJP)-led National Democratic Alliance during this decade, the economic policies pursued by the various governments in power showed a remarkable degree of continuity.[2] Thus the economic reforms introduced by the Narasimha Rao government in mid-1991 that replaced the old dirigistic regime regulated by licenses and permits was never reversed or even amended even when the INC lost power in 1996. The non-Congress formations that replaced the INC at Delhi themselves furthered the process of reforms.

Arguably therefore, there are today only two major issues on which there exist considerable differences of opinion between political parties; secularism and the question of distribution of powers among the Union, provincial and local governments. On the latter issue, regional parties are vociferous in their demands for greater powers to the states as well as an increased share of resources. National Parties are more reticent on this score although the INC finally pushed through legislation that promises to dramatically increase the powers vested in the Panchayati Raj Institutions (PRIs) but not the states.[3] The Left parties - the

Communist Party of India (CPI) and the Communist Party of India (Marxist) (CPM) - however not only advocate greater devolution of powers to the states, but are also practising votaries of devolving administrative powers and finances to PRIs and other local government institutions as they have demonstrated in West Bengal and Kerala (unlike most of the regional parties). However, the discussion on the redistribution of powers has not generated as much debate or passion as that on secularism. This neglect on the effect of decentralisation especially on the Indian economy (which is increasingly being integrated with the global economy) is unfortunate because redistribution of powers between the Union, the states and the PRIs will have dramatic implications and deserve to be studied in great detail.

The object of this chapter is to discuss the economic impact of the roles played by the Union government, the state government and Panchayati Raj Institutions (PRIs) in an economy that has accepted the market economy as well as integration into the global economy. It contends that, while the centralisation of powers witnessed today is a direct result of the strategy of growth followed by policy makers from the second five-year plan (1956-61) onwards, centralisation is ill-suited to the requirements of the global market economy because it robs the economy of much needed flexibility and put India at a disadvantage vis-à-vis its competitors by making it a high cost economy. In the same vein, a centralised form of government is also ill-suited to the requirements of sustainable development as conditions may differ from locality to locality, each calling for a different set of policies based on the peculiarities of the local case.

It will also be argued that neither the Centre nor the states of the Indian Union have yet geared themselves to the changed political, economic and technological environment of post-1991. One of the consequences has been the regression of India into a lower growth rate after the spurt of 7 per cent growth soon after the reforms were introduced. Thus although much has changed after 1991, yet nothing substantially has changed.

This chapter is organised as follows: in the first section the scope and role of the various levels of the government are discussed in the pre-1991 period, given the economic regime that existed. The second section describes the reforms and the new latitudes given to the various levels of government. The third section is devoted to the public good requirements of a market economy fast integrating with the global economy given the constraints of sustainable development and the constitutional/political structures that make such actions possible and the problems that arise in the absence of such structures. This chapter concludes with a discussion of the trajectory of India's development given the problems and challenges it faces in the absence of appropriate constitutional structures to tackle these problems.

Section 1: The Mahalanobis Model and the growth of centralization

It is well known that the Indian constitution displays a marked bias in favour of the Union government vis-à-vis the states in the division of powers. The economic model of development and growth that the INC opted for further strengthened this bias. The leaders of newly independent India, especially Jawaharlal Nehru, had made it very clear (even before India had attained independence)[4] that India would embark on a path of rapid industrialisation. In addition, they (certainly Nehru and Subhas Chandra Bose) had also indicated in no uncertain terms that industrialisation would occur in a socialistic regime, i.e. it would be State-led.[5]

The first aim was given shape and focus by the Mahalanobis Model (MM)[6] of economic growth and began to be implemented from the mid-fifties onwards. The MM belongs to a class of economic growth models called 'turnpike' models which seek to attain a level of income or a particular capital structure in the minimum possible time (instead of the more myopic goal of maximising current income). Turnpike models require the planning authority to invest primarily in the (capital-intensive) capital goods industry in the beginning of the planning period. Only later may the planning authority invest in the (usually labour-intensive) consumer goods industry. The second aim was to be implemented by the 'licence-permit Raj' a complex system of licenses quotas and quantitative controls exemplified by the Industrial Development Regulation Act (1955), which gave the Central government the necessary powers.

The implementation of the MM in a socialist framework applied to poor country like India meant that financial resources became increasingly concentrated. This was inevitable as the Union government in its role as the planner chose to invest in the (capital intensive) capital goods sector and chose to extend ownership over most of these industries to fulfil its aim to usher in a socialist pattern of society. This meant that the Central government had to raise vast amounts of resources from the economy and vest these resources in itself which led to concentration of economic power. The financial marginalization of the states became worse as inflation caused by budget deficits brought on by heavy Central government investment ate into the resources of the states that unlike the Centre could not monetise its deficits to overcome budget constraints.

However, it was not just the concentration of financial resources in the Centre that led to the disempowerment of the states. As Stated earlier this was accentuated by the licence-permit Raj already in place. Thus (as has been noted earlier) even modest efforts at autonomous industrial growth by the states on their own was now ruled out. This is because even if the states managed to raise finances to initiate industrialisation or persuaded businessmen within or without to invest, without Central government permission in the form of a licence, setting up even one plant would be illegal. The only way states could promote industrial growth was by lobbying with the Central government to set up an industrial unit locally or give a licence to an industrialist to set up a factory in the state. Thus industrial growth depended on the munificence of the Central government. It was enough for the state to have an efficient infrastructure or an investor friendly climate. Thus an important link between state government performance and economic growth was eliminated.

Agriculture was neglected and the economy would pay the price in the drought years of the mid-sixties when food shortages forced a plan holiday. Indeed, in the mid-sixties, when the monsoons failed for three years in succession, the Indian economy had come to a sorry pass. Where the people were concerned, it had not been able to generate adequate employment, nor keep food prices under control. For the policy makers, an acute balance of payments crisis was also an additional cause for worry. While this state of affairs was largely due to the policies followed by the Central government, the brunt of popular dissatisfaction was borne by the state governments even though they had neither the resources nor the power to foster growth or create employment. In 1967, while the INC was returned to power at the Centre, several states saw a change in guard as non-Congress governments came to power. Indeed as India experienced a 'Hindu rate of growth' of 3.5 per cent coupled with high rates of inflation, the states financially marginalized to begin with, found their real tax revenues being whittled down.

Indian policy makers decided to change certain parts of the strategy of economic growth in view of its shortcomings. The changes however did not call for a massive overhauling of the system or replacing it. The changes were the minimum required to keep the MM afloat. Since the twin problems of food shortages and inadequate foreign exchange had temporarily brought about a plan holiday, the policy makers decided to undertake those changes that would obviate specifically these problems. To increase food availability, the government decided to introduce a series of packages in the agricultural sector which would be collectively known as the Green Revolution.[7] What the Green Revolution comprised of was basically the introduction of High Yield Variety (HYV) seeds into Indian agriculture backed by heavy inputs of petrochemical fertilisers. However this mix was geared mainly towards wheat and would only work in those areas which had an assured supply of water. This necessity restricted the initial thrust of the Green Revolution to the irrigated areas of Punjab, Haryana, parts of Rajasthan and Western Uttar Pradesh which were well served by an existing network of canals. By choosing the most productive agricultural region in the country to launch India's Green Revolution, the policy makers were maximising the impact of the investment. In so far as the objective of the government was to increase the supply of food to make food imports redundant this policy was spectacularly successful. However, it must be remembered that the Green Revolution did not transform Indian agriculture, nor was it intended to do so. So while it ensured that inadequate food supply would no longer torpedo the planning process there was no major change in agricultural policy in the sense that it did not get the prominence that India's comparative advantage in this field merited it. With no all round thrust in agriculture, the institutional barriers in the form of un-empowered PRIs remained undiscovered and thus untouched.

On the industrial front, no serious overhaul was thought of. Policy makers wanted only those changes that would tackle the problem of inadequate foreign exchange. This called for an export promotion policy as exports, under the milieu of export pessimism, had stagnated and had not been enough to pay for India's imports. As India had by then become a high cost economy, these measures were in the nature of financial incentives to exporters and an increase in the supply of licenses to potential exporters. The license-permit regime was to stay in place. While these measures did succeed in boosting exports, states in general did not gain much. Their ability to pursue an autonomous economic growth policy was still as circumscribed as before given the continuance of the regulatory regime as well their continued reluctance to go in for an exclusively agricultural growth oriented strategy.

While GDP growth in the seventies was higher than it was in the sixties, it was still low and employment generation was by no means high, more so for a labour surplus country like India. While the INC was able to win the 1971 general elections with the help of populist slogans like 'Garibi Hatao' and actions like the nationalisation of banks and privy purses, dissatisfaction over inflation as well as low employment generation was quick to resurface. India was rocked by a series of agitations and ultimately emergency was imposed only to be lifted in 1977 when elections were called. In the elections, the INC was thoroughly defeated and the Janata Party came to power. However, the Janata interregnum was brief and marred by infighting and there were no breaks from the old policy regime.

The INC came back to power in the 1980 elections and remained in power throughout the decade. During this period, although the 'license Raj' was not discarded, licenses became easier to come by. Additionally, fiscal discipline also became lax as the Government started to rely increasingly on deficit financing. Thus demand creation combined with a more liberal economic regime started to raise economic growth, beyond the earlier Hindu rate of 3.5 per cent growth, to 5 per cent. But it came at the cost of higher inflation. Secondly, even as economic growth picked up, employment generation did indicate that this growth was in capital intensive sectors of the economy. At the same time pressure on the states to deliver on the employment remained, although as before the 'licence Raj' still existed. Additionally, their resources were being constantly being whittled down in real terms as inflation rose.

Faced with rising expectations, when resources were not rising as fast, States tried to cope with the situation in a number of ways. Some played into the populist camp by subsidising food grains (N.T. Rama Rao's Rs 2/- a kilo rice scheme from 1983 onwards), others wrote off bank loans (Devi Lal in Haryana from 1987 onwards), while others, as already mentioned, tried to bring a more comprehensive approach to agriculture (West Bengal and Kerala) by instituting land reforms and, more importantly for the present study, by devolving administrative and financial powers to the PRIs. So while private sector employment in the eighties hardly grew (from 7.4 million to 7.67 million in the organised sector) in spite of growth, public sector employment increased rapidly (from 15.48 million to over 19 million around the same period).[8] This was, in most cases, disguised unemployment resorted to under political pressure to create employment as productive employment opportunities in the eighties grew very slowly, even if growth rates soared. As indicated earlier, this growth comprised of demand creation by government consumption and investment financed by budget deficits and external borrowing. However, growth rates financed by borrowed money, both internal and abroad, could not last. This was especially true especially with regard to the foreign debt that India incurred during the eighties while it did not expand its capacity to export sufficiently to service this debt. This was clearly an unsustainable situation and was proved so by the balance of payments crisis of 1991.

Section II - Empowerment by default: The abandonment of the Mahalanobis Model and the consequences for the States

The crisis of 1991 proved to be a turning point in India's policy-making regime. It was triggered off by the Iraqi invasion of Kuwait that caused oil prices to skyrocket briefly while at the same time remittances dropped. The government had not only run down its reserves to finance imports for just few weeks, it was also on the verge of defaulting on its loan payments. But, by and large, this crisis was financial in nature and could have been tackled by adopting corrective fiscal steps alone. However taking their cue from the experience of the eighties, when a liberal dispensation of licenses helped growth, the reformers decided on a more comprehensive set of reforms rather than just put India's financial affairs in order. They decided on a course of structural adjustment aimed at changing the very nature of the functioning of the Indian economy, one that would be a market economy based on price signals and would be integrated to the rest of the world through increasing participation in world trade as well as international financial markets. The 'license Raj' was finally discarded ending the Central government's power to allow/disallow private agents or state governments to set up plants, factories and businesses.

With the formal abdication of the licence permit Raj and the unreserved embrace of market economics, competitiveness of Indian industry became all important. The crucial difference between how India looked at competitiveness in the post-liberalisation era and the one that had preceded it was this; before 1991 India had continued to look at exports as merely a device to pay for its imports with aggregate domestic demand being led by domestic actors, i.e. the state itself, the non-competitiveness of Indian industry mattered only in so far as there was a problem in meeting export targets. Thus, for example it mattered little that rice productivity in water abundant states like Assam and North Bihar was low and much of contribution to the rice pool came from relatively water scarce regions like Haryana and Punjab and at increasing cost. Therefore the state only tinkered at the margins of the economic regime in place to address this problem and never though of overhauling the regime itself. In the same vein the financial and political emasculation of the states and PRIs in the licence regime was not that important; it was the success of the Central government economic programme that was pertinent to the sustainability of the regime.

However, when India finally embraced economic liberalisation in 1991, discarding years of export pessimism, the high cost nature of the economy became relevant as export demand became increasingly the primary source of demand as the chart below depicts.

year	1991	92	93	94	95	96	97	98	99	2000
effective government consumption(i.e. Government expenditure minus interest payments) (in percentage)	12.16	12.16	12	10.95	10.95	10.95	10.95	10.8	11.36	12.24
Export/GDP ratio (in percentage)	9	9	10	10	11	11	11	11	12	14

The sectors (e.g. agriculture and garments) where India had a comparative advantage because of abundant labour became the dark horses. To amplify India's advantages in this field, the discarding of the license permit Raj, the introduction of unfettered competition and the winding up of state monopolies in several fields that have occurred after 1991 was obviously one set of ways of achieving that. While the latter has done well, the former has not yet lived up to expectations especially when compared to China after it introduced the 'responsibility system'. Indeed, Indian agriculture has fluctuated violently compared to the Chinese agriculture as the graph below depicts.[10]

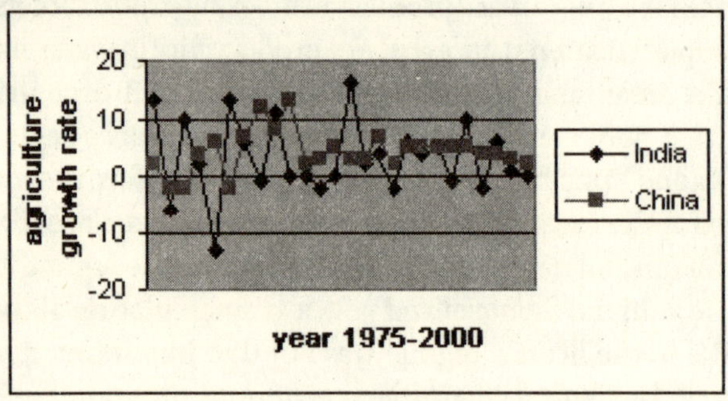

There a set of problems especially with regard to agriculture and the manner in which this sector's requirements impinge on industry, which cannot be taken care of by economic policies alone. Left to themselves, they will ensure that Indian agriculture and industry remain high cost in an integrated world economy. Indeed, it is argued below that political decentralisation, especially the empowerment of local self government provides a way out of this problem.

Economic Liberalisation and the Continued Impotence of the States

In a changed paradigm, where market economics had replaced the earlier 'command economy' administered by licences and permits, it became possible - at least in theory - for the states to pursue, if need be, an autonomous policy of economic growth. In actual fact, however, it came at a time when the financial health of the states were without exception precarious. While the Central government on its own volition had given up its monopoly to issue licences, it empowered the states to some extent by default but the financial marginalization continued in effect denying them much leeway in pursuing strategies of growth. The financial health of the states had become poor for two reasons, one related to the MM model. States during this period had generally tried to get on the industry bandwagon lobbying with the Central government to give them licenses to set up industrial units. Sometimes the states managed to set up these units by raising the required resources on their own. This obviously meant the shouldering of a financial burden that was aggravated on two counts: the fact that a resource scarce economy had to garner resources to set up a capital intensive project and it did so when it was already being financially marginalized by the Central government which had an industrial agenda of its own. In most cases the project promoted by the state governments failed but the states kept the concerns going financing their losses. Far from socialising their profits for future growth, the state governments, now by financially covering their losses, had less left over to finance development.

The second factor was that the eighties had seen the abandonment of fiscal prudence by both the Central and the state governments. Deficits as a proportion to receipts for the states shot up from 19.2 per cent to 28.2 per cent in the period 1980-81/1990-91 and in the year 2000-01 stood at 32.7 per cent.[11] The inflationary impact of Central government policies combined with their own burgeoning debt burden caused by populist policies left the states with very little investible resources. Thus the continued powerlessness of the states could be indirectly attributed to the MM and the manner it was implemented as well as to the unwillingness of most states to devolve power to PRIs and promote agriculture. Most states which had been largely left out of the development process had little funds left over to invest in infrastructure, like roads or power, necessary preconditions for bringing in private investment.

In the field of agriculture (as has been noted) there was not much progress. Agriculture in India has been as sensitive to '*other factors*' as price incentives.[12] In spite of considerable investment in irrigation projects, the total area under irrigation grew slugglishly with gross irrigated area rising from 22.6 million hectares to 78.5 million hectares in fifty years since 1950 which corresponds to an increase from 17 per cent of gross sown area to 41 per cent over the same period.[13] Meanwhile from 1970 onwards, agriculture, especially the HYV package, also became capital-intensive, thus closing one of the few routes that the states had to promote growth. The increasing capital intensity of agriculture had its origins in the requirement of the new technology responsible for the Green Revolution. One requirement was a regular supply of water that called for large irrigation projects often linked with multi-purpose dams. The capital requirements of these projects are enormous and generally beyond the capability of most states. Even if the financial constraint had been lifted, such a strategy would have been a high cost one with its implications for the competitiveness of the rest of the economy. Yet there was a way to promote growth in the state even without considerable additional help from the Centre and one where India had competitive advantage with the potential to participate profitably in the global economy.

Indeed this was the only sector that had been open for development to the states without Central government interference. In fact strategies of utilising under-utilised labour for capital formation were advanced by Nurkse[14] and adapted to Indian conditions by Vakil and Brahmanand[15]. What the Nurkse-Vakil-Brahmanand (NVB) thesis suggested was the following: Given the fact that much of labour in rural India was either under-utilised, idle or seasonally employed, they could be used to build capital in the form of small dams, dykes, tanks, irrigational canals and ditches without affecting adversely economic activity elsewhere. This thesis postulated that this labour although idle did not starve as their family members fed them although they were not gainfully employed. Employing such people by paying them wages did not therefore necessarily mean that these wages would be spent on food thus causing inflation. Even if it did, given the fact that this labour was being spent on investments that reduced agricultural bottlenecks, agricultural/food production would rise to meet this extra demand. Thus even the use of deficit financing in this case would be non-inflationary as increased productivity in agriculture would liquidate inflation caused by the rise in demand due to increased investment expenditure in the form of wages.[16]

There would be a number of problems if the states tried to implement the NVB strategy on their own. Firstly, the states that were strapped for resources, in a regime that called for resource concentration by the Central government, would have to take recourse to deficit financing to promote agriculture in a big way. However, for the states deficit financing could only mean issuing interest-carrying bonds and increased debt servicing costs in the future. The less expensive option of borrowing from the central bank is not open to them as it is to the Central government. While the investment as devised by the NVB may raise agricultural output, it will also in all likelihood push the State government into a debt trap. This is because the State government is not the beneficiary of the increased productivity in agriculture - the farmers are -, nor can it tax the beneficiaries to pay off debt incurred in financing that investment, as farmers do not pay income tax. Thus this investment that has to be financed either through taxes or borrowings - paying market rates of interest - would not have - and do not even today - increase the revenue base of the government.

While the difficulties of the financially constrained States in pursuing a strategy of agricultural growth have been outlined in the previous section there are certain non-financial problems associated with such projects as well. An agricultural growth strategy requires a certain degree of flexibility as crucial conditions like soil type, terrain, availability of water, availability of local labour may vary greatly across regions, districts and indeed even villages. For a centralised Planning Commission to take into account all these local peculiarities to form a plan, and for the state government to implement this plan, is no easy task, if at all feasible. This is because the agricultural growth plan would actually comprise of a plethora of plans each geared to a particular region, sub-region. These projects are best handled locally where the representatives of the local government have a better idea about local conditions and are likely to plan and execute projects of a local nature more efficiently than a remote authority.

However Indian states by and large did not empower their PRIs. Elections to these institutions were more often than not kept in abeyance and there was hardly any transfer of finance to the PRIs. Even regional parties who came to power in their respective States on a political platform asking for greater devolution of powers from the Centre to the States were reluctant to share power and resources with PRIs. As mentioned earlier, it was the Left alone that was consistent in calling for the greater devolution of powers from the Centre to the states while ensuring that PRIs also were empowered financially and politically and elections to these institutions held regularly in states where they had attained power, i.e. West Bengal and Kerala (Maharashtra and Gujarat being the only other States where the Left has no presence and where the PRIs had taken firm roots).[17] It is not entirely co-incidental that growth in these states have been above the national average (per capita incomes in West Bengal and Kerala rose (in the period 1991/92-1997/98) by 31 per cent and 32.7 per cent respectively compared to the all India figure of 28 per cent)[18] even without the kind of Central government investment in the form of a Bhakra-Nangal project that Punjab witnessed. Food grains production in West Bengal rose by 34 per cent in the 1990s compared to 16 per cent nationwide.[19] However as most states did not undertake agriculture-led growth strategies, the need to decentralise power was never quite felt. Thus PRIs in most states remained moribund institutions, and therein lay a problem. This is because crucial problems like adequate water availability are best tackled in a particular way. This combines traditional practices of water harvesting with the NVB thesis on capital accumulation in economies with surplus labour. The capital costs involved are much lower as an abundant resource, i.e. labour, is used and inexpensive check-dams/bunds are built. These projects however are micro projects and cannot be managed from the state capital. These projects are best handled at the village level. That however requires the institution of a local self-governing body at the village level or some form of PRI with some financial and administrative powers. It is precisely this institution that very few states allowed to take root and evolve. And the differences in performances of states with a flourishing PRI culture, and those without, has been telling especially in agriculture. For example, while the States of Maharashtra and Gujarat are prominent in public consciousness for their rapid economic growth, Kerala and West Bengal have also done very well despite impressions to the contrary. Indeed agriculture has been the key factor in pulling growth in these two states that has more than compensated for a lacklustre industrial performance. Decentralization at the village level has not only made targeting of poverty alleviation schemes better,[20] it has also made capital accumulation more effective[21] and helped solve the vexatious problems of water rights.[22] Assam, with the same advantages (abundant water and appropriate climate) as West Bengal, has not grown. It is clear that political and administrative decentralization have certain consequences for economic growth. However, this is not appreciated by most economists. While the end of the Mahalanobis Model with the 'license Raj' had meant that the reduction of states to glorified municipalities was no longer necessary, it was also not clear as to what economic logic demanded devolution of powers to self-local governments. Indeed votaries of local-self government had cited leakages in poverty alleviation schemes as a reason why they should be strengthened. Devolution of economic powers were generally advanced by those who valued participatory planning, economic efficiency was not necessarily a criterion.[23] As a result, ten years after economic liberalisation commenced, a sector that seemed to have so much promise has not yet delivered. On the contrary, vested interests in this sector by asking concessions for free power transfer costs to Indian industry and make the latter uncompetitive as the latter have to pay a higher price for a crucial input which in turn jacks up their cost of production.

Section III - Towards a theory of decentralization

What is the economic argument for decentralization? A case for decentralization may be made on the same grounds on which von Hayek[24] defended the market economy vis-à-vis the planned economy. In so far as one of the role of the State is to provide public goods like infrastructure where externalities are involved, a theory may be advanced. It must be recognized that most economies are not homogenous entities. There is a wide variation among various regions and localities within regions. Consequently, economic infrastructure that has to be created is not always standardized or uniform. Planning for infrastructure in a non-uniform environment, especially when local economic activity is especially affected by local factors, requires the collection of relevant data - available locally - and then processing this data into information. Ideally, it should be this information that is the basis of planning for certain kinds of infrastructure. This is especially true for agriculture and a host of agro-industries. To that extent infrastructure required to support that industry/ economic activity will be peculiar to the locality as its nature and quantum will depend on local conditions. Thus that portion of infrastructure will be best planned, executed and managed by the members of the locality itself. The reasons are simple. The members of the locality or their representatives being first hand observers of local conditions should know the best way to create an appropriate supporting local infrastructure and should be able to do so in the most economical manner. Indeed, for projects relating to watershed management, local self-governing bodies can mobilise free labour (by suitable innovation as regards distribution of benefits) from its citizens, which in the context of South Asia usually means unutilised labour.

If, on the other hand, the Central government is entrusted with the responsibility of providing all infrastructural requirements, then it has to collect information from all the localities, aggregate this information and process it to arrive at a plan to provide infrastructural support. This is obviously a monumental task and one that is not easily accomplished. Secondly, in the process of aggregating information, it is likely that some information of value will be lost. To that extent the plan created will be *faulty/sub-optimal.* Thirdly, given the magnitude of this exercise it is also likely that the *lag* between the perception of the problem and action will be larger. Fourthly the possibility is that the link between local public good requirement and a local solution will be broken. While local demands will be aggregated, the solution that is proposed will be a centralised one. Take the case of the construction of a multi-purpose irrigation dam to cater to the needs of a large number of people spread over a large area distributed into various localities. This solution, while at times the only and perhaps the best solution, may not always be so. For one, the capital costs of such projects are very high. Secondly, they can take a long time to complete. Thirdly, it has a tendency to submerge the most fertile areas and thus the most populated areas and displace a section of people 'for the greater common good.' However in the absence of effective decentralization, the solution like the one above will be the only solution. Before discussing the effect of the redistribution of powers, a look at the public goods requirements of the Indian economy integrating with the global economy is useful.

What are the public goods that the Indian economy requires now that it has decided to integrate with the world economy? Obviously the public goods that must now be provided must supplement the strengths of the Indian economy. Given the fact that India is a labour surplus economy, this means that public goods provided must be those that amplify the strengths of those sectors of the economy that are labour-intensive. This covers agriculture and labour-intensive manufactures like apparel/garment manufacture. In the future, it could also include assembly of electronic goods, that is the labour intensive component of manufacture of electronic goods. The latter sector generally is comprised of small firms[25] that have a tendency to agglomerate/localize in a particular region. For an economy the size of India, these firms will possibly spread all over the country, with different regions supporting different clusters of industries.

However, whether agriculture or industry, both these sectors have a set of common public good requirements. These include an efficient and economical transport system (the preserve of the Central and state governments), reliable supply of power at economical tariffs (the responsibility of the state governments). A crucial commonality is electricity. However, given the poverty of the agricultural class, this common requirement has acquired the form of a zero sum game. Electricity to the agricultural class has to be provided at rates that do not cover the cost of generating it. The burden of picking up this cost is borne by industry that does so but not entirely. The end effect of it is to strap the State Electricity Boards (SEBs) with financial losses rendering them incapable of investing in either extra generation capacity or maintenance of existing infrastructure. All this leads to rising costs of electricity as transmission and distribution losses mount. All this is in addition to widespread electricity shortages as supply falls short of demand. Industrialists use captive power to tackle this particular bottleneck, but that only serves increase costs.

Another common requirement is water. Apart from civic requirements, water is needed for irrigation and has industrial uses, and water supply must be predictable and regular. Now provision of water is, by and large, in the domain of the state and the Central governments and logically so as the usual mode of meeting requirements on a mass scale is met by the construction of large dams which is beyond the capacity of local civic authorities, be it urban or rural. However, such projects are highly capital-intensive projects and not without their share of controversies, not the least because of doubts over their long run cost-effectiveness. The alternative is to go in for decentralised solutions but one that depends on local participation, like roof top/rainwater harvesting. Given their nature they are best administered by the local civic authorities like the PRIs. If these schemes are successful, then not only are significant savings effected, the conflict between agriculture and industry over electricity can also be lessened. This is because if the experience of the Tarun Bharat Sangh (see below) is anything to go by, the rise in the water table reduces power consumed in pumping water to the fields. Lower power requirements from agriculture can only mean more and cheaper power for industry as SEBs with a lower financial burden will be able to invest more in power generation as well as maintenance of existing infrastructure. This will lead to a lowering of costs as well as a removal of an infrastructural bottleneck. Additionally money saved by the State due to the substitution of the capital-intensive water supply project can be spent on transport and ports to lower transportation costs and add to competitiveness.

The effects of centralised solutions on national competitiveness will be easy to measure. In so far as the costs have to be financed by taxes, a rise in indirect taxes will ensure that costs across the board rise affecting competitiveness. It is also possible, that the project; usually a mammoth multipurpose dam may have other benefits like the generation of hydel power[26], the vast enhancement of agricultural productivity which may more than compensate for the costs incurred. However, even if cost benefit exercises conclusively prove that cheaper decentralised alternatives exist, in the absence of effective decentralization, the centralised capital-intensive scheme will be the only feasible option irrespective of the cost-benefit calculations. Indeed, there are now cases that demonstrate what happens when infrastructural projects best planned and executed locally are executed Centrally.

The successes of the Tarun Bharat Sangh (TBS)[27] in Rajasthan in watershed development projects have opened the eyes of policy makers to the possibility of rainwater harvesting as a tool for ensuring the supply of water even in areas with scanty rainfall. It is best exemplified by the experience of Alwar district that had been declared a 'dark zone' (no ground water) in the 1980s by the authorities and activities like agriculture had almost ceased to exist. It is here that the Magsaysay Award winner, Rajendra Singh, the founder of the TBS, with the help of the villagers of Kaonta Bhaontala constructed the first check dam in 1985. In 1986, they constructed a *johad* (a traditional crescent shaped pond) at the source of the River Arvari which had become a seasonal rivulet. Other villages too followed suit constructing *johads* in the other catchment areas of the Arvari. When the number of ponds touched 375, the Arvari that had almost ceased to exist, revived and from 1994 became a perennially flowing river. What TBS has accomplished is a vindication of the NVB thesis, that in a labour abundant economy like India, labour combined with very little capital can bring about a remarkable economic transformation. The economic impact can be gauged for the effect of the investment made by the villagers of Neembi. On an investment of Rs 50,000/- to build two check dams, Neembi produces vegetables and milk worth Rs 3 crores. This is not the kind of capital-output ratio that can be easily ignored especially by states who are financially constrained.

However it was ignored till 2000 when large areas in India were struck by drought. It was suddenly discovered that the villages under the TBS's area of operations did not suffer from want of water, even though Rajasthan was suffering from drought for three consecutive years. Indeed in some areas the ground water lay only three feet from the surface. In the aftermath of the drought in 2000, the governments of Gujarat and Andhra Pradesh[28] decided to go in for check dam construction on a massive scale. However the approaches of the two governments were different.

The Power of Panchayats: A Tale of Two States

The state government of Gujarat launched the *Sardar Patel Participatory Water Conservation Programme* (SPPWCP) choosing to act through the PRIs. The state government invited proposals from the Panchayats and faced an overwhelming response. Initially, the state government had budgeted for approximately 2500 check dams at the cost of Rs. 100 crores. However the response and innovation of the PRIs in the state ensured that while the number of sanctioned dams quadrupled to 10,500, the budget only doubled to Rs. 200 crores. Impressingly enough, the state government did not bear the entire cost but asked the villagers to bear 40 per cent of the cost. Planning and execution of the project was done by the PRIs themselves. The results of the SPPWCP have been described as 'good'. While there have been cases of corruption, these have been limited. The best results have taken place in those villages where civil society was involved. The case of Andhra Pradesh is another matter altogether.

The Neeru Meeru Scheme in Andhra Pradesh, unlike the one in Gujarat, did not rely on local participation. Here the State relied on contractors and bureaucrats and the results have been poor. Being centralised, they have fallen prey to certain members of the ruling party who utilised the scheme to set a system of patronage. This is easy, as those managing and executing the scheme do not live amongst those who are its beneficiaries. It is also clear that states who have a long nurtured PRIs are also states where participatory schemes will be successful. Indeed, as in the case set out below a village may even take it upon itself to finance the entire project itself.[29]

Gandhigram in Kutch, in the face of state government inaction, decided to mobilise the resources it requires to build a check dam in the year 1999. It organised a 15 lakh loan from an NRI, a 5 lakh loan (at 16 per cent rate of interest) from the Kutch Gramin Bank and voluntary labour from the residents would contribute an additional 7 lakh. The loans are to be paid back in five years. Each resident agreed not to irrigate more than 5 acres of land and will share the maintenance costs. As this dam will help them to grow an additional crop, the profits from this enhanced income is expected to pay for the dam. Again the ability of the local government to encourage/enforce cooperative behaviour enables it to execute this project. State governments, who are far more remote from the villagers than the PRI representatives, will find it impossible to elicit cooperation of this magnitude and certainly not from all villages of the state. Thus, the link between decentralising power and effectiveness on infrastructural expenditures cannot be ignored. As the capital-output ratio declines with political and administrative decentralisation the foundations of an efficient economy are laid.

Legislation and Implementation: The Divergence and Consequences

However, the larger part of India's polity has not yet accepted PRI despite the 72nd amendment that has given PRI constitutional status. Indeed the reluctance of some states to constitute these bodies and hold elections to fill these forced concerned citizens to petition the courts.[30] In any case, even when these bodies have been constituted, the flow of funds to these bodies have been low. The amount that the states spend on local bodies is on average not more than 1.7 per cent of their total expenditure.[31] While PRIs have certain powers of taxation, they are reluctant to use them. This is because of two reasons. The main reason is the proximity of the Panchayat members to the tax payers (ironically the strongest factor in the effectiveness of Panchayats) and imposition of taxes are generally unpopular decisions.[32] The second is the lack of a body of civil servants to administer tax collection.[33] While the costs are borne at once by the villagers, the benefits generally follow with a lag. Thus raising resources by the Panchayat through taxation is not easily done. If, on the other hand, a project initially financed by funds advanced by a higher body turns out to be successful, then subsequent efforts may be funded by the villagers themselves, as the case of Gandhigram in Gujarat shows.

An initial flow of funds to the villages to assume the role of a provider of public goods may be advisable. Yet, in the absence of genuine decentralization, Nurkse's dream of using unutilised labour to increase capital formation remains unfulfilled. This is tragic because the SPPWCP shows that such a goal is both realistic and gettable. Thus, in the context of a globalising economy, India remains a high cost economy as the abundant factor remains under-utilised due to excessive centralisation.

Conversely, there are also goods that are best provided by State and Central governments. There are obvious examples like rail services and postal services, which on account of scale economies and coordination are best handled by a federal government and indeed in India this is the case. However, there are some items that require Centralisation but are currently in the domain of the states and PRIs. These are issues like power and education.

It is well known that the power sector in India, which is in the domain of the state governments, faces a grave crisis principally because states governments are loath to charge certain consumers realistic rates for electricity consumed. Generally these are interest groups that have managed to organize themselves politically into a lobby and are able to get concessions like free power as in Tamil Nadu and Punjab. The effect of these concessions has been to bankrupt the SEBs with the result that these entities have no money left for investment for either fresh addition to power generating capacity or maintenance of existing infrastructure. This leads to a shortage of power where industry is concerned which has to rely on captive power generation that is expensive and leads to rising costs and decreasing competitiveness in the context of a globalising economy. Environmentally too, the presence of free power has led farmers to deplete groundwater as pumping water with the help of electric tube-wells is inexpensive. Thus farmers are left with no option but go on boring deeper and deeper in subsequent periods to reach the water table that leads to higher costs in the long run.[34] Thus even agricultural products lose their competitiveness even though an input (electricity) is being subsidized. Such policies are not sustainable from the point of view of either sustainable development or economic competitiveness or financial resources.

It is clear that the state governments being close to these lobbies find it difficult to resist pressures regarding power tariffs. Here the role of the Central government is clearly crucial: By forcing the States to adopt proper tarification that ensures the SEBs an appropriate return on capital employed, so that addition to capacity can be made as and when the need arises. Secondly, states that have potential or actual overcapacity can sell power to power-deficient states. Thus states with hydel power potential or excess reserves of coal can set up plants and sell power to other states, instead of the purchasing states setting up inoptimal plants in locations far away from sources of coal producing high cost energy.

Similarly, giving Panchayats the power to appoint teachers is also fraught with serious consequences. Appointments are not likely to follow an appropriate or transparent criteria and appointments once made cannot be easily reversed. This is because the appointing authority are generally too close to candidates to make an objective decision. Additionally the power of feudal groups is most acutely felt at this level of government. Nor is it easy to monitor all Panchayats in this regard as their sheer numbers makes monitoring impossible. A more appropriate approach is for the state governments (the level of government which is sufficiently remote to conduct a fair recruiting process) take charge of appointments and create a roster of candidates who can be allotted to the requesting villages. Indeed it may be noted that in France, teachers are recruited by the Central government and assigned to the requesting local body. The consequences of a poor recruitment are long term and pernicious. The recruitment of poor teachers sees to it that human capital formation remains poor. This has its impact on the ability of economic agents in the rural economy to adopt newer technologies or indeed adopt organizational innovations that help to boost productivity. The implications for long-term competitiveness are obvious. It is clear that given the fact that no economy can remain dependent on abundant labour for an infinitely long period, human capital formation/development is all important in the long run if technical progress is to occur.

The Freedom from 'Plebiscitary Politics'

Decentralised democratic governance such as the kind that the PRIs should ideally represent also emancipates the local polity from the baneful effects of 'plebiscitary politics'.[35] In a situation where all power and resources was concentrated in the Central government, the party that ruled the Centre set an upper bar on the conditions that governed the lives of all of India's citizens. It was practically impossible for any constituent unit of the polity to improve upon Central government performance. The constituent units did not have the power or resources to even attempt such a task. Thus even the existence of a talented and enterprising pool of people receptive and indeed capable of innovative ideas could not do much in this milieu. Their ideas would be implemented only if they caught the attention of a powerful figure at the Centre. Consequently, even technological breakthroughs would be associated with politicians, and not seen as market induced (as the market was circumscribed). Thus computerisation in India was associated with Rajiv Gandhi, the telecommunications revolution with Rajiv Gandhi and Satyendranath (Sam) Pitroda, Operation Flood (that boosted milk production) with Verghese Kurien, etc. All of them were either State-sponsored or had the backing of the State. Without State backing, they would simply not get off the ground. Thus even while India was formally a democracy, functionally power was concentrated in the hands of the very few who were elected.

The liberalization of the Indian economy ended the Centre's monopoly over licensing. But where infrastructure was concerned, it transferred plebiscitary politics to the state capitals. Thus were crucial services like electricity and water was concerned, it was the state government alone that would decide what was to be done. If dedicated NGOs were fortunate enough to be close to the state government, their ideas would be given a hearing. But actual action and the ground and indeed the right to initiate action (some States have insisted) was the state government's alone. It is in this context that the success of the TBS has to be measured and analysed. The TBS transformed an area designated a 'dark zone' into a water abundant area with a thriving agriculture reversing the drain of labour into the cities. Indeed he also revived the once-dead River Arvari over the vociferous objections of the officials of the Rajasthan State government. Indeed, had it not been for the organized protests of the beneficiaries of the TBS's activities, the check dams constructed by the organization would have been demolished, the vast improvement in the lives of the people that has taken place not withstanding. Unlike Sam Pitroda *vis-à-vis* Rajiv Gandhi, clearly TBS did not have the ear of the Chief Ministers of Rajasthan.

What is eminently clear is that there must be an institution that incorporates social entrepreneurs in its functioning and uses their talents, rather than have such organizations/persons work outside the system and often against it while attempting to do something constructive. Such an institution obviously cannot be a 'distant' one buffeted by a host of 'societies' and NGOs spurious or otherwise, all claiming to have ideas that will revolutionise life. Such an institution will perforce have to be local and numerous. The Panchayat is no doubt one of the institutions that fulfil this criterion. Social entrepreneurs and activists will be able to interact with a tier of government capable of putting their ideas to work. Indeed, they may even chose to run for office to occupy one of these institutions as the number of voters to be convinced is low and thus election expenses low. Thus innovation will stand a greater chance of legitimacy and state support than under a centralized government. The implications for innovative labour-intensive and environmentally friendly social capital formation are profound. If the success of the TBS is replicated nationwide with

State institutions reinforcing local initiatives rather than suffocating them, the implications for economic growth are obvious. However as of now, things stand very differently. The Indian State which is effectively still centralized is unable to incorporate men and ideas and talent which could enable to provide it public goods at the lowest possible cost. Today, NGOs with proven track records as well as dubious ones jostle for State attention and funds at the Centre and state level. Effectiveness of action is not necessarily a criterion for survival; contacts are.

Conclusion

The nineties in India has been aptly described as a 'liberating' decade'.[36] As the Indian State decided to liberalise its economic system from a 'license Raj' system to a market economy as well as integrate it with the global economy, it potentially empowered its citizens to take on the role of entrepreneurs to use the global economy as their playing field while also exposing them to competition from firms without. To engage global competition effectively, the ability of Indian firms to use relatively abundant factor labour effectively is of paramount importance. Thus, it is extremely important that the labour intensive sector of the economy is able to expand in the most efficient manner. In so far as Indian agriculture is labour intensive, agriculture must be made efficient.

This is possible if the infrastructure that supports agriculture itself is available and created efficiently which in turn implies effective use of labour and knowledge of local conditions. It is clear that such services are best provided by local self governments as they are best placed to gather information to plan such a task and, given the proximity to local labour, the best authority to implement the same. Centralised authority fails both on the informational front - which leads to faulty planning -, as, on the implementation front as coordination on such a wide scale is not easily done. Very often a common centralised solution (regardless of local requirements) is imposed at great cost leading to the creation of a high cost economy. Thus the liberation of the Indian economy is incomplete without liberating the rural citizenry from the monopoly of power by the Centre and the states. This calls for the effective empowerment in the form of PRIs and their participation in providing public goods. In effect we argue that the liberalisation of the economy has its corollary in the decentralization of administrative power. If, indeed, India is to be a competitive economy, it will be aided in no small measure by effective local self government.

Notes

1. It may be argued that the Bharatiya Janata Party (BJP) had never subscribed to socialism (except for a brief flirtation with Gandhian Socialism) while the Communist Party of India (CPI) and the Communist Party of India(Marxist)(CPM) have not embraced the market economy with the fervour which the others have.
2. This was not unlike the Janata Party experience in 1977-79 where a change in the government did not lead to the dismantling of the existing economic regime.
3. The Constitution (Seventy-third Amendment) Act, 1992.
4. Baldev Raj Nayar, Globalisation and Nationalism, The Changing Balance in India's Economic Policy 1950-2000, New Delhi: Sage Publications, 2002.
5. This was confirmed by the Avadi session (December 1956) of the All India Congress Committee (AICC) when a resolution to that effect was adopted formally.
6. See P.C. Mahalanobis, 'Some Observations on the Process of National Income', Sankhya, 12 (4), 1953.
7. For a less than enthusiastic view of the Green Revolution see, B.H. Farmer, Green Revolution? ', London: Macmillan and English Language Book Society, 1977.
8. Manpower Profile India Yearbook, Institute of Applied Manpower and Research, New Delhi, 1999.
9. Constructed from WDI 2003 CD-ROM Query database, World Bank.
10. Constructed from WDI 2003 CD-ROM Query database, World Bank.
11. Calculated from States' Gross Fiscal Deficit and Its Financing '. http://www.rbi.org.in/sec7/37054. pdf
12. T. Palanivel, ' Aggregate Supply Responses in Indian Agriculture: Some Empirical Evidence and Policy Implications', Indian Economic Review, vol.

30 no. 2, 1995. For a more pessimistic view see, S. Storm S, 'The Unfinished Agenda: Indian Agriculture Under the Structural Reforms', Journal of International Trade & Economic Development, vol. 6 no. 2, 1997.

13. Calculated from 'Agricultural Statistics at a Glance 2003', Ministry of Agriculture, Government of India.

14. R. Nurkse, 'Problems of Capital Formation in Underdeveloped Countries,' New York: Oxford University Press, 1967.15 C.N. Vakil, & P.R. Brahmanand, Planning for an expanding economy, Delhi: Vora & Co., 1956.

16. A.P. Thirlwall, Growth and Development: with Special Reference to Developing Economies, Basingstoke:Macmillan, 1972.

17. Buddhadeb Ghosh & Girish Kumar, State Politics and Panchayats in India, New Delhi, Manohar, 2003.

18. See National Human Development Report, 2001, Planning Commission of India, March 2002.

19. Handbook of Statistics of the Indian Economy, Reserve Bank of India, 2000.

20. See P.Bardhan and D. Mookherjee, 'Poverty Alleviation Report of West Bengal Panchayats', Economic and Political Weekly, 25 November, 2003 for a qualified view on this subject.

21. See R. Crook and A.S. Sverrisson, Decentralization and Poverty Alleviation in Developing Countries: A Comparative Analysis, or Is West Bengal Unique?, Institute of Development Studies (IDS), Working Paper no. 130, 2001 and J. Litwack, J. Ahmad, R. Bird, Rethinking Decentralization in Developing Countries , The World Bank, Sector Studies Series, 1998.

22. See L.K. Joshi, Irrigation and its Management in India, Need for Paradigm Shift, http://www.iar.ubc.ca/Centres/cisar/JOSHI/J1.html

23. To be sure, there were exceptions, e.g, A. Dasgupta,, 'Panchayati Raj and Decentralised Planning in West Bengal '– in, Malcolm Adiseshah (ed)- Decentralised Planning and Panchayati Raj: Proceedings of the DT Lakdawala Memorial Symposium: Institute of Social Sciences, New Delhi, 1994.

24. von Hayek, F (ed), Collectivist Socialist Planning, London: Routledge, Kegan and Paul, 1935.

25. Small as is being defined here may not tally with the government of India's definition of what comprises the small sector.

26. For instance the Bhakra-Nangal Project or even the Sardar Sarovar project.

27. 'The Arvari, Coming Back to Life', Down to Earth, 15 March 1999.

28. 'Tryst with Rain, Gujarat and Andhra Pradesh', Down to Earth, vol. 9, no. 11, 31 October 2000.

29. 'Bank Loans to Harvest Water, A Community in Kutch mobilises Resources to meet its Water Needs 'Jalvani, vol. 3, no. 2, 2000.

30. B. Ghosh, & G. Kumar, op. cit.
31. Note that this figure is covered in official statistics under he heading 'Others' which includes compensation and assignments to local bodies and PRIs and reserve with finance departments, State finances. A Study of the Budgets of 2001-2, RBI, Jan 2002.
32. James Manor, 'Madhya Pradesh, Experiments with Direct Democracy', Economic and Political Weekly, 3 March 2003.
33. A. Mukherjee, Decentralisation: Panchayats in the Nineties, New Delhi: Vikas Publishing House, 1994.
34. Praveen Swami., 'Sunset in Paradise', Frontline, Volume 21 - Issue 05, February 28 - March 12, 2004.
35. L.L. Rudolph & S.H. Rudolph, 'Organisational Adoption of the Congress under Rajiv Gandhi's Leadership' in, Diversity and Dominance in Indian Politics, Vol. 1, Richard Sission & Ramashray Roy (eds), New Delhi: Sage Publications, 1990.
36. Gurcharan Das, India Unbound: From Independence to the Global Information Age, London: Profile Books, 2002.

Economic Reforms and a New Public-Private Development Model in India:

Joël Ruet

The years 1991-2001 symbolise a decade of economic reforms in India; providing the opportunity for a critical assessment. They are also the period separating the last two censuses, thus allowing a focus on the social front. The present article however aims at characterising the structural modes of regulation of the Indian economy, and lays a wager moreover on the dynamic emergence of India as an economic power, via its cities and services. In other words, this article will concentrate on 'India' seen as urban India, more than on 'Bharat', the rural and traditional India. The earlier development model, based on public expenditures under a technical, non people-oriented paradigm, had reached its limits. The beginnings of a change in the paradigm of development are already visible, while the consequences on the rural world remains the major question mark for the coming decade. Looking beyond a rapid survey of the macro-economic figures (section 1), what are the reality of the public sector and of its contradictions (section 2) ?, and how does the private sector articulate upon the deficiencies of the earlier model (section 3)? Finally, what are the wagers of reallocation in the India of tomorrow, which the emergence of the private sector gives rise to or strengthens (section 4) ?

Looking at macro-economic facts alone

'Facts', or a classic interpretation which creates its own meaning

In 2001-02, the per capita GDP in India was 480 $. The total GDP of the country was about half that of China. India therefore remains, on an average, a poor country, and moreover overwhelmingly rural (70 per cent of the population). But this should not mask certain disparities which sometimes throw a veil over what are some veritable trump cards specific to urban India. The successive Central governments since 1991 have pursued a more or less active policy of reforms. This policy was officially launched following a foreign exchange crisis during the first part of 1991. Before 1991, India's economy had been, by and large, a closed economy with a policy based on import substitution. The banking sector, including private banks, was very largely controlled in order to finance at subsidised rates public investments in what were called the priority sectors, leading to a large 'ousting effect', that is, a siphoning of investment for them, at the expense of other sectors, which suffered from investment scarcity. This analysis, expressed in terms of investment availability for the private sector, has structured the reforms, from 1991 onwards, through policies of opening up of imports, reduction of taxes, and incentives to private investment, both foreign and Indian. What has been their result ?

The reforms were initiated subsequent to the foreign reserves crisis, and India has indeed succeeded in controlling the problem of its debt, whose ratio to the GDP has declined from 37.7 per cent in 1992 to 21.4 per cent in 2001. Inflation, which was of the order of 15 per cent in 1991-92, seems to have been contained, and has remained since 1997 at 4 per cent, although it did shoot up suddenly in 1998-99 to 13.1 per cent! The public deficit of the government of the Indian Union ('the Centre') was of the extent of 8.3 per cent of the GNP in 1991-92. This came down to 5.9 per cent of the GNP in 1995-96 (World Bank, 1996), but has stabilised since then to remain at this level. Moreover, the combined public deficit of the federal government and of the governments of the states within the federation is higher and has structurally stabilised at 10 per cent of the GNP (and, if we add to it the deficit of the public sector enterprises, it is structurally even higher at 11 per cent, source: IMF). And this is so without taking into account the total deficit of the public enterprises, only a part of which is covered by subsidies budgeted within both the Central budget and the state government budgets. But above all, we are witnessing a marginal growth in exports, and the expected foreign direct investment (FDI) has not materialised, due partly to the complexity of the administrative system and partly to the absence of any clear rules on the matter.[1] The FDI, initially very small, at $ 150 million in 1991, crossed over to $ 2 billion in 1995-96 (World Bank, 1996) but has remained at just $ 2.3 billion in 2000-01. But this continues to be structurally small. Thus, while it has soared upwards in countries such as China, it has stagnated in absolute terms as regards India, and has hence, by comparison, fallen, relatively speaking. Ultimately, after a few good recovery years, there has only been a 5.5 per cent growth on an average after 1998. Hence, despite the reforms, we are not very far from the 'Hindu rate of growth' (around 4 per cent) of the earlier period.

Thus, on the macro-economic level, the reforms, undertaken following a liquidity crisis arising out of the fiscal situation, have been reduced largely to the management of the obverse side of taxation, through a distinct reduction of transfers from the Centre to the states, but without a real change in the fiscal or financial paradigm (with a reduction of almost 25 per cent of transfers between 1990-91 and 1996-97, which have stabilised since then). The states were not able to generate new revenues through tax reforms, and constitutionally they have little latitude in external financing, while not disposed to structurally lower the subsidies they distribute. This constraint has thus been translated for a large part in a reduction of investments in favour of short term expenditures. Thus, the investments of the states went down from 2.5 per cent of the GDP in 1990-91, to 2 per cent in 1997-98, and have remained stable after that, for a total level of expenses remaining stable at around 16 per cent of the GDP (source : MEF, 1998, & RBI, 1998). Thus, India is macro economically stable, but the establishment of the financial and fiscal conditions required for a rapid and sustainable development has not yet been initiated.

The care devoted to some macro-economic indicators has ended up by creating its own space of coherence and justification ('India has stabilised its inflation', 'India has reduced its deficit and restructured its debt') without this discourse being related to sectorial evolutions, which are discussed in sections 2 and 3 of this article, and which are, more than the financial and tax systems, the real determinants of a change in the economic organisation of the country and its system of accumulation. Let us demonstrate how the sole macro-economic interpretation leads to a cloaking of the developmental paradigm initiated in India.

1. An interpretation which ignores more complex realities

While they were triggered by the financial crisis, the reforms were actually long overdue, and Manmohan Singh, the then Finance Minister who formulated them, acknowledged subsequently that it was the crisis that had served as a catalyst. For, while the earlier system of accumulation had enabled, over a period of forty years, the setting up and the integration of a national economy, a relative industrialisation, and had, more than anything else, put an end structurally to the problem of food security, it had been very largely based on a controlled economy. We are not referring so much to the influence of the planned nature of Indian development, which has been vastly overstated, as to the working of its economy.[2] Indeed, it was and remains largely co-ordinated by discretionary interventions conducted by the state at different levels (Ruet, 1999 & 2001a). It had reached its limits in several key sectors (cf. Ruet 2001b, 2001c, as regards electricity; Ruet & Zérah, 2001, for water). Thus, in the early 1980s, the members of Parliament, for instance, had a discretionary budget for the allocation of cement, steel, even watches, with waiting lists and the consequent building up of a constituency. It was this system which Bibek Debroy, director of the Rajiv Gandhi Institute for Contemporary Studies, has called 'Indian socialism or soviets without electricity'. But, more structurally, Indian development has been characterised conceptually by the administered control over *budgeted expenditures*, more than by a real management of *public investments*. Indeed, the study of the strategies of decision-making in several 'utilities' and public enterprises shows that the projects revolve around *expenses*, and that no effort is made, either on the level of the project evaluation, on the level of its maintenance, or on the level of its operation, to arrive at a convergence between the expenses allocated and the returns achieved. In other words, no costs and benefits ratio is established, and hence there is no *investment* as such (cf. Ruet 2001d).[3] This functioning is moreover *administered* in the sense that it is totally subjected to centralised procedures and *in fine* subject to the discretion of the state, which moreover does not possess structurally any information system integrating costs and benefits, nor physical quantities of public goods or services and financial amounts. This has an immediate practical implication, in the sense that preference is systematically given to expenses on new infrastructure as compared to a management/maintenance of the existing one. Thus, there exist in the overall fields managed by the state considerable scope for creation of internal resources, which are often politically neutral in terms of implementation (cf. for instance Planning Commission, 2000, Ruet, 2000, Ruet & Zérah, 2001).

The public sector is structured on a model of expenditure. Its crisis is therefore always analysed in terms of absence of resources. Given the poor informational framework available in the public sector, never based on costs, the development of internal resources is structurally neglected. To sum up, we have a paradoxical situation. On the one hand, a macro-economic policy of reduction of expenditures and of recourse to private investment is not capable by itself to bring out the structural deficiencies of the earlier development model. However, on the other hand, such a policy is mechanically supported because of the expenditure-centred functioning of the public system. The reporting, the way the decision-making process is organised, converge in underlining the need for funds at the expense of any other line of explanation for the public sector's failures. The structure itself of the public sector, through these reports, produces a set of very 'narratives' sustaining the idea that funds only are required, and that a macro-economic policy may be enough. However, what this account does not reveal is why the private sector should participate in the public sector (section 2), nor what the private sector is doing in the meantime (section 3).

2. Changing the paradigm for the public sector

The earlier section has already given an idea of the obstacles inherent in a controlled organisation of the public sector. Let us re-examine for a moment the classic narration.

An impossible privatisation

There are 210 public enterprises, or more precisely 'public sector undertakings'[4], which are dependent on the central government, and 1020 which are dependent on the states. During the first five years of the supposedly 'pro-privatisation' BJP government at the Centre, six firms under the Union government have been privatised, and in another forty-six, the shares held by the State have been reduced while still remaining the majority shareholder. Privatisation at the level of the states has been negligible. The 2001-02 budget had fixed an ambitious objective in the matter of privatisation, since disinvestments were to be of the order of Rs. 120 billion (around $ 2.5 billion), of which Rs. 70 billion were to be used for reforms in the remaining public enterprises, and Rs. 50 billion for the social sector and for the infrastructure. By the middle of the financial year, hardly 2 per cent of this objective had been achieved and some severe setbacks had been experienced, among these being Air India which found no takers, or the exit of the American firm, AES, from a regional distribution company in the state of Orissa, privatised two years earlier in incredible circumstances.[5] In the field of energy, the opening up of the sector was badly conducted, as everybody acknowledges today. From 1950 to 1996, the electrical sector had represented from 17 to 20 per cent of the total five-year plans expenditures (Das, Parikh & Parikh, 2000). The reform in this sector has been restricted nevertheless to opening up production to the private sector, without restructuring the distribution of electricity. In 1998, after seven years of reforms and opening up to investment, a production capacity of 1.4 GW only had come from private projects (out of a total installed capacity of 89 GW), as mentioned by Das, Parikh & Parikh (2000).

Standing back to look at the problems of the public sector

The Indian public has the impression today that its enterprises are being 'sold for a song', as well as the more justified impression that the few buyers are not really ready to invest. The overall rationality of the process of privatisation hence needs to be restated. Keeping in mind their present controlled working, it is practically impossible for investors to valorise many PSUs; their value is therefore a matter perfectly impossible to base on the 'fundamentals' of economics (cf Ruet, 2001d). As Bibek Debroy has said, 'disinvestment has been driven by the tactical compulsion of financing the fiscal deficit. This is perhaps why the word privatisation has not been used until recently, the word disinvestment tending to imply a soft choice' (Debroy, 2000). Debroy rightly mentions that improved efficiency, competition, as well as the opening up and development of a capital market should be the other determinants for disinvestment. In this truncated context, potential investors have simply not found the disinvestment policies to be credible. With just a few exceptions discussed in the next section, the Indian State has not been able to establish a comfortable relationship with investors.[6] It has not been able to make an impact in the public sector either, since the income from the few sales has not been reinvested in the concerned sectors.

In this context, a reappraisal needs to be made of the relationship between the public and the private sector. After all, it is not so much private investment that the State needs, but rather a change in its methods of management, more likely to bring about a change of paradigm in the management of resources. Indeed, in the Indian public sector, it is not the decision-makers who are a problem, but rather the processes of decision-making. For instance, 40 per cent of the executives in the private sector Ambani group, have come from the public sector where, according to Mukesh Ambani, CEO of the Ambani Group, 'they were not allowed the freedom to manage and to lead'. It is not an issue of proposing the private sector as a solution *per se*, but simply of taking note of the fact that the public sector is no longer providing its services or its products in satisfactory conditions, that its users and clients have to devise strategies to confront the very expensive shortages and have to turn in fact towards the private sector or the illegal appropriation of public resources (corruption), and finally that the indiscriminate State subsidies are actually regressive in the sense that they benefit largely those sections of society which have the means to deploy their own techniques of supply from the State. A plethora of studies have been made on these points (cf. among others, TERI, 1999, Ruet & Zérah, 2001). In this context, though far from being ideologically-inclined towards privatisation, we should not rule out either the forms of decentralisation of the decision-making power (Mishra 2002, Ranganathan 2002), or the forms of contractual partnership in management (Ruet 2001e & 2002a).

The challenge to be met is therefore that of management. All the more so as the Indian public enterprises are called upon either to evolve global strategies to be able to compete with globalised enterprises, or to sustain the economic take-off of India. The good news is that now, after a decade of limited reforms having met with failure, the economic analysis of the Indian public sector has made some progress. There is a greater awareness of its complexity and of the impact of the various solutions; a learning process has taken place.

3. The private sector as an aid or a driving force of 'development'?

Let us discuss the way the private sector has evolved during the past decade as well as its linkage with the public sector. Let us bring out the difference between the communications and information technologies (IT) sector on the one hand, and the sectors of industry and the conventional services on the other hand.

Two sociologies of Indian enterprises

In the nineties, certain sectors of production or services have indeed witnessed a good deal of development; automobiles and the hotel industry being the most visible ones. But the perspective for the overall economy remains one of moderate development. While a market has developed in the big cities, it has been very largely catered to by imports (from China among others), and outside of the largest cities, there is no trace of the much talked about 'middle class' supposedly consisting of 100 to 200 million inhabitants[7]. With the measures permitting Indian enterprises to invest abroad remaining limited and still in the process of formulation, the financial structures remaining largely covered by banks which maintain links with the State, Indian capitalism conserves to a great extent its structure of (i) family, (ii) political power base, (iii) relatively centralised and hierarchised conglomerates, steeped in a sea of micro-enterprises (Dorin, Lachaier, Flamant, Vaugier-Chatterjee, 2000). These enterprises support the setting up of some reforms such as the removal of controls over enterprises, and an end to the 'licence raj', i.e. control through licences delivered by the administration. This part of the reforms has moreover been advocated and urged since long by Indian employers who saw the opportunity opening up to them in 1991 to tread this path. However, employers remain *in fine* satisfied with a slow opening up of the country, as it gives them time to launch into a restructuring of their finances and of their activities, pre-empting the too great exposure to external fusion-acquisitions that too rapid an opening up would render probable. Conglomerate groups, which have evolved this way because of the policies for restriction on monopolies, and which continue to be a peculiar trait of Indian capitalism, have not yet been restructured. Their present uncompatibility with the forms of capitalism world-wide, necessitates a transition period for them. The possibility of developing a real banking industry is something that industrialists and bankers are still hoping and praying for.

The telecommunications sector, for its part, has undergone a complete transformation. The opening up of telecommunications has been slow, lively debates have accompanied the working of the regulatory authority, and the original telecommunications services remained for a long time associated with the regulatory and licence delivering authority. But today this sector has become truly competitive, prices have been considerably reduced, and the mobile phone has made an important entry, in relative terms[8]. This has been made possible thanks to the recent technological revolution which has led to a considerable lowering of the costs of infrastructure and has put an end, the world over, to the dynamics and the character of natural monopoly that this activity had taken on. It is in the process of re-composition, and the industrial strategies relating to the local loop and connection to long distance communications or to local internet are in the process of being formulated (Bomsel & Ruet, 2001).

Within a few years, via software followed by services, the information technology sector has truly emerged as an export sector and has spectacularly 'climbed up the value-ladder'. Since 1994, the growth of this sector has varied between 40 to 50 per cent per year. It had a turnover of $ 8.7 billion in 2000-01 and is expected to reach $ 12 billion in 2001-2002 (around 2 per cent of the GDP). Nasscom (National Association of Software and Services Companies) has set for itself the objective of achieving $ 90 billion in 2008. While this sector initially undertook semi-skilled sub-contracting, the quality of services and consultancy it offers today are at par with the world level. Certain 'start-ups' adopt right from their creation an absolutely world-wide strategy and thus contribute to the emergence of a perfectly innovative model of growth of the enterprise. Thus, they start off right from the beginning with a contribution from venture capitalists who are

American (or of Indian origin who have grown wealthy in the USA), and contracts with large American software, telecommunications and consultancy firms. Their internal organisation and decision-making also follow a model that is new to India: a flat hierarchical structure, organised in a modular fashion, project-wise. The IT sector has not only acquired an undeniable maturity and world class but has, by itself, led to a chain effect on services, housing, the hotel industry and telecommunications, as is demonstrated, for instance, in the booming development of cities such as Bangalore, Hyderabad, or even Gurgaon, in the suburbs of Delhi (Bomsel & Ruet, 2001).

Bureaucrats and entrepreneurs

The IT companies avail of State support for their development. Conversely, this sector in turn can promote some of the State policies. Indeed, the Indian government has set up the Software Technology Parks of India (STPI) so as to help the development of the sector, along with the grant of some tax exemptions. This is an important tool in urban development, since eighteen zones have been identified for setting up an STPI. Conversely, the governments of some States which have demonstrated a political will, have been able to reap dividends: an interesting example is that of the southern State of Andhra Pradesh, whose capital, Hyderabad, has rediscovered its economic dynamism. The model adopted by this State is a very attractive one : indeed, the government of Andhra Pradesh has invested only 20 per cent in the construction of 'Cyberabad' - the STPI of Hyderabad -, the rest having been financed by private enterprises. Moreover, it can be estimated that for every job created in the IT sector, four or five others follow in the conventional sectors.[9] Thus, the new economy is basically financed by the development of the networks, and not through a model of planned expenses. Can this be transposed on to other sectors ? And can it constitute a new model of development ?

Let us examine the possible involvement of the IT sector in the management of municipal services, as well as the general issue of the overhaul of the public service in association with the private sector. The wagers of reallocation allied to this are discussed in the following section. On these matters, India and its cities can be considered, along with other countries or cities (Johannesburg, for example) as a laboratory in which interesting experiments are being conducted and in which some innovative models of co-operation between the public and the private sectors will evolve. The first issue at stake can be illustrated by the experience of the Bangalore Agenda Task Force (BATF), based in the capital of the southern State of Karnataka, which is moreover an absolutely first rate IT district (cf. Bomsel & Ruet, 2001). The BATF is an initiative set up by the largest IT firms of the district with the objective, in co-ordination with the government of Karnataka, to help the Bangalore municipality in determining the specifications, the formulation, and the production of a master plan for the development of the city. This help takes on a multiplicity of forms: it ranges from the regular (bi-annual) organisation of public meetings with representatives of the civil society and of the public services to give priority to short term measures and to define long term objectives, to the financial participation in certain projects, along with making manpower available for conducting certain studies. Launched in end 2000, the BATF is still by and large at an experimental stage, but its promoters are already toying with the idea of revamping the municipal services in Johannesburg, and are planning to serve as models for other cities in India. According to one of those in charge of the BATF, over and above the institutional and financial support, one of the major assets of this experiment is the possibility for private enterprises, to develop a much more flexible management than the one conducted by any administration. For example, when a specific expertise is required for a project, this framework allows for a flexibility of recruitment and decision-making which the strictly public framework does not provide. Thus, while waiting for the necessary internal reforms of the administration and the necessary change in the paradigm of development, such experiments can *a minima* ensure a smooth transition. Another example of the back-up role played by the IT sector, and which is common to all the Indian megalopolises, is the setting up of new models of training institutes dependent on private structures. Training enterprises are being created, with a growth model varying from a traditional teaching but imparted through computerised aids, or distance learning, to the management of training institutes meant to ensure a pre-recruitment, or again agreements entered into with existing universities. At the end of it all, it is the IT enterprises which provide a growing part of the production of higher education required to satisfy the demand (Bomsel & Ruet, 2001). Thus, on the basis of a more flexible internal organisation, the IT sector participates effectively in the necessary reforms of the public sector, by giving it an impetus as much as by temporarily marching ahead of it.

But the small-scale private sector also can have a role to play. Let us examine for instance some organisational and institutional innovations which have come into place during the last two years with regard to the distribution and purification of water in Chennai (formerly Madras), in a situation of extreme water shortage. They hinge around (i) the delegation of power, internally, (ii) in interface with the private sector, the delegation of the operation of some pumping stations, and agreements entered into with private water sellers, and (iii) outside the public sphere, a real segmentation of the distribution of water in an independent manner, with the creation of a private market for water. Several of these measures have led to a greater availability of water for the inhabitants as well as economies for the local municipal 'authorities' in charge of water distribution.[10] While in detail, the structural linkage of these measures may be somewhat restricted (Ruet & Zérah, 2001), this experiment proves here again that under certain specific conditions (here again, let us not be dogmatic[11]) the private sector can play a role in the matter of reforms in the public sector.

To what extent these measures are propagated, or on the other hand neglected in favour of more 'conventional' ventures, will determine the form of the private/public linkages in India, and will determine, in a sense, the effectiveness of the reforms undertaken by the State. The speed and intensity with which the 'new sociology of the Indian private sector' will spread to the rest of society will also constitute the wagers of reallocations.

4. The wagers of reallocation : India, the 'urban poor', and Bharat

Let us return to the broad indicators. In ten years, from 1991 to 2001, the literacy rate has crossed over from 52 to 65 per cent. The poverty rate has, at the same time, decreased from 36 to 24 per cent. Yashwant Sinha, when he was Finance Minister, had given the pledge that a sustained growth of 7 per cent over the next ten years would bring the poverty rate down to below the 5 per cent threshold. The tenth five-year plan is however less optimistic, as it plans to reduce poverty rate from 26 per cent in 2002 down to 21 per cent in 2007 (and this, by considering a non-credible economic growth of 8 per cent). Over and above the blinked view of growth, what is certain is that in those places where it is seen today, that is to say in the richer sections of the cities of 'India', it has shifted conceptually from expenses to investments, from the rural areas to the cities, from a certain balance between States to a growing imbalance.

Indians of the Cities and Indians of the Fields : India vs. Bharat ?

As already mentioned, India has a predominantly rural population. Farmers account for 67 per cent of the working population, but produce only 30 per cent of the wealth (Landy, 1993), in a situation in which the green revolution had already engendered a 'social and regional polarisation' (Landy, 1996). Indeed, the green revolution has brought benefits to the irrigable areas, and within these, to those peasants who had the means to invest in irrigation and in the new techniques. Ten years of reforms not centred around the rural world have not remedied this situation. For the Indian state, the problem of the rural areas is simple; it is financial and fiscal. For instance, the annual deficit of the electrical sector alone may represent twice the budget on health and education (this is so in Andhra Pradesh). When moreover its teachers no longer take their classes, or its hospitals practically no longer have an operational budget, the states have the choice between undertaking cosmetic measures (which they generally do), or radically innovative ones whose results will be known a few years hence. Thus Andhra Pradesh is giving a push forward to 'e-governance', whose effects are taking time to penetrate the countryside, and Madhya Pradesh (Central India) has launched its Education Guarantee Scheme. The latter consists in recruiting and giving on the spot training to some of the villagers who then impart primary education on a minimum salary.

Whatever be the success of such measures, and even if the state governments were to search for some sponsors (the Centre, the World Bank), it seems that implicitly the political choice has been made : the budget allocations for the rural areas will remain minimal as long as additional resources are not found. Will they be forthcoming from the cities (the tax collection mechanisms are quite poor) ? And will it be possible to convince the cities to agree to a reallocation? At present, it seems that the only economic chain effects are confined to local limits : while the large megalopolises are visibly changing, the rural areas remain as they are. And, while the population of the cities is growing rapidly, there is no massive rural exodus, and the population of the countryside is also growing (Landy, 1996). But simultaneously, while the cities in India account for only 28 per cent of the population, they produce 50 per cent of the wealth, although they shelter also 100 million of the urban poor.

The core of the cities

Sheltering the largest amount of wealth along with the largest amount of poverty, the cities thus constitute the wager of the social contract of the nation. Delhi, for instance, witnesses an annual influx of 500,000 additional inhabitants. Delhi attempts its re-development through the creation of satellite towns (Dupont, 2001), but while doing so neglects to keep intact, in tandem, the social fabric of the present Delhi (Tarlo, 2000 & Soni, 2000). True, the model adopted in the 1960s of small industry on the scale of the home, drawing its inspiration from Japan's experience, has reached its limits. It is in the process of being submerged by the arrival of manufactured goods arising out of globalisation. Nevertheless, this model of development has generated a very large geographic intermingling between social classes, and has given rise to the appearance of economic services in the chinks created by the deficiencies of the public machinery. The legitimate policy of re-orienting this model, is actually being done today in accordance with a process of social dualisation and of eviction of the poor towards the peripheral areas, which revives the now outmoded principle of the 1930s, i.e. the garden cities in the English manner. That is to say a city devoid of a socio-economic fabric, and hence, *in fine* devoid of an economic fabric. Over and above matters of policy, the management of Indian cities is moreover hindered also by the poor co-ordination of a bureaucratic machinery with its unnecessary multiplicity of administrative levels. Thus Delhi for instance is jointly administered by three municipalities (one of which shelters an army base), the Delhi state government and the Union government. To be illustrative on the impact, in order simply to set up a bus stop on an existing line, the Delhi state government is obliged to refer the matter to four Union ministries, then co-ordinate with the municipalities.[12] Thus, in the Indian cities and their satellites, a new class of the well-to-do is emerging, with probably a new identity (Ruet, 2002b), but the social bond is becoming weaker and *a minima* is forming anew.

From one state to the next

How does the matter stand, on the countrywide scale, between the various states in India? The decrease in the transfer of allocations from the Centre leads one to question the economic convergence of the different states. Indeed, Cachin & Sahay (1996) have shown that these transfers have enabled in the long term (1960-1995) to reduce the differences in the per capita income between states, despite the divergence in the per capita gross domestic product. Today, the historic situations are evolving imperceptibly. While Maharashtra (capital, Mumbai) remains industrially active, Tamil Nadu (capital, Chennai) has overtaken it in terms of investment. Bangalore, as also Hyderabad, are able to attract large investments. Apart from any hazardous prospective assessment of these end evolutions, we note over the nineties a correlation between the composite growth and the per capita GDP. Thus the richest states continue to get richer more rapidly. Nevertheless, certain states are going about the process of 'catching up', like West Bengal (capital, Calcutta) or Kerala (capital, Thiruvanamthapuram), which, with an initial per capita GDP level twice smaller have witnessed a composite growth over ten years equivalent to that of Maharashtra, while Punjab (capital, Chandigarh) which was the richest, demonstrates a growth half that of these states (MEF, 1998). Since then, slowdown in Maharashtra's industrial growth has been confirmed. The Indian states have begun to compete with each other.

Conclusion

The impression of economic and social change given by the Indian megalopolises is therefore both qualitatively true and corresponds to a radical change in some of the elements of Indian society, and at the same time quantitatively over-estimated on the scale of the country. That is how the macro-economy ('the scale of the country') is overshadowing the micro-economy.

In terms of balanced distribution, and in an India whose cohesion is secured politically only through the power of an idea which today evolves due to centrifuge forces (Khilnani, 1997), the mediation of the bond between the economic and the social has been effected by a ratio of production based on the massive integration of a manpower producing small goods and carrying out small services. The dimension of geographic near-intermingling with the middle classes marked their social acceptance of what was then nothing other than labour. In an urban India which wants to ignore the workers in its shanty towns, and in which new ideas are being formulated (Ruet 2002, & 2002b), the persistence of this social bond requires to be reassessed.

More than the monetary system, what is really changing in India today is the new forms of salary incomes, of competition, of integration in the international system, and to a smaller extent, of the nature of the State[13]. Boyer & Saillard (1995) show that these are the institutional forms which determine and condition a system of accumulation. A new system of accumulation is thus coming into place in India, which by itself is enough to justify the interest of economists and of the overall community of social scientists for this country. In this new system, the State is feeling its way, matters of reallocations are open to change ; in other words, a new mode of regulation is in the making.

The matter of deciding whether this metamorphosis will remain confined mainly to its cities and its well-off sections of society can also be seen under a different light. If economic globalisation produces a capitalism which arises out of the configurations of 'competitors' in territories competing with each other, of a decreasing number of 'protégés' and an increasing number of the 'vulnerable' (Giraud, 1996), then there are entire sections of capitalism in India which are in fact globalised. It is equally undeniable that this kind of globalisation creates wealth in India. Over and above that, there is no political inevitability and the governments conserve a large scope for reallocation manoeuvres (Giraud, 1998). What is more, politics is larger than the State (Lazarus, 1996), and the evolution in the living conditions of the middle classes and of the vulnerable can be linked to that between the former 'first world' and the 'third world'. From this point of view, the speedy development of a middle class in India, for example, helps for instance the middle class to remain in existence in France[14] (Giraud, 1996). Conversely, when the European middle class makes an earnest plea for equitable trade, Indian artisans derive benefit from it. Like 'what was good for General Motors was good for America, and vice-versa', 'What is good for French workers is it good for Indian workers, and reciprocally ?'. This hypothesis has to be put to the test, but, in a country which does not desert politics[15], it is striking and stimulating to see that producers, peasants, social workers, activists, NGOs, are undertaking an active co-ordination with their counterparts in the other parts of the South and in the 'first world'.

Notes

1. For example, in the electrical sector which is considered as a priority sector, Parikh (2000) points out that in the course of a few years the institutional pattern has passed through the stages of memorandums with the states, to open tender invitations, to tenders guaranteed by the states or the Centre, finally to the study of government to government bilateral co-operations, in its last form.
2. Including the implementation of the five-year plans.
3. During a conversation, an executive in charge of water management in the public system in Calcutta, asked me in reply to one of my questions on the investment policy of the city :'but what exactly do you mean by 'investment' ?'.
4. Indeed, independently of their legal status, their very nature as enterprises is debatable, if we consider that, limited rationality apart, the concept around which decision making is structured in an enterprise is primarily the cost, whereas these organisations are based on political arbitrages between heterogeneous objectives. This is the definition of an administration, cf. Banfield (1976) and this is so in the case of India (cf . Ruet, 2001, 2001a).
5. A first round of bidding had shown the interest of few companies, which finally retracted. Then a second round of negotiations began, to know if AES, already present in generation, could bid. Further, AES negotiated the securitisation of financial supporting schemes from the government of Orissa. After the privatisation, it again re-negotiated the timing of these disbursements with the government, to finally resign from the activity. An ex-post analyses shows that, in any case, the guarantees given by the government were neither sufficient nor credible enough given the information which finally emerged after the take-over.
6. We can regularly read in the press, for instance, assertions on the subject 'of the private sector not having fulfilled its commitments', demonstrating a misreading of its working. It is not because the Government or the Planning Commission desires it that investment is made; this only works with a controlled expenditure ...
7. Which is hardly surprising, when we consider that these are found in the fifty odd cities in India claiming to have 'millionaires' in their population, and that in all these cities the rate of urban poverty is of the order of 30 per cent, and

that in the remaining 70 per cent, everyone does not belong, not by a long shot, to the 'middle class'.

8. In absolute terms, let us not forget that we are talking of a country in which just 3 per cent of the homes possess a private telephone.
9. Source : conversation, STPI, Hyderabad.
10. Administratively : a 'Board'.
11. In particular, and on this precise example, one can praise the involvement of local enterprise, but express reservations on certain modalities of contract management with international firms. This is incorrect in other cases ; in short, pragmatism, based on a solid institutional analysis, is a must.
12. For a study of the impact of administrative red tape on water management in Calcutta, see Ruet & Zérah, 2001.
13. Which, according to the levels of Government, the various states of the Union, and the matter in question, still evolve largely ad hoc positions and are seeking a global identity.
14. By catching up with salaries and hence, for the vulnerable, a decrease in the salary gap, and therefore in their vulnerability.
15. According to Lazarus (1996), 'the disappearance of the class dynamics leads to confusion between State and Society insofar as it was the class struggle which kept them at a distance. This differentiation having stopped, there remain today the State, the economy, and, for society, its state of crisis in the social category, about which, society having left behind its difference, there remains only State control'. In India, this dynamics has not stopped, and has been renewed in a politically and economically instrumentalised communalism on the one hand (Khilnani, 1997), and in a debate between communalism and secularism on the other hand.

References

Banfield E.C. (1976), Corruption as a feature of governmental organization, Journal of Law & Economics, December 1976.

Bomsel, Olivier & Ruet, Joël (2001), "Digital India: report on the Indian IT industry", CFCE study report, 170p, CERNA, Paris & CSH, New Delhi.

Boyer, Robert, & Saillard, Yves (1995), Un précis de la régulation, chapter 5 : 58-68, in Théorie de la régulation, l'état des savoirs, edited by Boyer & Saillard, 568p, La Découverte, Paris.

Cachin, Paul & Sahay, Ratna (1996), Regional Economic Growth and Convergence in India, Finance & Development journal, IMF, March 1996.

Das, Anjana; Parikh, Jyoti, & Parikh, Kirit S. (2000), Power, the critical infrastructure, in Kirit S. Parikh, ed, India Development Report, 113:124, Oxford University Press, New Delhi.

Debroy, Bibek (2000), Privatisation in India, issue on Privatisation in South Asia, journal Liberal times, Vol. VII, Number 2, 9:16, New Delhi.

Dorin, Flamant, Lachaier & Vaugier-Chatterjee (2000), Le patronat en Inde: contours sociologiques des acteurs et des pratiques, CSH, New Delhi, June 2000.

Dupont, Véronique (2001), Noida : nouveau pôle industriel ou ville satellite de Delhi ? Le projet des planificateurs, ses failles et son devenir, pp 189-212, Revue Tiers Monde, n°165, December 2001.

Giraud, Pierre-Noël (1996), L'inégalité du monde, Gallimard, Folio essays, Paris.

Giraud, Pierre-Noël (1998), Economie : le Grand Satan ?, Editions Textuel, Paris.

Khilnani, Sunil (1997), The Idea of India, Penguin, UK.

Landy, Frédéric (1993), Campagnes et villes de l'Inde: deux cultures antagonistes, cahiers des sciences humaines 29 (2-3) 1993: 313-332, Paris.

Landy, Frédéric (1996), Réforme agraire et révolution verte: l'impossible synthèse indienne, Cahiers agriculture 1996; 5:271-81, Paris.

Lazarus, Sylvain (1996), Anthropologie du nom, 249p, Collection 'Des travaux', Le Seuil, Paris.

MEF (1998), Les Etats indiens: finances publiques et développement, note of the Economic and Financial Mission, French Embassy in India, 32p, October 1998, New Delhi.

Mishra, R.K. (2002), Internal audit as a reform technique in power sector in India, 15p, in Ruet, ed, Organisational Restructuration of SEBs in India : Decentralisation, Information Building, profit Centre and Management Contracts, to be published in 2002, Manohar Publishing, New Delhi.

Morris, Sebastian (2002), Restructuring Gujarat Electricity Board : outline of a strategy and proposal for action, 21p, in Ruet, ed, Organisational Restructuration of SEBs in India : Decentralisation, Information Building, profit Centre and Management Contracts, to be published in 2002, Manohar Publishing, New Delhi.

Planning Commission (2000), Annual report on the working of State Electricity Boards for the year 1999-00, Government of India.

Ranganathan, V. (2002), Profit centres as instruments of performance enhancement of SEBs, 8p, in Ruet, ed, Organisational Restructuration of SEBs in India : Decentralisation, Information Building, profit Centre and Management Contracts, to be published in 2002, Manohar Publishing, New Delhi.

RBI (1998), Finance of State Governments, RBI Bulletin, February 1998, Reserve Bank of India, New Delhi.

RIS (2001), Foreign Direct Investment, regional economic integration and introduction of restructuring in Asia: trends, patterns, and prospects, by

Nagesh Kumar, occasional paper n°62 of the Research & Information system for the non-aligned and other developing countries, 51p, New Delhi.

Ruet, Joël (1999), Administrations for sale: the State Electricity Boards; private vs. public "entreprisation", Cahiers du CERNA, 99-C1, Paris.

Ruet, Joël (2000), Investment needs and possible incomes in indian power sector to bridge the energy gap, working paper ; to be published in the Indian Economic Journal, New Delhi.

Ruet, Joël (2001), Winners and losers of the reform of SEBs, an organisational study, 85 pp, Occasional paper, CSH, New Delhi.

Ruet, Joël (2001a), The future of State owned companies: is privatisation the answer?, paper presented at the IIPA-CSH conference on administrative reforms, January 2001, New Delhi.

Ruet, Joël (2001b), La mondialisation limitée du secteur électrique : de la prééminence des etats au retour relatif du centre, in "Questions d'échelle: du mondial au local", ed. Chaudhuri, Basudeb & Landy, Frédéric, collection Sciences Sociales, CNRS, Paris.

Ruet, Joël (2001c), Le secteur électrique en Inde : réforme libérale ou persistance d'une forme de développement à l'indienne ?, Revue Tiers-Monde n°165, December 2001, Paris.

Ruet, Joël (2001d), La réforme du secteur électrique de l'Inde : administrations à vendre ; Transformer les State Electricity Boards en entreprises, Doctorate Thesis, 349p, CERNA, Ecole des Mines, Paris.

Ruet, Joël (2001e), A new paradigm for the Indian power sector: going beyond the 'silver bullet' privatisation, paper presented at the international conference "Indo-French perspectives on privatisation", Hyderabad, March 2000.

Ruet, Joël (2002), Information technologies and development: clusters as economic policy tools for India", 17p, article presented at the International Conference on "Communication for development", 6-8 February 2002, Madras University.

Ruet, Joël (2002a), Delegation of power in SEBs under management contracts, 23p, in Ruet, ed, Organisational Restructuration of SEBs in India : Decentralisation, Information Building, profit Centre and Management Contracts, to be published in 2002, Manohar Publishing, New Delhi.

Ruet, Joël (2002b), " A trans-regional network of e-identity ; information technology clusters in New India ", to be published in 2002 in the proceedings of the conference on "Material Vitality and imagined authenticities", 14/15 December 2001, Jadavpur University, Calcutta

Ruet, Joël & Zérah, Marie-Hélène (2001) Water supply and sanitation in Indian Metros : Bombay, Calcutta, Madras, 71p, research report for Ondeo Services, CSH, New Delhi.

Soni, Anita (2000), Urban conquest of the outer Delhi : beneficiaries, intermediaries, and victims, the case of the Mehrauli countryside, chapter 4 : 75 :96, in Delhi, Urban Space and Human Destinies, ed. Dupont, Tarlo & Vidal, 261p, Manohar Publishing, New Delhi.

Tarlo, Emma (2000), Welcome to history : a resettlement colony in the making, chapitre 3 : 51 :74, in Delhi, Urban Space and Human Destinies, ed. Dupont, Tarlo & Vidal, 261p, Manohar Publishing, New Delhi.

TERI (1999), A study on willingness to pay for electricity in Orissa, report of the Tata Energy Research Institute, New Delhi.

World Bank (1996), India Country economic Memorandum: five years of stabilization and reforms: the challenges ahead, August 1996, Report n°15882-IN, 215p, New Delhi.

The long and winding road from potential to great power status

Gilles Boquérat & Frédéric Grare

The one event of India's making which drew the world attention during a prolific decade in international politics, starting with the disappearance of the Soviet Union and ending with the epoch-making September 11 attacks, is undoubtedly the nuclear tests of 11 and 13 May 1998. For twenty-four years following the 'peaceful nuclear explosion' of 1974, New Delhi had resisted temptation to cross the threshold of nuclear self-assertion even if, in the meanwhile, while rejecting militarisation in the full sense of the term, India developed its capability in assembling weapons. The hurried decision to exercise the nuclear option - the first of major consequence taken by the Vajpayee's government after assuming power in March 1998 – was conceivable since the BJP had always been wanting India to act decisively in the debate within India's official and academic circles on the opportunity to move from ambiguity to weaponised deterrence. Furthermore, the BJP, as first-timer in government, was unburdened by any past baggage. Yet, it came as a surprise for many since the general impression was to doubt the will of any Indian government to resolutely face international opprobrium and the ineluctable new sanctions which would follow. The decision encountered large public approval, notably among the middle class.[1] Even political parties which had refrained from nuclear testing readily joined the euphoric chorus hailing the sub-soil tests. Such a landmark decision does not exist in a vacuum and, whatever the inevitable capitalization for political expediency, it was first of all in line with the new power equation at the global level arising out of the end of the Cold War, combined with a short-term element resulting from the expected entry into force of the Comprehensive Test Ban Treaty by September 1999.[2] Nuclear testing had indeed been seriously considered in December 1995 when the Congress Prime Minister, Narasimha Rao, was the head of government, demonstrating that the post-Cold War international environment has forced upon India to re-evaluate its stand on the nuclear issue.

That the world has changed for India can be assessed with one example: in August 1991, the 1971 Indo-Soviet treaty of peace, friendship and cooperation, with its security provisions originally directed at countering any unwanted US moves during the Bangladesh war of liberation, was extended (before *de facto* falling into oblivion). Ten years later, in May 2001, the Indian government was one of the few important countries to welcome the controversial US National Missile Defence proposal which in effect would reinforce American military domination in space and on earth; a country which had fought for years for a nuclear weapons- free world was now supporting a discriminatory global nuclear bargain.[3] From the 'time-tested friendship' with the Soviet Union, India moved, with the Vajpayee's government, to call the United States a 'natural partner', still a notch below Ayub Khan describing once the United States as Pakistan's 'natural friend'[4] but a far cry from the suspiciousness of the Cold War years. Non-alignment had brought in the course of time India closer to the Soviet Union, whereas the fixation on Pakistan had substantially distanced India from to the United States. Security reasons played a role in this rapprochement – to get the US on its side vis-à-vis Pakistan and China - as well as in the explosion of nuclear devices. The 1998 tests constituted an important shift in New Delhi's approach to its security indicating the transition from a recessed deterrent (unexecuted capability with the option to move on to the manufacture of weapons and the rejection of both the concept as well as the use of nuclear weapons) to a minimal deterrent (inflicting damages considered unacceptable by the adversary; no first use pledge).[5] But the May 1998 nuclear tests went also beyond the traditional task of safeguarding the unity and territorial integrity of the country, it primarily conveyed the message that India would muscle in on the big powers' group and this objective could not be attained without the United States giving its sanction. For decades, the United States were seen as determined to drag down India with the help of Pakistan, the calculation was now that going along with a domineering United States would haul up India at the high table in world affairs. This posture cannot be dissociated from the feeling of helplessness and the spectre of marginalisation which accompanied the un-advantageous balance of power resulting from the end of the Cold War. The nuclear tests were intended to give a clear indication of India's drum-up self-confidence and hence the capability to make unpopular choices in the international system.

The first part of this paper examines the contextual parameters lying behind the power-enhancing rationale for the tests. To assess these elements, one has to carefully look at the immediate post Cold War international scenario as it opened up in the early nineties and how India responded to it so as to preserve a capacity for independent decision-making. One did not have to wait long for seeing the effects of the nuclear tests on the Indo-Pak equation. The second part poses the hypothesis that the possession of nuclear weapons, instead of being a means of achieving global power through reinforcing the capacity for independent decision-making, has on the contrary increased dependence on foreign powers, on the United States in particular.

Prelude to the quest for international stature

Belief in the fact that India has a providential role to play in international affairs has always been there. During the third session of the UN General Assembly held in Paris in the autumn of 1948, Nehru remarked that 'India is considered as a potential great power and specially as a dominant power in Asia, apart from the USSR in the north. There is full realization of this and therefore a desire to cultivate India'.[6] A recently published article in *The Economist* had then comforted Nehru in thinking that appreciation of India was on the rise. The praising headline was 'India-A New Great Power'.[7] It was said that India possessed not only great manpower and resources but also a relatively advanced administrative and economic apparatus, directed by men of notable ability and energy and could stand on its own foundations in defence of independence, capable of using effectively whatever assistance may be forthcoming from elsewhere. In a decolonised Asia facing the Soviet threat, India was the 'natural linchpin', its size and solidity enabling it to create an Asiatic balance of power. Emphasizing the significance for Britain and the Commonwealth to maintain close links with upcoming India, the author was nevertheless careful to affix a farsighted reminder that 'India's status as a Great Power must vary according to the state of its relations with Pakistan'. Clearly, Pakistan could spoil India's ambitions since 'the two nations in close co-operation can be extremely strong; but as long as relations between India and Pakistan are those of hostility and suspicion, India will be vulnerable to all kinds of untoward events'.

Basking in 'all praise and adulation', Nehru admitted at the same time that he 'felt rather uncomfortable and somewhat out of place and counterfeit'.[8] He was no doubt pleased by what was written, for few months earlier in a speech at the Constituent Assembly, he had emphasized that 'because we count, and because we are going to count more and more in the future, everything we do becomes a matter for comment (...) It is not a question of our viewpoint or of attaching ourselves to this or that bloc; and it is merely the fact that we are *potentially* a great nation and big power'.[9] But the Indian Prime Minister also acknowledged that India was neither a great military power, nor an industrially advanced power and without uncontested power capabilities, India run the risk of inviting people to call the bluff. The build-up of industrial and scientific capacities would take precedence and make possible the development of armed forces. Since the acquisition of the 'hard' attributes of power were contingent upon a modernization which would inevitably takes time in a developing country, and in the absence of any security guarantee resulting from a military arrangement with great powers, diplomatic means rather than armed power was to be the first safeguard against a threat to the country's integrity. In a text written twenty years before Independence, he explained that if 'wars come unannounced and the best of neighbours fall out', '[India's] main strength will lie in our peaceful and friendly policy towards all countries and in the spirit of our people. We shall covet nobody's land or goods and there is no reason why we should have enemies outside'.[10]

If its resources and geo-strategic position would ensure that India was not forgotten in the emerging Cold War, a pragmatic non-aligned policy will not only mean that the foreign policy autonomy of a newly-independent country as well as the agenda of national economic development would not be encroached, but also ensure a maverick role in a bipolar world. India's global power status would primarily be based on the international situation and the balance of power and verbalized through a diplomatic activism (India as the most vocal exponent of decolonisation and democratisation of international relations and advocate of peace and disarmament) was not just for the sake of lecturing wayward nations from the higher ground of superior goodness but also a reflection of the deep-seated conviction that India, as a major power in the making, should not remain a passive onlooker of the evolving balance of power. Morality was not dissociated from power but rather a mean to achieve power because the country was objectively constrained by its relative economic and military weakness.

These were the heady days of post-colonial Asian assertiveness with India assuming a lead role as a fierce opponent of the dominant power structure in the international system which was leaving little room for independent positioning. A French ambassador wrote in the mid-fifties that 'Delhi has become a meeting point, the most important political centre on the Asian continent. It is symbolic of what India now means to the world. If the events follow their normal course, one can foresee India, in the near future, as a permanent member of the Security Council, officially sitting among the powers ruling international politics. An offer in this direction has already publicly been done by the Soviet leaders and cannot see how such event could be delayed for long'.[11] G.S. Bajpai, the first secretary general of India's external affairs ministry, acknowledged that 'India [was] the major stabilising factor for peace in Asia', but with an admonition: 'the measure of stability that she can impart even to this unsettled part of the world is not a matter of good intentions but of power. And if peace, like war, be indivisible, a strong India can be an effective guardian of peace in Asia and thus make a vital contribution to the peace of the world'.[12]

The divisions of the Cold War, internal weaknesses and external dependencies were to curtail Indian power and influence outside the subcontinent and got the better of India's aspirations for big power status. India regained some leverage as a regional and rising middle power after the Indo-Pak war of 1971, yet it did not 'make any claim to a global role, since a global role is basically a function of strategic capabilities or superior economic muscle'.[13] India had to contend itself with being a leading actor of the non-alignment movement, an organisation wooed more for the support it could generate than for its influence on world or regional politics. The eight years long Iran-Iraq war opposing two non-aligned countries stigmatised the impotence of NAM when it comes to security matters. If the threat of mutual assured destruction hanging over the planet was the dark side of the division of the world into two adversarial systems, the Cold War offshoots were all not uniformly bad from a third world perspective since it 'did hasten the emancipation of nations, and peoples, and provided the have-nots of the planet with opportunities to assert themselves'.[14] The socialist world was generally perceived as a much needed counterpoise to the Western bloc, challenging its support to non-progressive regimes in various parts of the developing world.

Coping with the pains of transition

In theory, India had good reasons to rejoice at the end of the Cold War for the termination of the division of the international community into power blocs had been wished for since Independence. India, a firm believer in the role that the United Nations could play in creating a more democratic and equitable world order, based on collective security, had regretted that the UN, and its many organs set up after the Second World War, were often paralysed for action by the rivalry between the two superpowers. In practice, the end of the East-West and Sino-Soviet cold wars was one of those traumatic experiences where events for India run contrary to where they stood before. It happened twice before. The first time was when India obliged Britain by placing in 1948 the Kashmir issue before the United Nations and ended with feeling let down by the Western powers after this question became engulfed in Cold War politics. The second trauma was the humiliating defeat suffered at the hands of the Chinese in 1962 after having diligently helped People's China to engage countries beyond the Communist bloc. In the third case, it became clear, even before the demise of the Soviet Union, that Moscow would not be anymore the countervailing power to the United States it used to be. The first Gulf War only confirmed that the Soviet Union was no more in a position to prevent events to which it did not concur from happening, and even less to defy the United States enterprise. The formal end of the Soviet Union also entailed the dislocation of extensive and long-standing arrangements for defence supplies as well as a significant share of India's foreign trade and an access to cheap loans. Bereft of the Soviet Union which had been the guardian of India's interests in the United Nations Security Council, India was at the mercy of US or UN interventionism.

Adjusting to the emerging unipolar world could not have come at a less propitious time since the country was undermined by secessionist challenges and its cohesiveness challenged by political instability and the exacerbation of caste and religious divides. Furthermore its economy was dragged down by a severe external financing crisis bringing the country on the verge of defaulting on payment in the spring of 1991. India, which on the regional front was completing the pitiful pulling off the Indian Peace-Keeping Force from Sri Lanka, found its foreign policy in disarray and its stature in world affairs lessened for having been close to the losing side of the Cold War. India's clumsy attitude during the Gulf War, torn between its non-aligned credentials, the fate of a large immigrant community in the Gulf, and a politically correct anti-americanism, left the impression that it was not ready to substantiate its condemnation of Kuwait's annexation.[15] In the absence of Cold War deterrence, the US-led coalition invasion of Iraq comforted those who considered that India's security would be better assured if it becomes a nuclear power.

Inevitably, relevance of non-alignment was questioned with the dismemberment of one of the two antagonistic power blocs at the end of 1991. For NAM, whose capacity to sustain some attention relied on power blocs rivalry, the post Cold War dramatically reduced its competing leverage. It dawned on many that reviving a disparate group might be less intricate if given an economic rather than a political thrust to the NAM (the G-15 had just been created in 1989 to foster North-South cooperation and provide input for other international groups, such as the World Trade Organization and the G-7). But bereft of competition coming from the Soviet bloc and an alternative developmental model after the near-universal adoption of market-friendly economic policies, there was no pressing need for the developed world to bail out the developing world, except on its on own terms. The overall atmosphere was less towards trying to reinvigorate an elusive third world solidarity to build-up collective self-reliance or to indulge in confrontation with the West as it was the case in the previous decades than to strike personal deals with the first world or to emulate South-East Asian countries in terms of economic performance. One commentator wrote in the wake of the Iraqi invasion of Kuwait that 'India would be well advised to work for a UN collective system of security in a multipolar world, than to prop up the non-aligned movement that has outlived its utility in a bipolar scene'.[16]

What could remain of the non-alignment mantra in India was the freedom of taking decisions and implementing actions in tune with its own perceived interests, a pursuit which was not unique to non-aligned countries, but which became more difficult to attain in a unipolar world with less room for manoeuvre. The quality of the relations with the lone superpower – with whom an improvement had already occurred during the eighties - became critical and subject to debates. The idea of embracing the United States did have a significant number of critics. Hence, the warning that 'despite temporary difficulties on the economic front that threaten India's political sovereignty, it is a 'big' if not a 'great' nation. Indian diplomats know the value of an independent Indian posture on the world stage. There is little to gain by tying itself to the American coat-strings, particularly now (...) Considering India's historical problem with the US and the even greater imbalance of negotiating positions currently available, India would be well advised to be wary of too hasty a move to the US'. The author of these lines ultimately recommended that 'notwithstanding many common interests in regional stability and commerce, India would be well-advised to talk to the US only from a position of relative strength. Any attempt to satisfy US world order concerns for short-term gains could have long-term negative consequences for India's global position'.[17] In other words, India, given its size and resources, deserved to be heard and its point of view given due weight internationally. Temporary difficulties were not to divert India from its quest to be accepted as a great nation.

India was not among the top most priorities for the United States. It hardly figured in the official document on the 'National Security Strategy of the United States' released by the White House in August 1991, or for the negative reasons linked to the dangers of intermediate range missiles deployments and nuclear proliferation in the subcontinent resulting from the Indo-Pakistan military competition. Also it was expected that a bilateral dialogue and the adoption of confidence-building measures would lower down the temperature between the two regional enemies.[18] This was a reminder of the Gates mission that President Bush dispatched to the subcontinent in the summer of 1990 to defuse the potentially explosive tensions between India and Pakistan over Kashmir. Washington had been putting pressuring India to accept international safeguards on its nuclear facilities as well as to curtail its missile programme. If New Delhi derided the hypocritical nature of the non-proliferation discourse of the lone superpower since it did not pursue a universal, comprehensive and non-discriminatory approach to the goal of complete nuclear disarmament, Delhi was to have a taste of US concerns over dual-use technology when, in 1993, Washington, calling upon a violation of the Missile Technology Control Regime (MTCR), wanted to block Russia's cryogenic rocket engine deal – it succeeded in getting the technology transfer part cancelled but could not forbid Russia from supplying engines. US authorities had also drawn up an entities list blacklisting Indian industries and institutions linked to the nuclear or space programmes. Besides, India was, on the economic front, on the receiving end of US criticism for insufficient protection of intellectual property rights.

In the early nineties, the Washington Bureau Chief of the Times of India noted that 'for the US, the subcontinent is almost like a void in Asia. It is vitally concerned about West Asia and it is commercially involved with East and South East Asia. There are the serious parts of the continent for the United States'. South Asia will matter only 'if events suddenly run out of hand in an unpredictable fashion, thus introducing an unwelcome instability to the area. Economically, India probably matters even less'. If Washington was essentially concerned about neutralizing India's strategic weapons capabilities and its unsafeguarded nuclear programme, there was still a silver lining since the US could see in India a long-term strategic partner as it 'would like to disengage from the region by striking a military rapport with India in the course of the decade or so. It is concerned about the region and would like a partner for maintaining peace. India can be that partner in course of time and talks towards reaching that ultimate end are already in progress between the two'.[19] The proposals named after Lt.-Gen. Claude Kickleighter, formerly of the US Army Pacific, for expanded military cooperation between the two countries by the end of the decade, and envisioning strengthened interaction at the level of services and defence policy making establishments, could look as a step towards a closer collaboration notably in view of convergence on geo-political and strategic interests in the Asia-Pacific region.

New Delhi could at least find some solace in US belated efforts to censure Pakistan for its nuclear weapons programme, through the Pressler amendment adopted in 1990 leading to the suspension of military assistance, and for Washington coming to favour a solution within the Shimla agreement framework rather than by reference to obsolete UN resolutions. The end of the Cold War and waning US interest in Afghanistan had made Pakistan relatively inconsequential to the West. As the larger country in the region, India has far more promising potentialities than its western neighbour. South Block was nevertheless finding the US government's view rather indulgent on the issue of Pakistan-sponsored terrorism in Punjab and Kashmir. Speculation was rife that a section of the Indian policy makers would go to any extent to have India filling the vacuum left by Pakistan's shrinking place in US geo-strategic plans in the region even if that meant a shift 'not only from non-alignment to its opposite; (...) from a global to a regional role; and from the moral high ground to a cynical and timid brand of 'political realism'.[20]

Onlooker of an unbalanced world

As the world moved from the certitudes of the Cold War, with its well-defined adversaries and spheres of influence, to a 'New World Order' that President George Bush propounded during and after the Gulf War, what would be left of India's capacity for defending the necessity for a more equitable international system and of its traditional opposition to interferences in the domestic affairs of sovereign nations ? For if the more powerful countries were exhibiting an unrelenting determination to retain their superior military might in preventing the possession of weapons of mass destruction and the acquisition of lethal technology through the Nuclear Suppliers Group guidelines or the MTCR, the US-led Western world seemed earnestly engaged in bending the developing world to the their own values or worldview, notably through the multinational financial agencies and even the UN. Issues like good governance, human rights, market reforms, environmental and social concerns, potentially gave an open-ended right to infringe on one's own decision-making on aspects ranging from the economic to the security policies and also put a question mark on one's sovereignty by emphasizing the right to self-determination or in leaving the door open to intervention on humanitarian grounds. For instance, the IMF fiscal guidelines and insistence on structural adjustment ensured that defence expenditures would have to be kept on hold after the buying spree of the eighties in India.[21] The New World Order has 'now come to mean a world order in which one particular political power attempts to set all the rules of the game and then plays it according to its will' summed up a former diplomat.[22] An expression of concern at a new world order perceived as heavily tilted in favour of 'international oligarchies' could be found in the principles enunciated at the conclusion of the visit to New Delhi of the Premier of the Chinese State Council, Li Peng, in December 1991: these were the right of every country, strong or weak, to participate in the decision-making and settlement of international affairs on a footing of sovereign equality, the need for effective disarmament and to bridge the growing economic gap between the North and the South, and the indivisibility of human rights. Rao recalled that there should not be any 'imposition of non-economic conditionalities to development assistance'.[23]

International relations expert, M.S. Rajan, commented that 'if the bipolar world and the Cold War between the two sets of cold warriors were bad, the present unipolar world is worse in some respects for the rest of the world community (...) This "unipolar" world has threatened, if not deprived, the independence/ sovereignty of the vast majority of other states and, what is worse, these states have lost the even little manoeuvrability they had during the cold war years'.[24] Loss of assertive self-confidence by Russia and China linked to their dependence on the United States for economic and technological assistance, when it was not collusion in order to preserve the nuclear monopoly of the P-5, was contributing to give the USA a free hand in world affairs. An example was the US-inspired ideas of the creation of 'no fly zones' in northern and southern Iraq, acquiesced by UN organs, which seemed to ignore the sovereignty of States. The oil-for-food deal came also for criticism as it encroached on basic human rights of the Iraqi people because Washington had developed allergy to its ruler. The apparent subservience of the United Nations to the United States was a matter of concern for a country facing a renewal of insurgency in Kashmir, a critical issue which had been on the UN agenda in the past.

In an international environment characterized by the break-up of former composite States (Soviet Union, Yugoslavia) and the assertion of ethno-nationalist claims, India was in the front burner given its sensitivity on issues of self-determination and the insurgency problem in Kashmir and Punjab. At the first Security Council summit in early 1992, Prime Minister Narasimha Rao proposed that the parameters for human rights should be delineated to harmonize the defence of national integrity with respect for human rights, adding that contents and nature of human rights were conditioned by social, traditional and cultural forces that form different societies and not be determined unilaterally and externally. Rao also took on the practitioners and supporters of terrorists acts, an obvious reference to Pakistani support for cross-border terrorism.[25] India was looking to every visiting foreign dignitary to endorse its position on Kashmir. Islamabad indeed jumped at the new awareness sweeping the West, placing self-determination at the centre of global concerns, to get India condemned for its human rights record in anti-insurgency operations. The redeeming feature was that Pakistan's main sympathizers on Kashmir showed with the passing years less inclination to antagonize India on this issue, and in March 1994, Islamabad was even forced to withdraw from a move in the Political Committee of the UNGA in Geneva to involve the Secretary-General in the Indo-Pakistan imbroglio. By the mid-nineties and apart from occasional statements sure to raise a hue and cry, as when Robin Raphael, the US Assistant Secretary of State, questioned in October 1993 the validity of the instrument of accession of Jammu and Kashmir into the Indian Union, Kashmir became less of a liability in international fora, especially after the world attention got drawn to ethnic cleansing and massacre of civilian populations in Africa (Liberia, Sierra Leone, Somalia, Rwanda), in former Yugoslavia and in Chechnya. The decision to hold elections for the State assembly in the autumn of 1996 helped also to relieve external pressures for the self-determination of the Kashmiris.[26]

If promotion of democracy was a guiding principle of international relations as it was supposed to be in the new world order, India did not miss a chance to argue that it should include the world premier organization, by allowing for wider representation in the security council to ensure its moral sanction and political effectiveness. In the 1994 session of the UNGA, India put forward its claim, without gathering much support, to be a permanent member of the UN Security Council (Japan and Germany were then the two favourite contenders for seats), arguing that it would notably reflect the vast changes at the UN, including a three-fold expansion of the general assembly over the years, and would be a step towards the process of democratisation of the international system as a whole, reminding also the active participation of India in UN peacekeeping operations in Asia, Africa and Latin America. The discriminatory nature of the veto power given to the P-5 - even if it had at least served India's interests during the Cold War - could neither be really equated with a democratic functioning.

Making known its disapproval of a new world order based on inherent inequality, intrusive politics and discriminatory regimes, India also admitted that it could hardly afford to be unreservedly sanctimonious and indulge into gratuitous rhetorical internationalism. When asked about the new thrust of India's foreign policy, J.N. Dixit, who had been appointed Foreign Secretary in November 1991, answered that 'instead of our foreign policy being related to some hypothetical norms of India's role and importance in world affairs (...) the government of Narasimha Rao has decided that our foreign and economic policies will be realistic in relation to the world around us and it will be practical in terms of its objectives'.[27] Pragmatism was to rule the day, calling for adjustments and compromises to save the essential, and waiting for better days when India could realize its full potential and get its due place in the world. Domestic developments did not bring much relief. The demolition of Babri Masjid in Ayodhya in December 1992, soon followed by the blasts in Mumbai and the ensuing communal riots were reminiscent of India's darkest hours and New Delhi had to work overtime to assuage doubts about India's future stability and commitment to secularism. There were objective constraints to India seeking to walk tall on the world stage, especially at a time when it was speculated that the economic power would be the key to other kinds of power and would determine the degree of autonomy of nations more than any other factors. Reflecting on which country whose interplay will pattern the new world order, the *Economist* disqualified India even if it will be 'a power in its own neighbourhood, but its frail economy and its physical isolation between the Himalayas and the sea will almost certainly keep it out of the global competition'.[28]

The Indian establishment was keen to dismiss such dire predictions. It was indeed acknowledged that economy would hold the key to a brighter future and economic diplomacy was given a distinctive feature unknown in the past, precisely to gather international support to the economic reforms package and eventually to counter pressures on political issues at the bilateral level with a special mention for the United States which were India's single largest trade partner and the largest source of foreign direct investments. These were the years when fanciful figures about the ever-growing Indian middle class were flying around the foreign diplomatic representations in order to catch private investors' attention.

Ways and means of upping the ante

The mid-nineties were critical with India taking two momentous decisions showing its determinations not to succumb to external pressures when pushed too hard, heralding the nuclear tests of 1998. The first one was the refusal to go with the indefinite and unconditional extension of the NPT in May 1995.[29] The Clinton administration's decision to help pass in September the Brown amendment to ease the restrictions of the Pressler amendment mocked the anti-proliferation commitment and the sanction system. It is also no surprise that otherwise in the context of renewed pressures on India's capacity to determine independently its security requirements, the Indian Prime Minister is said to have been very close to issuing an authorization in December 1995 for nuclear testing in the Rajasthan desert. The second decision was taken in spite of the political instability which followed the defeat of the Congress in the 1996 general elections, starting with the thirteen days first Vajpayee government and then by the eighteen months United Front governments of H.D. Deve Gowda and I.K. Gujral. The former was Prime Minister and the latter foreign minister when India refused to join the Complete Test Ban Treaty (CTBT) when it was finally approved by the UN General Assembly in September 1996, a treaty whose draft proposal India had originally co-sponsored with the US in 1993. For India, obligations could not be one-sided on the nuclear have-nots and any conclusive treaty needed to be linked to the process of nuclear disarmament. To add salt to injury, an element of coercion was added when it was decided that the entry into force of the CTBT would be conditional on its signature and ratification by India – among some other countries - before 24 September 1999.

While it challenged the near-universal consensus on the nuclear treaties which would legally perpetuate indefinitely the P-5 monopoly over WMDs, but reiterated its intentions to remain a threshold state and not to cover the extra mile, India was fostering good-neighbourly relations by establishing trust and confidence under what came to be known as the 'Gujral doctrine'. It meant first of all offering unilateral concessions to improve relationships with the immediate neighbourhood - except Pakistan with whom the door to dialogue were nevertheless kept open - in a spirit of accommodation rather than obdurate reciprocity, as witnessed the trade treaty with Nepal and the signing of a thirty-year treaty on the sharing of Ganges waters with Bangladesh in December 1996. To those who criticized this policy as being too soft, it was answered that this was based on realism and aimed at liberating India to play a larger role in the world. In return these neighbours had to show respect for India's security concerns. Then came the next concentric circle, that is the extended neighbourhood comprising South-East Asia, Central Asia and the Indian Ocean region. India has land and maritime borders with South-East Asia and its EEZ spans the waters almost from the Persian Gulf to the Straits of Malacca. In all these regions, advances had been made under the Narasimha Rao government to take advantage of the new geopolitical openings. For instance, there were the signing with Nepal in February 1996 of a treaty on the integrated development of Mahakali River on the basis of equal partnership, the Prime Minister's visits to many Central Asian Republics and India's accession to the status of full dialogue partner with ASEAN in 1995, followed next year by its admission to the ASEAN Regional Forum as a fallout of thc 'Look East Policy' initiated in 1991. If the end of the Cold War had not brought about a more equitable world order, at least it allowed India to resume contacts with estranged regions because of affiliations with one of the blocs.

With Gujral, the focus on neighbouring regions and the promotion of regional cooperation (the Indian Ocean Rim for Regional Association was founded in March 1997 and a new trans-regional pact called BIST-EC (Bangladesh, India, Sri Lanka and Thailand Economic Cooperation) came into being in June 1997) were elevated to top priority in India's foreign policy. The goal was first to start first with the inner circle, then move to the next concentric circle to achieve new partnerships so that India can take its place in the world on a more advantageous basis. 'Indian diplomacy and foreign policy are making an entry into world politics through these concentric circles' expounded Gujral.[30] The rationale being that India could not skipped over a peaceful and constructive environment in its immediate neighbourhood without compromising its rightful place in the international community. India's standing in the world and its credibility as a major player would be in direct proportion to the degree of its acceptability in the region, apart from its internal strength. As a matter of fact, the regional baggage carried by India has been a major drag in its dealings at the global level.

A regional diplomacy, furthermore implying an asymmetric dimension, could not please those for whom India should not be overtly preoccupied with inconsequential or adverse countries. In a penetrating analysis foreseeing what was to happen few months later, left-wing journalist Praful Bidwai wrote that 'the Indian elite cannot even countenance global isolation, let alone deal with it in a dignified way. It deeply craves for external approbation, especially from the Great Powers. This craving is integral to its self-esteem and *amour propre* (...) Seeking Great Power status for India far outweighs the elite's engagement with burning issues: poverty and social deprivation, illiteracy, vicious gender and caste discrimination, or environmental degradation. There is another dissonance here. India can never command the world's respect so long as it remains a land of disease and disaster. In this regard it is rapidly falling behind even Southeast Asia, North Africa and many other Third World countries. Our elite's grandiose ambitions can only lead it to search for a military short-cut to high status (...) the elite wants the short, soft route to an exalted "image" and "status", not the harder option of becoming a major and responsible world player that is quietly confident because it is building an open, equitable, prosperous, democratic society for all its people'.[31] Impatience about India not being given due consideration and the place in the world community befitting an old civilisation and an emerging power because of an unassuming leadership falling short of taking forceful decisions, was reflected in the BJP election manifesto of 1998: 'In the recent past we have seen a tendency to bend under pressure. This arises as much out of ignorance of our rightful place and role in world affairs as also from a loss of national self-confidence and resolve. A nation as large and capable as ourselves must make its impact felt on the world arena'.[32]

BJP strategists took up a bet that the sanctions which would inevitably follow tests were bound to be transitory (they were lifted in September 2001). History taught that the US did not take long to make up with Communist China after it became nuclear in 1964 and India would not brake any international commitment since it was not a member of the NPT and had not signed the CTBT. Furthermore, economic interests precluded skipping over India at a time when the country was registering some of its highest growth rates ever (7+ per cent between 1994 and97). Here India might have learned a lesson or two from China who in spite of being regularly accused of human rights violations and for proliferation of nuclear and ballistic technologies was still being wooed by the great powers.

The motivations underlying the nuclear posture

In the wake of US pressures on India for signing the CTBT, the wrestling match between the United States and Saddam Hussein over the vexed questions of UN inspections in early 1998 and the thinly veiled threat that countries which do not abide by stipulated international disciplines on non-proliferation matters should be ready to forfeit their sovereignty, if necessary under pressure of superior military force, gave grain to grind to those favourable to forego the nuclear restraint. By then nothing was really expected from the United Nations to redress an unbalanced world order as there was no evidence that the expansion process would gather momentum in the near future. In October 1996, India had been decisively defeated by Japan for a seat in the Security Council as a non-permanent member by winning 40 votes against Japan's 142. Also there was a large consensus across the political spectrum to consider that the United Nations had become more of an instrumentality of the foreign policy objectives of the United States and its allies. 'The UN has been used either as a cosmetic umbrella, or a fig leaf, for the USA's political and military moves in reordering the world with the support of other important powers. The manner in which the crises in Yugoslavia, Somalia and Iraq were handled leads one to this conclusion. If we add to this list the powerful multilateral financial institutions operating on the policy orientations of western advanced countries, it becomes obvious that the emerging world order would remain subject to the overarching influence of the United States and that it will remain unfairly competitive and acquisitive' wrote J.N. Dixit.[33]

The immediate justification for the nuclear tests was the Chinese threat, cited by Prime Minister Vajpayee in his letter of May 11, 1998 to the American president, Bill Clinton. In effect, the 1998 tests can be interpreted as a manifestation of the rivalry between New Delhi and Beijing. Both countries see themselves as Asian giants and aspire to the status of global powers. If a pact on the maintenance of peace and tranquillity along the line of actual control and an agreement on confidence building measures along their disputed borders had been signed respectively in September 1993 and November 1996 so as to ensure that no force is used against the other, the border differences remained still unresolved: Beijing, for instance, did not recognize Sikkim as an integral part of India and had laid claim to a significant portion of Arunachal Pradesh, whereas India claims territories in the north-western tip of Kashmir annexed by China since the Sino-Pakistan border agreement of March 1963. Tibet, moreover, was a latent bone of contention between the two countries. More importantly, however, the rapprochement between China and Burma was causing India growing anxiety. Beijing apparently trained the Burmese army and had a monitoring base in the Coco islands, less then thirty nautical miles from the Andamans. Of course these dangers were not a new phenomenon, but the context had changed, especially in South-East Asia where the closure of the American bases in the Philippines in 1992 caused apprehension that the development of a power vacuum in the region would be to China's advantage[34]. At last, from the Indian perspective, the NPT regime formalized and perpetuated the imbalance with China.

Despite the fact that the importance of nuclear weapons declined in the immediate post-Cold War period, it did not result in the complete abolition of nuclear weaponry, a central element of Indian politics or at least in its discourse on the subject. Neither Russia nor the smaller powers, such as France or the United Kingdom, were prepared to reduce their arsenals as part of a larger process, which could eventually culminate in the complete eradication of nuclear weaponry. In every case, the old arguments on deterrence were combined with considerations regarding the great power status of each of the nuclear states and apprehension over the prospective proliferation of 'rogue' States as also of non-state actors.[35] As there existed no agreement on the principle of a denuclearisation schedule, India had no other choice except to ensure its security through nuclear means.

Of greater interest to our problematic is the link between the possession of the bomb and the status of a global power. The five permanent members of the Security Council were the five officially recognized nuclear states and the two prime contenders for permanent membership were Germany and Japan owing mainly to their economic weight. A nuclear India aspiring to the status of a major economic power in the coming century could score on both these attributes of uncontested power. In Perkovich's words, for the Indian leaders and backed by the entire nation, the bomb represented 'modernity, international rank and transcendence of the colonial past'.[36] The nuclear device confirmed its mastery of hi-tech and reflected the technological potential of the nation, placing it at par with the most developed nations. In the aftermath of the tests, Indian analysts, echoing the sentiments of the director of the DRDO, Abdul Kalam, were convinced of the fact that 'might respects might' and that "when a country is technologically strong, other countries respect it'.[37] It was, therefore, not surprising in their opinion that the five officially recognized nuclear States were also the permanent members of the United Nations Security Council. Consequently, India's determination to prove that it was capable of being a fully independent State, one moreover convinced of its moral superiority, had considerable influence on the reformulation of its nuclear policy. From this point of view, the 1998 tests were in keeping with its policy since Independence, but had an element of ambiguity. The new leaders wanted the power and prestige associated with nuclear capability, even as they maintained a posture of moral superiority, not by stressing their revulsion for the bomb and the concept of deterrence itself, in contrast to their predecessors, but by a doctrine of no first use. It is interesting to note that if a number of commentators endorsed the government's decision by rejecting a moralism inherent in Indian foreign policy and attributed to Nehru, Prime Minister Vajpayee, in his post-test speech, was at pains to reiterate the appeal for universal nuclear disarmament. The new India intended to adorn itself with the prestige bestowed by power as well with the virtues of morality.

The nuclear factor in Indo-Pak relations and the doctrinal ambiguities

The strains that the possession of the bomb injected into the Indo-Pak dispute, is a good indicator of the real impact of the nuclear posture on Indian foreign policy.[38] What is at stake here is the possibility of a conflict of the conventional type, limited or not, in a nuclear environment, and the political consequences that arise from this. For Pakistan, the possession of the bomb would prevent India from any attempt to escalate the conflict and transform it into a sub-conventional one. Consequently, the 1998 tests did not deter Pakistan in the slightest from backing Islamist groups operating in Kashmir. The guarantee of impunity ensured by the possession of the bomb is however not absolute and, from the Indian point of view at least, a conventional war remains a possibility up to a certain degree of intensity. From such a perspective, the entire difficulty resides in the assessment of the opponent's nuclear threshold. It is therefore never possible to completely eliminate the risk of escalation.

Such a situation straight away narrows the spectrum of conflict – ranging from terrorism to a nuclear conflict and including guerrilla and conventional warfare – to its two extreme options. In so doing it is likely to paralyse the side enjoying conventional superiority, in other words India, for fear that a Pakistan with its back to the wall might be tempted to use the bomb. In turn, this paralysis is not without political repercussions, for New Delhi cannot hope to extricate itself except by appealing to a third power - the United States in this instance - capable of exerting sufficient pressure on Pakistan to compel it to stop sponsoring Islamist groups operating in Indian Kashmir. Thus far from paving the way to greater autonomy of decision, the shift to a nuclear posture, on the contrary, reinforced its dependence on America and contributed to the internationalisation of the Kashmir imbroglio.

It is difficult to talk of an 'Indian nuclear doctrine' in the absence of a document enumerating the fundamental principles governing the use of nuclear force in the service of national interests. The document prepared by the National Security Advisory Board, a group of experts mandated by the Indian authorities, published on August 17, 1999 under the title *Draft Report of the National Security Advisory Board on Indian Nuclear Doctrine* has no official standing. Nevertheless it does give some indications as to the orientations of the Indian nuclear programme. The latter is not explicitly directed at Pakistan and does not target any country in particular. Its primary objective is to 'deter from the use and the threat of use of nuclear weapons by any State or entity against India, and its armed forces'. This programme is not meant to be offensive. The passage cited above thus affirms that 'India will not be the first to initiate a nuclear strike but will reply with punitive strikes if deterrence fails'. Lastly, it contains the pledge not to use, nor threaten to use the bomb against States that do not have nuclear weapons or are not aligned with nuclear weapon States.[39]

It can, however, be seen from the history of the Indian nuclear programme, and also from that of the Pakistani programme, that both are intimately linked to the regional situation. As George Perkovich remarks : 'Had China not defeated India in the 1962 war and acquired nuclear weapons in 1964, India might not have built upon the nuclear weapons capabilities made possible by the projects planned and initiated in the 1950s. Had India not declared its possible nuclear weapon ambitions in the early 1960s, Pakistan might not have pursued countervailing nuclear weapon capabilities, which in turn, intensified India's motivations to build nuclear weapons in the 1980s and 1990s'.[40] The National Security Council Advisory Board's draft report indirectly affirms that India could, if necessary, have recourse to nuclear weapons against States having the same weapons, that is to say, amongst others, against China and Pakistan. It is therefore illusory to delink the Indian programme from the regional context.

Pakistan has, on its part, stressed the strictly deterrent nature of its nuclear arsenal without going as far as to publish a doctrinal text. Nevertheless, it did pose a certain number of specific conditions that would compel it to use its nuclear arsenal. Namely, if the survival of the nation is in jeopardy or its conventional forces collapse in the event of a war with India, or yet again if its territorial integrity and nuclear installations come under attack. The conditions underlying the use of the bomb by Pakistan are thus to a large extent linked to its conflict with India and directed against the latter.

By the same token, Isabelle Cordonnier and Bruno Tertrais maintain that the pledge of no first use made by India with regard to nuclear weapons contains a number of ambiguities, thereby giving New Delhi some room for manoeuvre. These two authors point out that the assertion that India would not take the initiative of a nuclear strike is different from an unqualified commitment of no first use. Similarly, the decision to resort to punitive action in case of the failure of deterrence is not the same thing as an explicit pledge to retaliate only in case of a nuclear strike by the adversary. Lastly, the suggestion that the security guarantees proposed by the Indian government would not hold if the State in question were aligned to a nuclear power in fact provides a loophole allowing India to initiate a nuclear strike.[41] For both protagonists the nuclearisation of any future Indo-Pak conflicts fall within the realm of the possible.

The stability-instability paradox in South Asia

Over and above the doctrines relating to the use of nuclear weapons by the two protagonists, the debate on the importance of atomic weapons for Indo-Pak relations revolves around the 'stability-instability paradox'. This supposes that 'the nuclear option renders sterile the risk of any major conventional conflict but does not prevent low intensity warfare and can even encourage it, for neither protagonist can afford to let the situation degenerate to a level that would compel the other to cross the nuclear threshold'.[42] The stability-instability paradox has been used to advantage by Pakistan. Whatever the legitimacy of Islamabad's territorial claims on Kashmir, it is Pakistan that is calling the present status quo into question. The Pakistani scenario (at least such as it is presented by some Indian analysts) is as follows : Pakistan foments trouble in Kashmir until India is provoked into escalating the conflict to which Pakistan will retaliate with added intensity. This escalation will continue to spiral until India eventually intrudes into Pakistani territory. Once the Indian tanks cross a particular line, Islamabad will declare that the nuclear threshold has been crossed. At this stage India will have no other choice but to draw back. Its conventional superiority will thus have been neutralised. Admiral Menon counters this logic with the fact, for example, that a country can engage in nuclear war while a conventional war is going on. As a result, the shift to the nuclear option will prove extremely painful for the anti-status quo State, which will then abstain. From the Indian perspective, it is therefore advisable to envisage a flexible response from the beginning in order to discourage a conventional attack from the anti-status quo State, in other words, Pakistan.

The possibility of a major conventional war cannot however be ruled out a priori. It can result in particular from an inadequately controlled escalation or a miscalculation by one of the parties. It has been shown elsewhere that nuclear deterrence can play the same role in Asia as it did in East-West relations.[43] This in no way signifies that India and Pakistan will always be able to avoid a confrontation with a nuclear dimension. In this regard, it seems obvious that the nuclear environment in South Asia is particularly unstable. At this point a comparison with the situation that prevailed during the Cold War era is called for. During this period, in effect, Soviet and American leaders were constantly preoccupied with finding ways and means to minimise nuclear risk and worked in concert to implement the steps needed to prevent a catastrophe. Comparing this situation with that of South Asia, Michael Krepon identifies nine steps which were taken to reduce nuclear risk between the United States and the USSR :

1) a formal agreement to change no territorial status quo in sensitive zones through military means;
2) a tacit agreement not to practice brinkmanship in each others neighbourhood;
3) an agreement to minimise or avoid dangerous military practices;
4) special safety measures with regard to ballistic missiles and nuclear armament systems including, besides inducting the habit of transparency, the undertaking not to launch any weapons of mass destruction in space;
5) belief in the strict observation of obligations resulting from the treaties and confidence-building measures;
6) verification procedures;
7) establishing reliable communication lines between the political and military leaders of both countries;

8) installing command and control systems;
9) a mutual undertaking not to be satisfied with the existing measures.[44]

Although we are fully in accord with the author that these measures can be applied to South Asia, it is apparent that to date they are not even in the initial stages of realisation. Calling the territorial status quo into question through military or paramilitary means in a highly sensitive zone, Kashmir, is the crux of the problem between India and Pakistan, while dangerous military practices along the border are the rule and the two sides engage in brinkmanship at regular intervals. The two States are of course not responsible for their geographical contiguity but this renders the situation potentially explosive. Moreover, measures for minimising nuclear risk behoves a collaborative attitude from the parties concerned, which to say the least is often missing between India and Pakistan. Lastly, the rhetoric of peace that each State indulges in essentially for political ends by attempting to force the other into a defensive posture, cannot be a substitute for treaties or even for the confidence building measures that the two States undertake to negotiate after each crisis, but whose impulsion vanishes just as rapidly.[45] Therefore, it is not at all an exaggeration to conclude that the South Asian nuclear environment is an unstable one and that there exists a real risk of nuclear war if a conventional war were to break out between India and Pakistan.

The nuclear factor in the Kargil crisis of 1999

It is interesting to examine the role of the nuclear factor in the successive crises in Kashmir.[46] This has been and continues to be much debated. In 1990, the crisis coincided with the publication of an article by an American journalist, Seymour Hersh, claiming that India and Pakistan were on the brink of a nuclear war with Pakistani F-16 nuclear missile delivery aircraft in a state of high alert. This thesis was refuted by American diplomats posted in the region but was widely believed in the United States where it helped to underscore the risks of proliferation and to throw light on the role of American diplomacy in the settlement of the crisis.[47] According to other studies, the nuclear capability possessed by both India and Pakistan in 1990 effectively prevented these border incidents from degenerating into an open war.

Nevertheless it is the Kargil imbroglio that has provoked the most heated debates on the role of nuclear weapons. Early in May 1999, Indian troops found that several hundred Pakistani fighters, comprising both regular troops and irregular elements,[48] had infiltrated the heights overlooking Kargil town, thereby controlling the road between Srinagar and Leh. Less than three months after the 'historic' meeting between Atal Behari Vajpayee and Nawaz Sharif and the ensuing Lahore declaration, India and Pakistan were at war. The vicissitudes of the conflict are of little import here, but ultimately, American intervention and Chinese neutrality forced Pakistan to retreat. In this instance too several conflicting theses exist with regard to the nuclear factor. One such thesis refutes the notion th at it had any role in the crisis :

1) Kargil supposedly demonstrated that the nuclear status was not enough to prevent an open conflict between the two countries. According to the authors 'this proposition is not very credible, in the sense that the crisis was of much lower intensity than earlier confrontations [...] and did not perhaps merit, if violence is the yardstick that qualifies the relationship between the two countries, the appellation of open conflict'.[49] Nevertheless, it should be noted that it is the status of 'open conflict' that is in question here rather than the role of the nuclear factor;

2) A second thesis also denies the role of nuclear deterrence in the way the crisis developed for it did not put the vital interests of the two countries into jeopardy. On this point we can only concur with Isabelle Cordonnier and Bruno Tertrais that Kashmir is at the heart of the differences that oppose India and Pakistan and that in consequence it is difficult to affirm that their vital interests were not in cause;

3) Other observers, on the contrary, felt that the possession of the bomb by the two actors prevented the conflict from degenerating into an open war;
4) Lastly, a fourth thesis states that the nuclear status of both countries enabled Pakistan to re-open the Kashmir debate by correctly anticipating that the fear of a nuclear skid would impel the international community to intervene promptly.

The last two hypotheses appear all the more plausible as they echo the Pakistani strategy. However, only the release of the military and diplomatic archives will provide some definite answers to these questions.

There is no doubt that for India, the nuclear status was a constitutive element of the crisis, as much in its initiation as in its unfolding. The *Kargil Review Committee* notes that one of Pakistan's primary motivations was its keenness to 'internationalise Kashmir as a nuclear flashpoint requiring urgent third party intervention'.[50] Pakistani firing on the LOC was thus aimed at projecting a volatile situation in South Asia. Islamabad thus intended to blackmail the international community into forcing India to accept a cease-fire and mediation on the Kashmir issue.

The same report also draws attention to attempts by Pakistani spokesmen, official and non-official, to convey an implicit message of impending nuclear danger[51] in mid crisis, with at least one missile base activated and several missile systems probably ready for launching.[52] It seems a little doubtful that the threat was taken seriously and influenced the restrained nature of the Indian riposte. In reply to the hints dropped by the Pakistani Foreign Secretary, Shamshed Ahmed, the Indian army, apprehending a pre-emptive Pakistani nuclear strike, activated all its three types of nuclear delivery vehicles, keeping them at Readiness State 3, meaning that the bombs could be coupled with the delivery vehicles within a short time. The air force was asked to keep its Mirage aircraft on standby, while the scientists of the Defence Research and Development Organisation (DRDO, the organisation responsible for the development of the Indian army's missile programme) proceeded to the deployment sites of the Prithvi missiles, and four of them were prepared for a possible nuclear strike.[53]

Pakistan may not have achieved its immediate military objectives and may have paid a heavy political price for its military adventurism, it nevertheless managed to internationalise the issue thanks to the nuclear factor. It is certain that American political intervention in the conflict, as well as the overall renewal of American interest in the region was largely a direct consequence of the nuclearisation of the latter. Moreover, it confirmed the permissive role of nuclear weapons for Pakistan, which could thus pursue its objective of weakening India by means of low intensity warfare. These two consequences indubitably convinced Pakistan of the necessity of diversifying and reinforcing its nuclear arsenal, as well as, at the beginning of any new crisis, mobilising its nuclear reserves, thus giving India a clear indication of the seriousness of Pakistani deterrence. At the same time it would continue to catalyse international intervention to resolve any future crisis. On the Indian side, the Kargil crisis, far from substantiating New Delhi's choices, served to demonstrate the necessity of developing capabilities as well as undertaking institutional re-organisation to ensure a minimum credible deterrence.

The nuclear factor in the Winter 2001 and Spring 2002 crises

In the Winter 2001 and Spring 2002 crises, from all appearances the nuclear factor played a much more subtle and decisive role. In the aftermath of the September 11, 2001 attacks, in effect, India tried to develop a strategy of tension with the aim of putting an end to the relative impunity of Pakistan sponsored terrorism that the possession of the bomb by Islamabad seemed to guarantee to the Kashmiri militants. It took advantage of the new American rhetoric, designating terrorism as pernicious in itself independently of any political causality, which it was necessary to eliminate under any circumstances, to stop Pakistan from supporting Kashmiri militant organisations. This strategy was decided in the wake of the American decision to use Pakistani and not Indian bases as New Delhi had proposed.

By doing this, India showed that it had retained the lessons learnt from Kargil, namely that because of its very nature the nuclear risk alone could mobilise the attention of the international community and that the latter, if it was made to focus on Pakistani cross-border terrorism in Kashmir, could be positive for India. During the Kargil crisis, in fact, international opinion had more or less unanimously recognised Pakistan as the aggressor and called for mutual restraint and a bilateral settlement of the problem, as well as for a revival of the Lahore process. Its stand on Kashmir in general, and Kargil in particular, was in India's favour. The American reaction, which had forced Pakistan to retreat and lauded India for the restraint it had shown, had especially surprised the Indian authorities[54] and also demonstrated Washington's capacity to curtail Islamabad's military and diplomatic options.

A series of attacks against India between October 2001 and May 2002 heightened tensions and legitimised mobilisation but was not really the cause of either. During this period India applied indirect nuclear blackmail. None of the limited conflict scenarios formulated by the Indian army offered any guarantees against escalation with possible nuclear consequences. In Kashmir, India could claim only very limited conventional superiority in comparison to the Pakistan army that commands excellent defensive positions. The Indian army could envisage air strikes against training camps and military installations, but these can easily be rebuilt, whereas combined air and ground attacks were likely to suffer heavy damages.

Under these conditions, India could not count on significant gains except by going around Kashmir and by launching a major attack so that it would be in a position to deploy its numerical superiority to advantage. But the very fact of Pakistan's weakness and limited strategic depth inevitably raises the question of the use of nuclear weapons.[55] Although observers agreed that Pakistan would be able to resist long enough (one week) before international mediation could take place, the nuclear risk was considerable.

The Pakistani response only served to endorse the reality of a nuclear threat. Islamabad delivered a number of threats, initially implicit and later explicit, in a cleverly orchestrated crescendo. To the Indian Prime Minister's declaration of a 'decisive battle' the Pakistani Foreign Minister replied with the warning that 'any misadventure by India will be met with full force' and that this would be a 'major miscalculation leading to grave consequences'.[56] This reference, devoid of all subtlety, obviously did not go unnoticed in Delhi, along with the series of medium and short-range missile tests by Pakistan at a time when the crisis was at its peak. Islamabad had of course informed the Indian authorities beforehand and explained that these tests were not in any way linked to the current stand off. Despite the prior advice they were nevertheless taken as a supplementary warning. Even more explicit were the declarations of the Railway Minister, Javed Ashraf Quazi, ex-chief of the ISI, who stated : 'If it ever comes to the annihilation of Pakistan, then what is this damned nuclear option for, we will use it against the enemy', adding, 'if Indians destroy most of us, we too will annihilate parts of the adversary'.[57]

The threat of a limited conventional conflict was enough to shake the Western chancelleries. Their intervention was all the more probable because an Indo-Pak war would in all likelihood interfere with the American anti-terrorist operations in Pakistan and Afghanistan, whereas on the other hand any pressure on Islamist activists by the Pakistani president was likely to facilitate them.

Conclusion: the lure of greater independence

The decade under review saw India trying to adjust to the post-Cold War world dominated by the unequalled power of the United States whose aspirations and adverse reactions to them were to give the pitch to the international relations. It opened with the call for a 'New World Order' which, according to the words pronounced by President George H.W. Bush on 11 September 1990, was to usher in a new era, 'free from the threat of terror, stronger in the pursuit of justice, and more secure in the quest for peace, an era in which the nations of the world can prosper and live in harmony'.[58] Eleven years later, terrorist attacks on the twin towers and the Pentagon were a dramatic reminder that goodwill rhetoric could be seen as imposition of one's own set of values and clash of interests often leads to frustrations. These were indeed challenging years for a country whose independent stand had for decades been nurtured by the equilibrium of power ensured by the Cold War. In this regard, one can recall the words of an Indian official: 'the forces driving to war can be checked only by the most persistent and patient effort to bring and hold all sides together – not by helping to build up the preponderance of one side, which in itself, and through its example upon others, can have no other result than that of widening the cleavage, pulling down the bridges and pushing the world a little nearer to the brink.'[59] By the end of the decade, India's foreign policy-makers appears to have been somewhat dismissive of this advice when one considers that in 1991, India was shying away from being seen as supporting the US war effort against Iraq's Saddam Hussein and ten years later the Indian government was displaying a disturbing propensity to eagerly support US initiatives.

If the ultimate goal of India's foreign policy was and remains to make the country an important player in the international arena as an independent centre of power, three ways, sometimes complementary, were thought of during this decade: Gujral's concentric circles' approach establishing a steady regional foundation upon which India could back up a larger role in world affairs, the multipolar idea challenging US predominance through the existence of multiple centres of power and accommodation with a US-centric unipolar configuration. The 1998 nuclear tests were to signify the transition 'from the past emphasis on the power of the argument to a new stress on the argument of power' as C. Raja Mohan put it up.[60] It was a first step meant to deride the widespread notion that India had an unrealistic perception of self, earning a reputation for talking rather than doing. The nuclear explosion was supposed to create a confidence-boosting wave which would extend to the other attributes of power and would elevate the country to a position of strength allowing to negotiate an equilibrium with the new power centres of an emerging multipolar world. If the nuclear tests earned India negative reactions in the guise of all-round condemnation and sanctions, it also attracted world attention and the ensuing flurry of diplomatic activity was seen as an acknowledgement, even if rather grudging, of India's importance. New Delhi could extol the virtues of a multipolar world as the P-5 stood divided on the issue of sanctions which had moreover little economic impact. In the wake of the apparent success of the 'bus diplomacy' with Pakistan, India felt even encouraged during the Kosovo crisis to take a strong view of NATO air strikes in Yugoslovia in March 1999 and the propensity of NATO to act outside the UN system and to extend its areas of operation beyond the territory of the alliance.

After the Kargil conflict, if it was occasionally good form to emphasize the need to address the world's 'asymmetries which demand a coalition of interest amongst equals, rather than alliances build around a hegemony, however well intentioned'[61], the impression was gaining ground that India's was tilting in favour of an alliance-like relation with the United States germinating on a series of meetings held between Foreign Minister Jaswant Singh and the US Deputy Secretary of State Strobe Talbott between June 1998 and early 2000. The willingness of the United States to rein in Pakistan had been first met with incredulity in India - a hangover from the Cold War which assumed that Washington would always favour Pakistan in crisis situation – and then interpreted as an historic opportunity to have the United States on their side vis-à-vis its two biggest security concerns: Pakistan and China. After Washington put relentless pressure on Pakistan to unconditionally step back from the Kargil heights and finally accepted that cross-border terrorism should take precedence over human rights violation in Kashmir, the Indian government might have foreseen the possibility of bringing the United States to now pressure Islamabad in stopping its military support to the Kashmiri militants, especially because of the risk induced by the nuclear factor. While Washington was still keen to cap India's nuclear programme, New Delhi argued that the priority should moved from non-proliferation *per se* to sources of proliferation, unambiguously pointing an accusing finger at China. Besides New Delhi expressed a readiness to cooperate with Washington in containing the ever-growing Chinese ambitions in Asia.[62] It led to think that India has reconciled itself to smaller ambitions, settled for operating under the US hegemonic umbrella and to play the role of a strategic asset for the latter. Other 'poles', like Russia and the European Union, were often left with a secondary role and whose partnership is useful in case it can help to trigger India's prestige in the eyes of Washington. Whether it is the Kargil conflict or the Indo-Pak tension following the 13 December 2001 attack on the Indian Parliament, the shift from a 'recessed deterrent' to a 'minimal deterrent', in other words a declared and open nuclear capability, has not really strengthened its autonomy of decision, which was the implicit objective of the 1998 chest-thumping nuclear tests.[63] The threat of a nuclear exchange during the spring of 2002 was exaggerated so as to ring an alarm bell in Washington to force the US to intervene in favour of India vis-à-vis Pakistan. If September 11 validated India's oft repeated appeal to the international community to address vigorously the issue of terrorism,[64], it also signified its dependence on the United States to confront the sources of terrorism in Pakistan. Ironically, the nuclear tests were to trigger a 'big power diplomacy' based on more realistic foundations than Nehru's supposed indulgence for moralistic overtones but yet one would still be at a loss to put forward deeds showing that nuclear India counts for more in the world that post-Independence India. More enduring image-boosting successes were to be found during the nineties in the realm of economics. India at the beginning of the millennium is undoubtedly a power in the world to be reckoned with but not yet a world power.

Notes

1. In an opinion poll conducted just after the tests in six metropolitan cities in India, 91 per cent of the respondents approved of the nuclear tests. Times of India, 13 May 1998.
2. I.K. Gujral commented that the tests were both 'foreseeable and unavoidable' and that he had hinted at this possibility to President William J. Clinton and President Jacques Chirac during meetings with them. I.K. Gujral, Continuity and Change: India's Foreign Policy, Delhi: Macmillan, 2003, p. XXI. One can gather that this was during Gujral's meeting with Clinton in September 1997 and during the French President's visit to India for the 1998 Republic Day.
3. If there is one link to be found between the two stands, it is in their potential to cope with a Chinese threat.
4. Telegram from the Embassy Office in Pakistan to the Department of State, 11 March 1964. US Department of State, Foreign Relations of the United States, 1964-1968, Vol. XXV, Washington D.C., 2000.
5. Isabelle Cordonnier and Bruno Tertrais, L'Asie nucléaire, Paris : IFRI, 2001. p. 52.
6. To Vallabhbhai Patel, 27 October 1948. Selected Works of Jawaharlal Nehru, Second Series, Vol. 8, New Delhi: Jawaharlal Nehru Memorial Fund, 1989, p. 285.
7. The Economist, 23 October 1948, pp. 650-652.
8. To Indira Gandhi, 28 October 1948, Selected Works of Jawaharlal Nehru, Second Series, Vol. 8, op. cit., p. 432.
9. 8 March 1948. Selected Works of Jawaharlal Nehru, Second Series, Vol. 5. New Delhi, Jawaharlal Nehru Memorial Fund, 1987, p. 503.
10. 13 September 1927. Selected Works of Jawaharlal Nehru, Vol. 2. New Delhi: B.R. Publishing Corporation, 1988 [repr.], pp. 359-360.
11. Annual report of the Embassy of France in India, sent by the Ambassador, Stanislas Ostrorog to the Foreign Minister, Antoine Pinay, le 28 January 1956. Archives du Quai d'Orsay, Nations Unies- Organisations Internationales, Vol. 540.
12. G.S. Bajpai, 'India and the Balance of Power', The Indian Year Book of International Affairs, 1952, University of Madras, pp. 7-8.
13. Baldev Raj Nayar, 'Regional Power in a Multipolar World', in: John W. Mellor, India, A Rising Middle Power, New Delhi: Selectbook Service Syndicate, 1981, p. 151.
14. I.K. Gujral, 'The Hinges of Global Change', Challenges of the Twenty-First Century, New Delhi: Indira Gandhi Memorial Trust, 1993, p. 347.
15. See, Gilles Boquérat, 'Indian Response to the Gulf Crisis of 1990-91', International Studies, 38 (4), October-December 2001, 427-440.

16. Rikhi Jaipal, 'Future of Non-alignment', The Hindustan Times, 17 September 1990. During a BJP executive meet in September 1991, A.B. Vajpayee said that 'the BJP would like the world to be multipolar. The Non-Aligned Movement has to be given a new thrust in this context'. The Times of India, 30 September 1991. By 1998, no mention of non-alignment was even made in the election manifesto of the Congress Party for the general elections, even more so in the case of the BJP.

17. Manoj Joshi, 'In a sea of change', Frontline, 14-27 September 1991, p. 45. India's decision in December 1991 to go along with the two-thirds of the NGA's membership in revoking the 1975 resolution 3379 equating Zionism with racism marked a significant change in India's West Asia policy traditionally pro-Palestinian. If Narasimha Rao defended this vote as motivated by India's desire to remove a major impediment to UN involvement in the Middle East peace process, some saw in it was an act of sheer opportunism to please the Americans - especially to get the support of the powerful Jew lobby - and to benefit from Israeli experience in anti-insurrectional operations. In January 1992, India established full diplomatic relations with Israel.

18. http://www.globalsecurity.org/military/library/policy/national/nss-918015.htm

19. Gautam Adhikari, 'India Isolated', Times of India, 24 November 1991. The National Security Strategy of the United States of America released in September 2002 by the George W. Bush administration acknowledged (p. 27) that the United States 'has undertaken a transformation in its relationship with India based on a conviction that US interests require a strong relationship with India (...) Differences remain, including over the development of India's economic reforms. But while in the past these concerns may have dominated our thinking about India, today we start with a view of India as a growing world power with which we have common strategic interests. Through a strong partnership with India, we can best address any differences and shape a dynamic future.'

20. Praful Bidwai, 'India Lurches Towards U.S.: Foreign Policy Without A Doctrine'. The Times of India, 24 September 1991.

21. During the eighties, defense expenditures as a proportion of the GDP had more than often crossed the 3 per cent mark, peaking at 3.6 per cent in 1987-88. They regularly declined in the nineties to stand on the eve of the nuclear tests at 2.45 per cent in 1997-98. Jasjit Singh and Swaran Singh, 'Trends in Defense Expenditure', Asian Strategic Review 1996-97, pp. 50-51.

22. 'India's Foreign Policy Objectives', Mani Shankar Aiyar, World Focus, Nov-Dec. 1992, vol. 13 (11-12), p. 16.

23. The Hindustan Times, 17 December 1991.

24. 'The Emerging New World Order', M.S. Rajan, World Focus, Nov-Dec. 1992, Vol. 13 (11-12), pp. 3-6.

25. The Times of India, 1st February 1992.
26. Within the US Congress, support for Pakistanis and Kashmiris lobbying activities fizzled out and it became progressively difficult to gather support for passing resolutions condemning India on its human rights records. The increasing clout of the India Caucus created in the early 1990s also played its part.
27. Sunday, 9-15 August 1992, p. 20. Elsewhere J.N. Dixit, who served as Foreign Secretary till February 1994, expounded that 'the most important effort in our thought process should be to carefully assess our strengths and weaknesses and then to create our foreign and domestic policies in a rational and practical manner, where our interests are served, where we do not get isolated and where the external and environmental inputs to safeguard our territorial integrity, unity and our developmental objectives are met'. 'India and the Post-Cold War World'. The Hindu, 31 March 1994.
28. The Economist, 'The New World Order: Back to the Future', 8 January 1994, p. 19.
29. K. Subrahmanyam was to argue that NAM lost all credibility regarding its commitment to global nuclear disarmament when on 11 May 1995, 178 nations of the international community – a majority of whom were non-aligned – allowed a declaration of consensus to be adopted in the extension conference of the NPT, legitimizing in perpetuity weapons of mass destruction in the hands of a few. 'Non-alignment Revisited', Economic Times, 31 May 1995. The demand for the total elimination of nuclear weapons at the 11th NAM Summit in Colombia in October 1995 sounded more like pious wishful thinking. To add to NAM's dillydallying, the final document of the 12th Summit in South Africa in September 1998, noted the complexities arising from the nuclear tests in South Asia and to accommodate India and Pakistan remarked that the tests would have to be seen as underlining 'the need to work even harder to achieve the disarmament objectives, including elimination of nuclear weapons'.
30. Interview with I.K. Gujral, Frontline, 4 April 1997, p. 10.
31. Praful Bidwai, 'India's schizophrenic elite', Frontline, 27 December 1996, pp. 98-99.
32. Bharatiya Janata Party, Election Manifesto 1998, New Delhi : BJP All-India General Secretary, p. 29.
33. J.N. Dixit, 'The Problem', Seminar, no. 472, December 1998, p. 16.
34. Partially compensated, it is true, by an agreement signed in 1990, authorizing the United States navy to use Singaporean ports.
35. Ashley Tellis, India's Emerging Nuclear Posture : Between Recessed Deterrent and Ready Arsenal, New Delhi, Oxford University Press, 2001, p. 25.

36. George Perkovich, India's nuclear bomb : the impact on global proliferation, New Delhi, Oxford University Press, 2000, p. 448.

37. Quoted in Waheguru Pal Singh Sidhu, Enhancing Indo-US Strategic Cooperation, Adelphi paper 313, Oxford, Oxford University Press/ International Institute for Strategic Studies, 1997, p. 127.

38. The close relationship between Beijing and Islamabad takes on special significance in this context. The relations between the two countries, along with apprehensions caused by the greater presence of the Chinese navy in the Indian Ocean in its search for new sources of hydrocarbons, and consequently, the need to protect the sea lanes of communications, has added to India's encirclement complex. In this context China is increasingly seen as a strategic threat. India perceives Pakistan as a threat in itself as well as a constituent of the Chinese threat. As a result, Chinese assistance to Pakistan's nuclear programme has for a long time been a source of tension between the two countries. Kashmir, however, plays a specific role in their relationship, even as it forces India into a permanent confrontation with its neighbour and corners a part of its political, economic and above all military resources. Moreover, the recurrence of Indo-Pak crises that it occasions, affects India's credibility as a major international power, confident, responsible and a future– permanent – member of the United Nations Security Council. This has resulted in limiting it to a role as a regional power, something that entirely suits Chinese designs.

39. Draft Report of the National Security Advisory Board on Indian Nuclear Doctrine, art. 2.4, 2.5.

40. George Perkovich, India's Nuclear Bomb: The Impact on Global Proliferation, New Delhi: Oxford University Press, 1999, p. 477.

41. Isabelle Cordonnier and Bruno Tertrais, op. cit., pp. 56-57.

42. Ibid., p. 110.

43. Ibid.., pp. 75-79.

44. See Michael Krepon, 'Nuclear Risk Reduction : Is Cold War Experience Applicable to Southern Asia?'; Michael Krepon and Chris Gagne (eds), The Stability-Instability Paradox: Nuclear Weapons and Brinkmanship in South Asia, Report No. 38, Washington DC: The Henry L. Stimson Center, June 2001, pp. 1-7.

45. Michael Krepon, op. cit., p. 11. During the 1988 Islamabad SAARC Summit, both parties had agreed not to attack each others' nuclear facilities. In the Lahore Declaration on 21 February 1999, India and Pakistan decided to inform each other in advance of all military exercises and ballistic missile tests to avoid any misunderstanding, but no nuclear risk reduction talks were held before June 2004 when it was decided to establish a hotline between the two foreign secretaries.

46. The nuclearisation of South Asia led to a renewed concern for the Kashmir issue as a nuclear flashpoint. At the 12th NAM summit in Durban, Nelson Mandela's reference to Kashmir in his inaugural address was resented by the Indian delegation. Soon after, it was the turn of Kofi Annan, in its report to the UNGA, to put on top of the world's zones of violence Kashmir and lent its voice to the demand for India and Pakistan to sign the CTBT and the NPT.
47. Isabelle Cordonnier and Bruno Tertrais, op. cit., p. 109.
48. According to the Research and Analysis Wing (RAW) and the Border Security Forces (BSF), the ratio of regulars/irregulars was 60 per cent : 40 per cent. According to the Intelligence Bureau, this ratio was 70 per cent : 30 per cent. The Kargil Review Committee, From Surprise to Reckoning, New Delhi: Sage Publications, 2000, p. 97.
49. Isabelle Cordonnier and Bruno Tertrais, op. cit., p. 109.
50. Kargil Review Committee, op. cit., p. 89.
51. Kargil Review Committee, op. cit., p. 183.
52. Mentioned in Ashley Tellis, C. Christine Fair, Jamison Jo Medby, Limited Conflict Under the Nuclear Umbrella : Indian and Pakistani Lessons from the Kargil Crisis, Santa Monica, RAND Corporation, 2001, p. 56.
53. Raj Chengappa, Weapons of Peace: The Secret Story of India's Quest to Be a Nuclear Power,.New Delhi, HarperColins, 2000 p. 437.
54. Ashley Tellis, C. Christine Fair, Jamison Jo Medby, Limited Conflict Under the Nuclear Umbrella : Indian and Pakistani Lessons from the Kargil Crisis, Santa Monica, Rand Corporation, 2001, pp. 21-23.
55. For a discussion on the military balance between India and Pakistan, see Anthony H. Cordesman, The India-Pakistan Military Balance, Washington DC, Center for Strategic and International Studies, May 2002, pp. 3-4.
56. The Hindu, June 8, 2002.
57. Ibid.
58. US Department of State, Current Policy Document no. 1298. Quoted by Dipankar Banerjee, 'A New World Order: Trends for the Future' in: Security in the New World Order: An Indo-French Dialogue, Dipankar Banerjee (ed.), IDSA, New Delhi, 1994, p. 4.
59. An Indian Official, 'India as a World Power, Foreign Affairs, July 1949, 27 (4), p. 548.
60. C. Raja Mohan, Crossing the Rubicon: The Shaping of India's New Foreign Policy, New Delhi: Penguin Books India, 2003, p. XXII.
61. Speech by Jaswant Singh, 17 February 2000. India and France in a Multipolar World, Proceedings of a Seminar, New Delhi: Manohar/Centre de Sciences Humaines, 2000, p. 216.

62. In the wake of the Kargil conflict, Jaswant Singh declared that 'a politically stable and economically thriving India has the potential to emerge as the fulcrum of Asia', Jaswant Singh. The Hindu, 31 July 1999. In incriminating China and its arms-selling activities with Pakistan as the first reason for the nuclear tests, New Delhi expected to attract some positive consideration from Washington.
63. On American intervention in the Kargil crisis, we refer to Bruce Riedel's work, American Diplomacy and the 1999 Kargil Summit at Blair House, Policy Paper Series, Philadelphia, Centre for the Advanced Study of India, University of Pennsylvania, 2002.
64. A year before, A.B. Vajpayee, in New York to address the United Nations General Assembly at the 'millenium summit', had recall that India has been the victim of state-sponsored cross-border terrorism for more than a decade and he appealed to the international community to adopt the draft of a comprehensive convention on international terrorism that India had proposed. The Hindu, 9 September 2000.

Indian Television - A Model of Cultural Appropriation in the Context of Globalisation

Camille DEPREZ

For several decades, the term 'globalisation' has been used to identify and explain the social, cultural and technical changes experienced by societies, a trend that is moving towards an inevitable homogenisation of the world along the lines of the American model. However, the removal of distances and the homogenisation of the world through the new mass communication technologies, as proposed by MacLuhan in the 1970s, constitute too simplistic a vision of the 'global village'. For such thinking raises doubts about the capacity of societies to adapt themselves and respond with their own cultural weapons to the influence of the globalised world. This article endeavours to show how Indian television, while being permeated with the globalisation wave, is steeped in its own local culture of images and which has actively created new, strictly Indian audiovisual cultural forms since the advent of satellite channels in the early nineties.

Indian society in images

The status of images in Indian society

In 1976, after seventeen years under a common body, the radio and audiovisual sectors separated into two distinct organisations. While the first retained the name of *All India Radio*, the second, pertaining to television, took on the name of *Doordarshan.* This almost literal Hindi translation of the term 'television' also alludes to a particular moment of the Hindu ritual, during which the devotee looks upon the divinity, while being seen by it. This reciprocal relationship can also be transposed to the viewer—and to the images the latter can see unfolding on the screen. The image has to make itself visible to the viewer, who has to see and understand whatever comes before his eyes: the latter does not receive the *Darshan* (literally, the grant of a vision of Himself by God, and His worship) passively, but appropriates it and instils it within himself (Grimaud, 1997: 67-84). This long-standing cultural attitude may explain why Indians are so enthusiastic about particularly powerful TV programmes, such as the *Ramayana* and *Mahabharata*, which were broadcast at the end of the Eighties on *Doordarshan*. Their unequalled popular success played a role in transforming television, which was until then essentially limited to city-dwellers, into a mass phenomenon. Viewers watched these programmes as if they were truly a religious experience. The actors tended to be viewed as the Gods they were playing, in the light of the Hindu belief that God exists even in images depicting Him, and they were even worshipped as Gods. While the power of images is remarkable in the Indian subcontinent, it is not as if the images broadcast on TV and in the movies are systematically worshipped or the actors playing the role always deified. Furthermore, one must also avoid the temptation of considering the *Darshan* as the only relationship between the viewer and the image. Anyone who has gone to see a film in India would attest to the diverse reactions of the viewers, who appropriate the film in order to better appreciate it. But this is still a civilisation in which images are loaded with a specific meaning, which springs back to Indian society as a whole.

The film world vis-à-vis the audiovisual world – The distinctive Indian identity

Indian TV has always drawn inspiration from *Bollywood* films. Since the advent of television in 1959, it has had at its disposal a rich and varied catalogue of over 50 years of movie making, and it is still a major outlet for popular cinema. As for movies themselves, they have always provided entertainment for TV. The passion for any programmes related to films that reigns among all the channel managers has to do with their low broadcasting costs. TV brings renewed popularity to old films, but also promotes those that are shortly to be projected on the big screen. Effective marketing techniques sell the original soundtracks of these films before they are screened, supported by the continuous broadcast of trailers and other forms of advertising on TV channels. But there is also some cross-fertilisation, as producers often choose new faces from among popular TV announcers, compères and actors, known for their young and 'fashionable' image. Filmmakers sometimes adopt the 'MTV style' in the way they shoot their films, for instance, by favouring jump cuts—short shots in which the actors find themselves in a series of very different sets during the dance sequences, with no visible transition between them. An increasing number of Bombay's big studios, whose problems go back to the advent of independent producers in the Fifties, are agreeing to shoot TV serials as a way of offsetting their desertion by filmmakers, who are now more attracted to location shoots.

An undeniable ally of films, TV is nonetheless a tough competitor. The programmes themselves have to be considered as one of the reasons why viewers have moved from the big screen to the small screen. After all, the latter offers them novelty, as compared to the 'formula-based' Bollywood films. The tone of TV serials, with their social content, is often more incisive than that of the *masala* movies, not hesitating to break with certain filmmaking conventions, such as the traditional 'happy ending'. By opting for originality and a certain freedom of expression, against the taboos raised by traditional Indian society about inter-caste relations, sexuality and relations between men and women in general—a trend that is largely inspired by American soap operas—satellite channels have been able to attract viewers from the urban middle class.[1] Doordarshan came up with its first soap operas in the mid-1980s, to provide programming for its new entertainment channel, Metro. Thus, during the 1984-1985 season, the serial *'Hum Log'* ('We'), inspired by South American *telenovelas*, was filmed in India for a specifically Indian public. It was aimed at delivering a message of 'modernity', based on the idea of a small family, aspiring for a better life through education and consumption.

The advent of video players (VCRs) undoubtedly complicated relations between movies and TV further in India. In the context of the public sector monopoly of TV in the 1980s, videos were the only alternative to Doordarshan programmes. The success of videos strengthened the place of TV, both as an outlet and as a rival for films. Films could be re-broadcast on TV, which was a good thing, but at the same time, people were less inclined to travel to cinema halls, since the same titles could be watched at home, almost at the same time as the films came out on the big screen. In 2003, film producers and distributors were warring with the big private channels—including Zee TV, which, in the absence of any regulations, were broadcasting hit films sometimes just two months after they came out. These legislative shortcomings, which remain to be settled to this day, did not help in creating peaceful relations between the two sectors. Video also made it possible to overcome the lack of equipment. Thanks to video, rural populations were able to have access to their favourite TV programmes or movies, and cable operators did not hesitate to hold out the prospect of being able to see them on the small screen, in order to convince villagers to subscribe to their cable network. Of course, the resulting rise in audiovisual broadcasts in India also brought in considerable income. By giving birth to inventive and often very lucrative experiments (video parlours, video restaurants, video clubs, video buses, etc.), video competed strongly with movie halls (Johnson, 2000). Faced with this situation, the Indian film industry increasingly started viewing multiplexes as a possible solution to win back prosperous urban viewers, without endangering the survival of smaller halls, which were more affordable for the less prosperous sections of the population,[2] as cheap movie tickets had been the reason behind the success of popular cinema. This was a fairly recent initiative, as the first complex, the Priya Village Roadshow, came up in Delhi only in 1997 with the financial assistance of an Australian firm, and took full advantage of the opening of the Indian market to American films. Since then, forty multiplexes have been or are in the process of being built in the country, not only in the four major cities, but also in mid-size towns like Chandigarh or Ahmedabad.[3] This recent and rapid development was largely favoured by a reduction in the entertainment tax imposed for this kind of project,[4] and the determination of a small number of large Indian or foreign companies (Adlabs, Shringar, Inox, Imax, etc.). These developments are changing the way films work in India, along with the way individual and mediocre cinema halls work —even comfortable halls using the latest technologies and screening several films at the same time. Furthermore, the process is governed by a handful of powerful firms. Private channels like Zee TV have also showed interest in this kind of activity. But however complex the relations between the audiovisual and movie sectors, the images they project are, above all, the fruit of the socio-cultural context in which they have taken shape.

Development of the Indian audiovisual sector - Reflecting a multi-faceted society?

Every linguistic, ethnic or religious community wishes to assert its own specificity, whether it is acknowledged at national level or simply at local level. Movies and TV too are subject to this trend, or at least, such claims. While Indian cinema was born in Bombay, the assertion of regional identities engendered a fractioning of the market as early as in the 1930s. Today, the majority of films are made in Hindi (246 films in 2003), closely followed by productions in Telugu (155 films) and Tamil (151 films).[5] Hindi films are often dubbed in regional languages in order to ensure their success with the public. TV too has been affected by the regionalisation of its channels (like Asianet in Kerala or Sun in Tamil Nadu) and the popularity of regional channels is undoubtedly linked to the distribution of films. The current shortage of stocks and the growing demand of TV are creating a considerable market for regional film production.

When images of the First Gulf War were broadcast in India by CNN, they marked the death knell of Doordarshan's monopoly. In 1992, Subhash Chandra established Zee TV and Rupert Murdoch started broadcasting Star TV programmes in India. Doordarshan, faced with the new competition from the private sector, expanded in 1994, adding 11 regional language channels and specialised sports, news or educational channels. But the quality of its regional channels as compared to the private channels was inferior, resulting in just a moderate success. Nonetheless, its programmes retained the highest viewership at an all-India level, as most rural areas did not yet have cable. On the other hand, private cable channels started offering serious competition in urban areas (cf. Table 1).

Table 1

Advertising income per TV channel or competition offered by private channels to Doordarshan

	Doordarshan	Zee-TV	SONY	Star-TV	Sun-TV
1996-97	133 M $	49 M $	16 M $	26 M $	16 M $
1997-98	113 M $	69 M $	42 M $	36 M $	32 M $
1998-99	92 M $	90 M $	59 M $	47 M $	43 M $

Source: Singhal and Rogers, 2000

Satellite broadcasts led to new viewership trends, making a better response to various regional demands possible. They are now turning towards the Indian diaspora on the one hand, and strictly local level populations on the other.[6]

But the mushrooming of movie halls and TV channels does not necessarily mean diversification. Hit 'formulae' are reproduced on the basis of various linguistic, religious or ethnic specificities. In the end, all the channels have a high content of movies, serials, games and news, and just the form in which these programmes are screened changes. However, these programmes clearly stand out for their specifically Indian content, which cannot be seen anywhere else in the world. And it is popular far beyond the country's borders. One could, perhaps, speak of local standardisation (at national level), but global differentiation (at the international scale). But this attempt to meet public demand — that too, an increasingly segmented public —is essentially limited to urban areas. Today, the TV network covers a major portion of Indian territory, though differences between the city and countryside and between different regions nonetheless remain (cf. Table 2). It is true that the number of viewers living in rural areas (297 million) is now higher than in urban areas (239 million), and TV is the medium that is the most extensively available to the Indian population as a whole. However, several villages still do not have access to any network other than Doordarshan, which is the only one authorised to beam its programmes through earth-based transponders. In 2000, just 6.5 per cent of all rural households had access to the cable and satellite network. The lack of infrastructure —too expensive for mass installation in villages—makes it difficult

Table 2

Audiovisual hardware facilities in Indian households in 2003 (in lakhs)

	Urban areas	Rural areas	Total
Indian households	561	1357	1918
Households with TV	429	386	815
Non-TV households	132	971	1103
Households with Cable/Satellite	272	133	405
Households without C & S	157	254	411
Cable TV penetration	63.4%	34.3%	49.6%

Source : Prasar Bharati, Doordarshan (2003)

for these populations to have access to private channels retransmitted by satellite. Hence, there is a vast market that remains to be conquered by cable channels, but there too, conditions vary depending on the means available to the various states.[7] It is true that rural viewers are barely taken into account by cable channel programming, which essentially focuses on the interests of the prosperous urban middle class, with its higher purchasing power. But from the viewpoint of the total number of individuals, the rural category nonetheless constitutes a major market share. In fact, between 2000 and 2001, a 53 per cent rise in rural households with cable and satellite TV was observed. These developments are the fruit of the technical efforts made by channels, whose aim is to be watched by a maximum number of people. But all Indian TV viewers stand out for their preference for local programmes.

Indian Television vs. Globalisation

From global to local, from local to global

Indian TV shows signs of having being swept up by the globalisation of the media, without, however, being absorbed into the worldwide homogenisation wave. Since the Eighties, but especially since N. Rao took over the reins of government in 1991, the Indian economy has been following the worldwide trend of liberalisation and media deregulation, and the choice to do so seems to attest to its commitment to globalisation. In 1991, the advent of CNN marked the entry of major international audiovisual groups —such as Time Warner, News Corp., Disney or Viacom —on the Indian audiovisual landscape (Page and Crawley, 2001). The context of globalisation made India adopt the path of strategic alliances, with the result that the interests of the public and private sectors began to intersect increasingly. Doordarshan no longer produced all its programmes, but took recourse to private Indian producers or overseas firms. Advertising began to take up an increasing amount of space in the sources of income of the channels, and the broadcast of India's first soap opera, '*Hum Log*' (1984) accelerated the public network's mercantilism. Another indication of the fact that Indian TV had started down the path of globalisation was the transformation of TV channels into multimedia groups. Private channels continued to diversify their activities and tended to turn into octopus corporations, present in all the key sectors of the mass communications industry. For instance, Zee TV developed branches in TV, cinema, radio, the press and, more recently, the Internet. By asserting their multinational inclinations, the biggest Indian channels —such as Doordarshan and Zee TV —followed along the lines of globalised media operations, in the tradition of major international audiovisual groups. In fact, they sought to establish bridges of communication with Indians living abroad and to show them their country of origin, its culture, values, traditions, modernity, diversity and so on. They provided news and entertainment programmes (music, films, serials, games, etc.) essentially targeting the diaspora, but which could, at a secondary level, appeal to the entire world.[8] This dual success created a link between the diaspora and the people of these foreign nations, as well as between India and the rest of the world, not only in India's traditional zones of influence (Middle-East, Asia, Africa, etc.), but also in Western countries. Zee TV, Doordarshan India, the Indian Star TV and MTV India networks established themselves as veritable laboratories for audiovisual experimentation and innovation, and constituted an effective instrument of influence for Indian culture at an international scale.[9]

But the indications of the increasing influence of globalisation failed to wipe out the importance given to local concerns. In India, government control over the audiovisual network did not prevent socio-economic actors from seizing autonomy. Thus, the absence of a legal framework enabled anyone who wished to do so to establish himself as a cable service provider in his district. In fact, *cable-wallahs* worked at a local level, re-transmitting the channels their neighbourhood wished to watch, and some even created their own channels in the light of the needs of their subscribers. These alternative organisations are not unique to India. In Asia, cheaper technologies have enabled the development of a sector —albeit clandestine —for minorities that were ignored by TV. In Taiwan, these pirated cable channels are symbolic of the subversion of the audiovisual sector, as they broadcast all sorts of programmes without ever bothering about their copyrights (Richards and French, 2000). Nevertheless, the current multiplicity of small cable operators in India is unique in the world. It would be impossible to paint an exhaustive picture of the TV channels broadcast here. The effect of these channels is completely opposite to that of the globalising multinationals —or, rather, the former distort the system, as they are solely interested in the tastes and interests of a specific local audience. But local media combine issues of identity with motivations of commercial profit, promoted by the capitalist global culture. And the independence of these small cable operators is threatened by an increasing business concentration. A few major companies compete with each other over the establishment of their hegemony on the cable sector, buying up small local units.[10] Thus, the audiovisual sector remains, above all, the stronghold of powerful captains of industry and politicians. Indian programmes are sometimes inspired by ideas from outside the country,[11] which could lead one to conclude that they were swept up by the wave of worldwide homogenisation. However, the government keeps a close watch on the content of programmes and never hesitates to censor them. TV groups that fail to adapt to Indian cultural habits are likely to fail in their attempts to conquer this vast market. In 2002, the French channel, Fashion TV, was obliged to Indianize its programmes (it had been accused of being pornographic) under the threat of being penalised by the Ministry of Information (so now it shows Indian fashion shows as well, fewer bare bodies on screen, etc.). Nevertheless, recent changes in the law governing the audiovisual sector can be observed: since 2002, 36 Indian TV channels have been authorised to beam their programmes from Indian soil—a sign of opening up by the Indian government to private channels, but the taxes and duties levied on foreign broadcasters are still very high and dissuasive. Direct to Home (DTH) services facilitate the broadcasting of private programmes, which would be beamed to small screens directly through an antenna and a decoder, but the Ministry of Information is still watchful and endeavours to ensure that issues of national security, morality of vertical distribution are borne in mind.

The impact of television on the Indian population

The penetration of TV in the daily life of people irreparably raises the question of what impact it may have on their lifestyles.

Would Indian TV viewers be swept away by the winds of globalisation, another name for the standardisation of human cultures and the Western model of consumption? The influence of advertising through private satellite TV channels is at the heart of such upheavals. Indian TV echoes the emergence of a majority world culture linked to commercial symbols (major international brands), promoted by the use of English (the international language). TV advertisements transcend the traditional division of Indian society into casts and target social groups that are defined by their level of consumption. TV viewers allow themselves to be persuaded into buying products that they did not use habitually in the past, and succumb to the era of consumerism, promoted by the economic liberalisation of the nineties. Free time and entertainment are largely monopolised by TV and cinema, as these are the most accessible to the people, both because they are broadcast or screened throughout the country and are not very expensive. Even with its growing middle class, India spends just one-tenth of the total amount spent by the USA on entertainment. The entertainment industry is nevertheless expanding rapidly in India, rising from Rs. 166 billion in 2002 to Rs. 190 billion in 2003.[12] Some talk shows like the *Kiron Joneja Show* or the *Priya Tendulkar Show* engender new points of view on subjects that were considered taboo, such as sexuality or relations between individuals, which were hitherto governed by traditional social norms, largely borrowed from religiosity (cast barriers, submission of women to men, of younger children to older siblings, etc.). Serials like *Saans* ('Breath'), *Kyonki Saas bhi kabhi Bahu thi* ('Because the mother-in-law was once a daughter-in-law too') or *Kahani ghar ghar ki* ('The story of a house') are playing a primary role in changing mind sets with regard to women, in the sense that they have novel characters —independent, working women who no longer live solely for their husband and children (*Viewer's Voices*, 1998/1999). In urban areas, serials like these have received some of the highest ratings.[13] The infiltration of Western ideas in India's audiovisual sector has not necessarily favoured women. TV commercials no longer hesitate to use degrading and stereotypical images of women, often reducing them to mere sex objects or foils to set off products (bikes and cars, beauty, hygiene, etc.). The urban middle class seems to aspire to external symbols of wealth, as in the West, and to emulate the success of their fellow-countrymen who are now settled in North America or Europe. Indian satellite TV also unites all Indian communities dispersed the world over through their original culture. Thus, the cultural invasion does not work only in one direction —from Western countries to India—but also from India to the countries in which the Indian diaspora can be found. A new form of cosmopolitanism is emerging in major Bollywood productions, like *Dil chahta hai* ('Heart's desire') or *Kabhi khushi kabhi ghum* ('At times joy, at times pain'), and in certain TV serials like *Hum pardesi ho gaye* ('We're foreigners now'), *Dollar bahu* ('Dollar daughter-in-law') or *Sansaar* ('Life on Earth'). This cosmopolitanism illustrates the emergence of the new multinational class, which navigates between the Indian universe and that of the West, where everyone knows how one should dress, what the best travel destinations are, etc. Today, the Indian diaspora accounts for over twenty million people, reflecting the social, ethnic, religious and cultural diversity of their country of origin. In the West, they enjoy a relatively high standard of living —in the USA for instance, an Indian family's average income is 25 per cent higher than the average for American families. This kind of life becomes a sort of ideal life that the Indian middle class aspires to achieve, for which the movies and TV are the preferred medium for this urban middle class elite to portray themselves. We already know that the Indian diaspora —caught between its native culture and its host country's culture —often suffers from an identity crisis. It is true that the diaspora is composed of a heterogeneous group of communities, but they converge and meet in Indian TV programmes and popular cinema. Indeed, the latter, owing to its economic might, has influenced the content of these media over the last ten years and programmes such as 'The Kumars at No. 42', broadcast on Star Plus, have been very successful in Europe or the USA.[14]

But quantitatively, the middle class remains a minority group in the audiovisual audience, in relation to the majority of the population living in rural areas, which constitutes a major force of resistance to the rising wave of globalisation, as it is largely faithful to local and ancestral traditions. Moreover, Indian society is also known for its vigorous opposition to outside influences. A field survey conducted in February 2001 and February 2003 in two villages in Rajasthan, Goner and Lalwari, attempted to discover the capacity of this rural population to resist change and its ability to adapt external factors to its traditional socio-cultural norms. Indeed, Western values do not seem to have caught on in the villages surveyed, which tends to modify MacLuhan's 'global village' thesis, within which Western society would reign triumphant. These new observations also modify the findings of the few studies carried out on the impact of TV in India's rural areas.[15] These had concluded that TV had caused an upheaval in the daily life of the villagers. But all the respondents agreed that TV programmes did not determine their schedule. They watched TV when they had free time and their working day still revolved around the work being done and the efficiency of local infrastructure: '*jab hamare pas vaqt hai, jab bijli hai, tab ham TV dekhte hain*' (we watch TV when we have time and when there's electricity). While most of the inhabitants asserted that they enjoyed the advertisements, they were often unable to afford the products whose praises they sung. The new forms of consumption promoted by advertisements do not translate into support for the social systems that give rise to them. Indeed, the consumer revolution remains a distant dream, with needs changing on the basis of essentially local factors. People remain focussed fundamentally on their local environment. The frontiers of the outside world often remain somewhat blurred — what is considered to be external or foreign in a given area is anything 'outside' (*bahar*), whether the other place is just 100 km away or on another continent. English programmes are ignored and those in Hindi are preferred, although programmes in the local language —Rajasthani in the case of the survey —are given the highest priority. TV viewers here first wanted to be able to understand what was being said on the screen and were far from interested in foreign programmes. The villagers also enjoyed the soap operas, particularly the women, but they all bore in mind the fact that they depicted an urban lifestyle. No one imagined that the situations evoked in these serials, in which the women are shown as independent, working women, could be reproduced in Goner or Lalwari: women wearing clothes that were too revealing or any other posture deemed immoral were immediately censured, with the viewers not hesitating to switch off their TVs whenever they were too shocked by the images shown. Technically, TV provides direct access to forbidden images or situations, but these were filtered by the viewers.

TV even promoted a certain durability of traditions and social restrictions. The programmes were often viewed in groups, but caste barriers remained. Thus, a *Harijan* said that he did not have the right to attend group viewings or to go over to his neighbour's place, because he was considered impure. According to him, purchasing a TV gave him the opportunity to enjoy the same social status as the others, the same material comforts, and have access to the same information and the same entertainment as the others: '*abhi mere pas TV hai, to main dusre gaonvalon se baraabar hun*' (I have a TV now, so I'm equal to the other villagers). But it is not really a democratising factor, as he still remained confined to his own four walls, excluded from the rest of the community. In a similar context, *Rajput* women bound by the *purdah* (veil), who were not allowed to leave their homes alone, also had access to the outside world through TV. But their access remained virtual, as they themselves were still confined to their home compounds. TV had also failed to make any changes in the highly hierarchised traditional family relations. Most villagers lived within joint (extended) families, in which relations between different generations and genders were governed by very specific statutory rules. The traditional hierarchy still continues to function. For instance, women from the high Rajput class still wore their *gunghat* (veil) lowered over their faces, even when they watched TV in groups, in order not to attract male eyes. However, they did so even when they were on their own homes and what they were watching made them uncomfortable. TV has also led to the emergence of new forms of social domination, copied from local traditions: the community distinguished between those who had a TV and those who didn't, in the same way that they made a distinction between landowners and the landless; the size of the antenna used also marked the social status of the house concerned in villages and homes were no longer linked by common activities but by cables. Hence, TV has helped perpetuate traditions. Villagers appropriated the technology and inserted it in their daily lives in such a way as to ensure that it did not change their social and cultural habits.

India, a tradition of resistance

Defending national identity in the face of foreign interference is at the very heart of the stands India has taken since the rise of nationalism during its colonisation by the British (whence the *Swadeshi* campaign, foreswearing the purchase or use of foreign goods), then while India was forming itself into an independent State (a domestic policy of self-reliant development and a non-aligned foreign policy). Since the Eighties, India has further developed its assets in the hi-tech field and has established high technology poles.

The Indian nation has also been able to resist the cultural invasion. Whether emanating from the elite or the masses, a strong current of national identity has always helped in maintaining or adapting a certain cultural specificity in the face of penetration by foreign cultures. In the nineties, the advent of American serials and multinationals like McDonalds or Coca-Cola even led to a nationalist withdrawal on the part of certain groups. In India, the political leadership soon understood the opportunities TV offered as an effective medium to get its voice heard by the masses and, today, any opening to the outside world is still controlled by the authorities. Indeed, during the World Trade Organisation (WTO) meeting in Seattle in 1999, India joined with the countries that were protesting against America's cultural hegemony. Along with the French, they also defended the right to 'cultural exception', especially for the cinematographic sector, faced with the unrelenting advance of major American productions in its market. Hence, the move did not merely consist of passive resistance by social actors, but also expressed a certain political will in the international arena. The 'spectre' of globalisation therefore appears to have retreated before India's strong identity —political, economic and cultural. And while the most minority cultures and languages may be endangered, most manage to adapt themselves to the society's development and sometimes even take on totally new cultural forms.

Indian TV or cultural appropriation in action

Foreign TV channels soon understood that to break into the Indian market, they had to adapt the content and form of their programmes to India's cultural reality. The case of MTV was, without doubt, the most striking example of this trend, when the channel entered the Indian market in 1994 and tried to broadcast its own programmes. In 1996, given the lack of interest shown by the subcontinent's viewers, the channel decided to review its entire programming grid, aware of the high stakes involved in conquering the South Asian market.[16] Thus, in 2000, 12 million Indian homes watched MTV India, which became a point of reference for the identity of India's urban youth. The channel thenceforth offered a remarkable case of the transformation of a foreign TV model into a channel that retained some Western traits, but was specifically aimed at India's urban youth. The channel's logo adopted the colours of the Indian flag, 70 per cent of its programmes were devoted to Indian pop music (Indipop) and extracts of the original soundtracks of *masala* (popular) films, while the remaining 30 per cent still broadcast Western music. Such cases, taking the support of established cultural references and an American-style approach, which had not yet been seen on Indian channels, was called the 'Indianization' of programmes. And its success transcended India's borders, as it spread to the

Indian diaspora all over the world, playing a role in creating a homogenous social class worldwide, even if it is confined to the urban youth. Some foreign TV programmes can still be seen on India's small screen, but transformed —Indianised, in order to optimise their chances of success among local audiences.[17] The most popular Indian programme recently was *Kaun Banega Crorepati*, the local version of 'Who wants to be a millionaire?', which started broadcasting on *Star Plus* during the first half of the evening, at the start of the school year in 2000.[18] This programme of American origin is broadcast in several countries in the world, but adapted to the local context in each case. While this type of programme was quite common in North America and Europe at the time, it was truly innovative in India's TV landscape. No programme had been televised before in which so much money was at stake. The contents of the game were completely Indianised, as it was essentially based on Bombay's film-world, cricket and Hindu myths. But its principal asset was that it was compèred by Amitabh Bachchan. It was true that the popularity he enjoyed in the Seventies and Eighties had waned somewhat by the nineties, but the 'Big B' remained Bombay's biggest superstar for many Indians. Indeed, the programme led to a revival of his film career. It is the only version of this programme to use a movie star —a way of asserting its own identity in today's globalised audiovisual landscape. The success of *Kaun Banega Crorepati* (KBC) was such that it led to a sort of programme war between the major private channels and an escalation in the amounts of money involved. Take for example the case of '*Jeeto Chappar Phaad Ke*', a similar game compèred by Govinda —another Indian movie star —broadcast on Sony Entertainment, in an attempt to benefit from KBC's success. For a long time, Indian TV was a by-product of its film industry and based its successes on popular movies. But for the last ten years or so, in order to be competitive, TV channels have had to innovate and improve the content of their programmes. Every channel has to create its own identity and the three most popular networks (Star, Sony and Zee) are developing fresh formats and attempting completely new experiments in order to win additional viewers. Sony, for instance, has introduced a new 'reality show' (a fairly new genre in India) called '*Shubh Vivah*' (happy marriage), since marriages are a major focus of attention in the country.

The cultural appropriation of foreign programmes by India also affected the language in which they were broadcast. Given the need to adapt to the Indian context, foreign channels initially opted for bilingualism,[19] broadcasting programmes in both English and Hindi. This then led to a certain linguistic hybridisation. On private Indian channels, announcers and compères began to speak in 'Hinglish' or 'Zinglish' —with reference to Zee TV (Thussu, 2000). Faced with the challenge of globalised programme models, India responded by producing its own common language. It is true that 'Hinglish' only worked for the urban middle class in North India, specially the youth, but it nonetheless constitutes a model of true cultural appropriation. The strong cultural and identity-related claims of South India gave rise to a Tamil version of 'Hinglish' on Tamil Nadu's private TV channels, called '*Tamenglish*' or '*Tanglish*'. As you can see, 'Hinglish' was created by the Indians, for the Indians.[20] It even helped in reaching out to the vast diaspora market, as its members did not understand Hindi fully and only a rudimentary version (partially thanks to Hindi films). Advertisements, mostly promoting the merits of foreign consumer goods, constituted a major support for the spread of 'Hinglish'. TV announcers sold the new language as a brand — with a fully-fledged identity of its own.[21] Some observers found that this model of linguistic hybridisation constituted progress on the path of globalisation and towards a gradual linguistic homogenisation, but we see it, rather, as a local way of appropriating English, the 'international' language, and as a stage that helped overcome India's linguistic diversity. This linguistic hybridisation would then be akin to an adaptation of the globalised model, dominated by English, to the Indian socio-cultural context.

Conclusion

One of the recurring clichés about Indian civilisation is that it has always been able to assimilate the diverse incursions into its territory, thereby proving its immense capacity to mix and change foreign influences and forge new cultural forms, which are incorporated by the society as a whole over the years. The rapid technical progress made by television in the recent past has enabled it to extend its reach to the country's remotest areas, turning it into the foremost vehicle for social and cultural change among the Indian people. The latter are now faced with globalisation, and the mass media have become a favoured means for its spread. But the linguistic, religious, ethnic and social diversity of Indian society is such that it would seem difficult to subject it to the unified system of globalisation. While some aspects of globalisation may have fond their way to India, they remain largely limited to the urban areas, each community reacting and adapting itself on the basis of its own cultural identity. In the Indian cinema and TV sector, this Indian aptitude to digest everything coming from beyond its borders has led to the emergence of completely new cultural forms, broadcast through MTV, games or 'Hinglish'. Indian TV is therefore a model of cultural appropriation, which puts an end to the idea according to which the world is currently witnessing a process of homogenisation of all its societies.

Annex

Chronology of TV in India

1959 - Television was introduced in Delhi under the aegis of UNESCO.

1975-1976: The SITE programme was launched in 400 Indian villages through NASA's ATS-6 satellite —the first attempt in the world at the mass use of TV for socio-educative goals. The government set up *Doordarshan* (DD), and TV separated from the radio broadcasting authority.

1980: Start of advertising in the audiovisual sector.

1982: Technological efforts made to cover the Asian Games held in Delhi — expansion of transmission network, beginning of national programming and introduction of colour TV.

1984-1985: Creation of the second public sector channel (*Metro*) to entertain viewers in major cities. Soap operas and mythological serials gain popularity: *Hum Log* (84-85), *Ramayana* (87-88), *Mahabharat* (88-90)...

1990: The *Prasar Bharati* bill for the autonomy of *Doordarshan* was adopted by the Parliament, though it had not yet come into force.

1991-1992: CNN transmitted images of the Gulf War, marking the entry of satellite and cable TV in India. Cable operators mushroomed to cope with the demand. Competition with *Doordarshan* for viewership and advertising contracts began.

1993-1994: Reorganisation of *Doordarshan* into several channels to fight against the new competition. The *Metro* channel was retransmitted by satellite, regional language and theme-based channels launched.

1995: Launch of *DD-International*, aimed at the Indian diaspora.

1996: Cable channels proliferated in South India, its way of asserting its cultural identity vis-à-vis North India. Emergence of pay channels: *Star Movies*, *HBO*, *Zee Cinema*, etc.

2002: Over 500 million Indians watch TV regularly, i.e. almost 50 per cent of the population. *Doordarshan* broadcasts around 20 channels by satellite, while its 1000 terrestrial transmitters enable it to provide access to 90 per cent of the population, thereby constituting one of the biggest audiovisual broadcasting networks in the world. Almost 40 private audiovisual networks broadcast their programmes.

Notes

1. For instance, the serial '*Tara*', broadcast on Zee TV, was based on the life of four young women who, on moving to Bombay, discover independence, or '*Saans*' (Breath), programmed on Star Plus, relating the life of a nuclear family and the husband's adulterous adventures.
2. Multiplexes are still few and far between in India and are primarily limited to urban areas, which are the only areas that can attract a prosperous audience.
3. Cf. FICCI 2002 Report.
4. These decisions have to be made by the regional governments themselves, with some regions offering incentives while others are still waiting for the laws to be changed.
5. Cf. FICCI, 2004 Report.
6. Cf. Impact of Television on the Indian Population.
7. Rural areas in South India, which are richer, are better equipped in cable and satellite than those in the North and, particularly in the North-West.
8. For instance, the Doordarshan India channel was launched in 1995. It is now available in nearly 150 countries across the world.

9. Cf. Indian TV or cultural appropriation in action, p.18.
10. The cable industry is composed of six major companies: SitiCable, InCable, Sumangli Cable Vision, Hathway Cables, RPG-Netcom and ORTEL Communications.
11. In India, the idea of soap operas was inspired by the South American telenovelas, TV games by American quizzes and news bulletins are modelled after the American style of presentation.
12. A growing number of industrialists are taking interest in the sectors of live shows (which accounted for Rs. 3.4 billion in 2003) and of amusement parks (almost 280 million visitors in 2002), attracted by the purchasing power of the middle class. Cf. FICCI, 2004 report.
13. Cf. Figures given by TAM on www.indiantelevision.com
14. This show, produced in the UK, revolves around an Indian family that hosts various British celebrities (singers, writers, etc.) in a sort of chat show at their homes, using a great deal of satire while interviewing them.
15. Cf. Behl, 1988; Johnson, 2000; Kaur, 2002.
16. Today, it is a major asset for the group, as its audience rating is one of the highest in the world in this part of the globe. Today, the channel enjoys as 58 per cent market share in the music channel section and is therefore ahead of Channel V, Zee Music and B4U Music (cf. www.indiantelevision.com).
17. The influence of local culture was not limited to India alone. In most Asian countries, viewers welcomed programmes that were broadcast in local languages most (India, Pakistan, Taiwan, Singapore, etc.). Some countries even managed to impose their own TV programmes, not only within their borders but also beyond (such as the manga in Japan).
18. An Indian version of 'Pop Star' in Hindi was also screened on Channel V (also belonging to the Star TV network). It too was an example of the local adaptation of a programme broadcast in different versions in several countries, just like '*Kamzor Kadii Kaun*' (The Weakest Link) or '*Ji Mantriji*' (Yes, Prime Minister).
19. MTV, Channel V, Disney, Discovery, Star News, Star Plus, Zee TV, Star Sports, Cartoon Network, etc.
20. This model of linguistic hybridisation is not unique in the world. In Hong Kong, the middle class often speaks in '*Chinglish*' – a mix of Chinese and English.
21. Which is how Coca-Cola sold itself with the slogan: '*Coca-Cola, life ho to* aisi " (Coca-Cola - That's the life!).

Bibliography

Audience Research Unit, 1999, *Doordarshan 99*, New Delhi, Doordarshan Prasar Bharati, Broadcasting Corporation of India, 79 p.

Audience Research Unit, 2002, *Doordarshan 2002*, New Delhi, Doordarshan Prasar Bharati, Broadcasting Corporation of India, 77 p.

Audience Research Unit, 2003, *Doordarshan 2003*, New Delhi, Doordarshan Prasar Bharati, Broadcasting Corporation of India, 121 p.

BEHL N., 1988, 'Equalizing Status: Television and Tradition in an Indian Village', in J. LULL (dir.), *World Families Watch Television*, New Delhi, Sage, pp. 136-157.

ECK D., 1996, *Darshan, Seeing the Divine Image in India*, New York, Columbia University Press.

Federation of Indian Chambers of Commerce and Industry, 2000, *The Indian Entertainment Industry, Strategy and Vision*, New Delhi, 57 p.

Federation of Indian Chambers of Commerce and Industry, 2002, *Indian Entertainment Industry: The Show must go on...*, New Delhi, 72 p.

Federation of Indian Chambers of Commerce and Industry, 2002, *The Indian entertainment sector in the spotlight*, New Delhi, 93 p.

Federation of Indian Chambers of Commerce and Industry, 2004, *The Indian Entertainment Industry: Emerging Trends and Opportunities*, New Delhi, 99 p.

GRIMAUD E., 1997, 'L'ébullition de la représentation, l'ordre visuel du cinéma indien populaire' *in Gradhiva*, No. 22, p. 67-84.

GRIMAUD E., 2001, *La spirale prolifique, ou l'histoire du processus cinématographique dans l'Inde contemporaine, du script à la mise en théorie du mouvement*, Ph.D in Ethnology, Université Paris X.

JOHNSON K., 2000, *Television and Social Change in Rural India*, New Delhi, Sage.

Medias en Inde, l'actualité de la Télévision, de la Radio et du Cinéma en Inde, 1998-2001, New Delhi, bimonthly letter of the Cultural Section of the Embassy of France in India.

KAUR K., 2002, *Impact of Mass Media on Rural Social Life in Ferozepur District of Punjab*, Ludhiana, Master of Science in Sociology, Department of Economics and Sociology, Punjab Agricultural University.

PADOUX A., dir., 1990, *L'image divine, culte et méditation dans l'hindouisme*, Paris, CNRS.

PAGE D., CRAWLEY W., 2001, *Satellites Over South Asia, Broadcasting, Culture and the Public Interest*, New Delhi, Sage.

RICHARDS M., FRENCH D., 2000, 'Globalisation and Television: Comparative Perspectives' *in Cyprus Review*, Volume 12.

SINGHAL A., ROGERS E., 2000, *India's Communication Revolution, from Bullock Carts to Cyber Marts*, New Delhi, Sage.

THUSSU D. K., 2000, 'Language Hybridation and Global Television: The Case of Hinglish' *in Cyprus Review*, Volume 12.

Viewer's Voices, 1998-1999, *Report of the Viewer's Forum*, New Delhi, Human Resources Development Foundation.

Index

B

Q

R

S